कालीपूजा

Kali Puja

Translated By

स्वामी सत्यानन्द सरस्वती

Swami Satyananda Saraswati

Published By

Devi Mandir Publications

Devi Mandir Publications
5950 Highway 128
Napa, CA 94558 USA
Communications: Phone and Fax 1-707-966-2802
E-Mail Swamiji@shreemaa.org
Please visit us on the World Wide Web at
http://www.shreemaa.org/

ISBN 1-877795-68-2
Library of Congress Catalog Card Number
CIP 96-72539

Kālī Pūjā, Swami Satyananda Saraswati
1. Hindu Religion. 2. Goddess Worship.
3. Spirituality. 4. Philosophy. I. Saraswati,
Swami Satyananda

Saṁskṛta and Computer Layout
by Vittalananda Saraswati

Kālī

Kāla means Darkness; Kālī takes away that Darkness. She takes away the darkness from every individual who strives in the path of perfection by performing the spiritual disciplines of purifying austerities. Just as all the colors of the spectrum mix into black, yet still black remains black, so too, Kālī, who is completely Dark, Unknowable, takes away all the Darkness, yet She, Herself, remains unchanged.

Kāla means Time and ī means the Cause; Kālī, the Cause of Time or She Who is Beyond Time. All existence has its perception in time, and therefore the Cause of Time, She Who is Beyond Time, activates Consciousness to perception, allows Consciousness to perceive.

She wears a garland of the heads of impure thoughts, which She has severed from the personalities of Her devotees. She cuts down all of the conflicting concepts which debate their various ideologies within the arena of mind, silences the tumultuous roar of mental conflict and the anguish of egotistical attachment, takes the physical manifestations to Herself, and makes a garland of perplexity. Thus She wears all karma as an ornament, while She stops the chattering voices of the active mind, so that Her devotees can experience the purity of inner peace in the absorption of solitude.

As the Destroyer of Madhu and Khaiṭabha, Too Much and Too Little, She puts Her devotees in the balance of divine meditation.

She is called Cāmuṇḍā, the Slayer of Anger and Passion, who cuts down all the angry thoughts and impure passions along with their tremendous armies. When Caṇḍa and Muṇḍa, Anger and Passion, hurled thousands of discuses at Her, She merely opened wide Her mouth, and all of those terrible opposing weapons entered the gateway to infinity, absorbed into Her being without effect.

She took all the horses of the cavalry of thoughts, along with their chariots and charioteers; elephants along with their drivers, protectors and armor; and uncountable thousands of warriors of the army of thoughts; She put them into Her mouth and hideously began to chew. She took all the soldiers of the armies opposing divinity, the entire army of thoughts, projections, speculations, and immediately She digested them all.

Witnessing the destruction of confusion, the Gods experience extreme joy! See how many contemplations, prejudices and attitudes from which we have been freed! Having given up all the difficulties, all the thoughts, the very ego itself, to Kālī, the mind experiences the utmost peace and delight!

Raktabīja, who performed great austerities, was awarded the boon that whenever a drop of his blood would touch the ground, in that very same place a new Raktabīja would be born with the same vitality, courage and strength, the same capacity to captivate the mind. Rakta means red, the color; it also means blood and passion; most specifically, a passion for something - Desire. Bīja means the seed; Raktabīja literally translates as the Seed of Desire.

See how he manifests in action. In order to accomplish his desire, he multiplies into countless new desires with the same intensity, the same capacity of captivating the mind, all of which seek fulfillment as well. As we find desire for one thing, one drop of blood has touched the ground, and immediately, automatically, a new "something" is required in order to fulfill that desire. Another drop.

This goes on indefinitely, causing a continual necessity to act. Every time a Seed of Desire touches the ground, a new Seed of Desire is born in that very same place. Ultimately the entire earth has been filled with Seeds of Desire.

Seeing this and understanding fully well the tremendous importance and significance of the all-pervasiveness of desire, the Gods became extremely dejected. In great alarm we all called to the Divine Mother for help. "Oh Compassionate Kālī, stick out your tongue and drink up all the desires of existence. Only your mouth has sufficient capacity to consume all desire! And when you will have digested all desire, then the Gods will be free from desire."

This is why She shows Her very lovely, red, protruding tongue - in order to make all existence free from desire.

Kālī is most often depicted as standing upon the corpse-like form of Lord Śiva, dancing upon the stage of Consciousness. She is the perceivable form of Consciousness. Consciousness is awareness. Rather than the actor, Consciousness is the witness of all action. That is why Lord Śiva is shown as a lifeless corpse: still, immobile, his eyes are fixed, trained on the image of the Divine Mother. All that Consciousness perceives is the dance of Nature.

She is dancing to infatuate Him, causing Him to direct His attention to Her. But Śiva does not forget that it is Nature who is dancing, not I;

and He remains the silent Witness. This body is Nature. I am Consciousness, the silent witness of the actions of Nature. I am not the performer. This body acts according to its nature, because that is its nature. Remembering this, I am free, one among the audience in a theater watching the drama of life.

Kālī is Nature personified - not necessarily the dark force of Nature, but all of Nature: Mother Nature, as She dances upon the stage of Consciousness. As all of the qualities reside together, the three Guṇas: Sattva, Rajas and Tamas; activity, desire and rest, Kālī embodies the Three. However, She is more frequently associated with Tamas.

Tamas means darkness, but not necessarily in the sense of ignorance. There is a darkness which obscures external perception. And there is a darkness which exposes the light. Kālī as the personification of Tamas, is the Energy of Wisdom.

She spreads Her darkness over worldly desire, makes seekers oblivious to the transient externals, totally self-contained within. Pure Consciousness knows that the world of matter will continue to revolve according to its nature, in a cyclical flow of creation, preservation and transformation - the wheel of life. It goes on of its own accord.

When one can reside within, without identification or attachment to the ever-changing externals, then the supreme truth can be realized.

Kālī is jñānaśakti, the energy of Wisdom, the intuitive illumination within, as compared with the intellectual contemplation of the external. Knowledge is conceived, wisdom is intuited. When Kālī takes away the darkness of the outside world, She grants illumination of the inner world. Such is Her Grace.

With Kālī's Love we become unattached, free from reaction, the silent witness of the stimulus and response which action and interaction bring. We cease to react emotionally to the circumstances of life, and rather plan our actions for the optimum efficiency; so that all the sooner we can complete our necessary contributions to creation according to our karmas, and spend the balance of our time delighting in Universal Consciousness. This is the path that Kālī shows.

The following translation includes a booklet of the basic elements of the worship of the Goddess Kālī, which we published in 1989, called Kālī Dhyānam. That book contained Her Gāyatrī mantra, the Meditation on Her form and its meaning, the bīja mantras of Her nyāsa, Her japa, and the famous Ādyā Stotram, Song in Praise of the Foremost. This is most interesting as it identifies all forms of the Divine Mother as differing manifestations of the One Supreme Śakti. At the end came the Closing Prayers and Praṇāma to the Goddess.

To this original material has been added almost two hundred pages of other mantras intrinsic to the advanced worship of the Goddess: The Hundred Names of Kālī, The Thousand Names of Kālī, The Armor of Kālī, as well as the establishment of life in the deity, and the mantras and procedures for consecrating all of the offerings to the Goddess, including the elaborate offerings of bhāṅga and alcohol, and the mantras for engendering dharmic children.

The original text is presented in Saṁskṛta, followed by the Roman phonetic transliteration, and the English meanings. It is impossible for a translator to maintain pure objectivity in composing an English interpretation of the glorious Saṁskṛta mantras. No matter how hard one might try, some part of his own experience, his own philosophy, his own intellectual understanding, will no doubt creep in. For this reason the original text is presented without alteration.

But if there be any prejudice on the part of this translator, let it be that he strives to convey the purest devotion, the most joyous inspiration, and the greatest unconditional love of which he is capable, for the Divine Mother, for his beloved Guru, Shree Maa, and to the sādhana to which he has devoted his life.

Swami Satyananda Saraswati
Devi Mandir, 1996

What a privilege to be writing a preface to the third edition so soon. It surely indicates how popular the worship of the Divine Mother is becoming in various countries around the world. Both the Indian edition and the American edition are completely out of stock, and with great sincerity I humble myself before the devotees of the Divine Mother. Shree Maa, herself, has recorded the *Thousand Names of Kālī* on a beautiful CD, with music scored by Richard Sales.

Several devotees with busy schedules have asked for smaller pūjās which they can perform on a daily basis, allowing for the performance of the entire book of *Kālī Pūjā* on weekends and holidays when they have more time. We recommend the Invitation and Vow of worship, pages 6-27; Purification of Water and Flowers, pages 36-42; Establishment of the deity within, pages 57-59; Offerings to the Goddess, pages 72-82, and the Closing Prayers, pages 227-233. This practice can be completed in approximately half an hour, and can accompany regular meditation practices.

The object is to continually expand our practices until they consume our entire lives, and I pray that the Divine Mother Goddess blesses us all with the sole contemplation of Her in our every action.

Swami Satyananda Saraswati
Devi Mandir, 1998

Changes in printing technology and the globalization of Hinduism have necessitated this fourth edition. Our website is regularly receiving visitors from 81 countries, and our books are being used in many more places than I can name. It is so rewarding to find that devotion to the Divine Mother in many forms is being appreciated and practiced around the world.

Again we are performing an extended austerity in seclusion, and we pray that everyone feel the blessings of peace and welfare that come from sincere worship to the Divine Mother. Again and again we bow down to Her with our greatest intensity of love, and pray that She continues to bless us all with the highest and the best.

Swami Satyananda Saraswati
Devi Mandir, 2005

Table of Contents

श्रीमन्महागणाधिपतये नमः

śrīmanmahāgaṇādhipataye namaḥ

We bow to the Respected Great Lord of Wisdom.

लक्ष्मीनारायणाभ्यां नमः

lakṣmīnārāyaṇābhyāṁ namaḥ

We bow to Lakṣmī and Nārāyaṇa, The Goal of all Existence and the Perceiver of all.

उमामहेश्वराभ्यां नमः

umāmaheśvarābhyāṁ namaḥ

We bow to Umā and Maheśvara, She who protects existence, and the Great Consciousness or Seer of all.

वाणीहिरण्यगर्भाभ्यां नमः

vāṇīhiraṇyagarbhābhyāṁ namaḥ

We bow to Vāṇī and Hiraṇyagarbha, Sarasvatī and Brahmā, who create the cosmic existence.

शचीपुरन्दराभ्यां नमः

śacīpurandarābhyāṁ namaḥ

We bow to Śacī and Purandara, Indra and his wife, who preside over all that is divine.

मातापितृभ्यां नमः

mātāpitṛbhyāṁ namaḥ

We bow to the Mothers and Fathers.

इष्टदेवताभ्यो नमः

iṣṭadevatābhyo namaḥ

We bow to the chosen deity of worship.

कुलदेवताभ्यो नमः

kuladevatābhyo namaḥ

We bow to the family deity of worship.

ग्रामदेवताभ्यो नमः

grāmadevatābhyo namaḥ

We bow to the village deity of worship.

वास्तुदेवताभ्यो नमः

vāstudevatābhyo namaḥ

We bow to the particular household deity of worship.

स्थानदेवताभ्यो नमः

sthānadevatābhyo namaḥ

We bow to the established deity of worship.

सर्वेभ्यो देवेभ्यो नमः

sarvebhyo devebhyo namaḥ

We bow to all the Gods.

सर्वेभ्यो ब्राह्मणेभ्यो नमः

sarvebhyo brāhmaṇebhyo namaḥ

We bow to all the Knowers of divinity.

खड्गं चक्रगदेषुचापपरिघाञ्छूलं भुशुण्डीं शिरः
शङ्खं संदधतीं करैस्त्रिनयनां सर्वाङ्गभूषावृताम् ।
नीलाश्मद्युतिमास्यपाददशकां सेवे महाकालिकां
यामस्तौत्स्वपिते हरौ कमलजो हन्तुं मधुं कैटभम् ॥

khaḍgaṁ cakra gadeṣu cāpa-
parighāñ chūlaṁ bhuśuṇḍīṁ śiraḥ
śaṅkhaṁ saṁdadhatīṁ karai
strinayanāṁ sarvāṅga bhūṣāvṛtām
nīlāśmadyutimāsya pāda-
daśakāṁ seve mahākālikāṁ
yāmastaut svapite harau kamalajo
hantuṁ madhuṁ kaiṭabham

Bearing in Her ten hands the sword of worship, the discus of revolving time, the club of articulation, the bow of determination, the iron bar of restraint, the pike of attention, the sling, the head of egotism and the conch of vibrations, She has three eyes and displays ornaments on all Her limbs. Shining like a blue gem, She has ten faces and feet. I worship that Great Remover of Darkness whom the lotus-born Creative Capacity praised in order to slay Too Much and Too Little, when the Supreme Consciousness was in sleep.

अक्षस्रक्परशुं गदेषुकुलिशं पद्मं धनुः कुण्डिकां
दण्डं शक्तिमसिं च चर्म जलजं घण्टां सुराभाजनम् ।
शूलं पाशसुदर्शने च दधतीं हस्तैः प्रसन्नाननां
सेवे सैरिभमर्दिनीमिह महालक्ष्मीं सरोजस्थिताम् ॥

akṣasrak paraśuṁ gadeṣu kuliśaṁ
padmaṁ dhanuḥ kuṇḍikāṁ
daṇḍaṁ śaktim asiṁ ca carma
jalajaṁ ghaṇṭāṁ surābhājanam
śūlaṁ pāśa sudarśane ca
dadhatīṁ hastaiḥ prasannānanāṁ
seve sairibha mardinīmiha
mahālakṣmīṁ sarojasthitām

She with the beautiful face, the Destroyer of the Great Ego, is seated upon the lotus of Peace. In Her hands She holds the rosary of alphabets, the battle axe of good actions, the club of articulation, the arrow of speech, the thunderbolt of illumination, the lotus of peace, the bow of determination, the water-pot of purification, the staff of discipline, energy, the sword of worship, the shield of faith, the conch of vibrations, the bell of continuous tone, the wine cup of joy, the pike of concentration, the net of unity and the discus of revolving time named Excellent Intuitive Vision. I worship that Great Goddess of True Wealth.

घण्टाशूलहलानि शङ्खमुसले चक्रं धनुः सायकं
हस्ताब्जैर्दधतीं घनान्तविलसच्छीतांशुतुल्यप्रभाम् ।
गौरीदेहसमुद्भवां त्रिजगतामाधारभूतां महा-
पूर्वामत्र सरस्वतीमनुभजे शुम्भादिदैत्यार्दिनीम् ॥

ghaṇṭā śūla halāni śaṅkha
musale cakraṁ dhanuḥ sāyakaṁ
hastābjair dadhatīṁ ghanānta
vilasacchītāṁ śutulya prabhām
gaurīdeha samudbhavāṁ
trijagatām ādhārabhūtāṁ mahā-
pūrvāmatra sarasvatīm anubhaje
śumbhādi daityārdinīm

Bearing in Her lotus hands the bell of continuous tone, the pike of concentration, the plow sowing the seeds of the Way of Truth to Wisdom, the conch of vibrations, the pestle of refinement, the discus of revolving time, the bow of determination and the arrow of speech, whose radiance is like the moon in autumn, whose appearance is most beautiful, who is manifested from the body of She Who is Rays of Light, and is the support of the three worlds, that Great Goddess of All-Pervading Knowledge, who destroyed Self-Conceit and other thoughts, I worship.

या चण्डी मधुकैटभादिदैत्यदलनी या माहिषोन्मूलिनी
या धूम्रेक्षणचण्डमुण्डमथनी या रक्तबीजाशनी ।

शक्तिः शुम्भनिशुम्भदैत्यदलनी या सिद्धिदात्री परा
सा देवी नवकोटिमूर्तिसहिता मां पातु विश्वेश्वरी ॥

yā caṇḍī madhukaiṭabhādidaityadalanī yā māhiṣonmūlinī
yā dhūmrekṣaṇacaṇḍamuṇḍamathanī yā raktabījāśanī
śaktiḥ śumbhaniśumbhadaityadalanī yā siddhidātrī parā
sā devī navakoṭimūrtisahitā māṁ pātu viśveśvarī

That Chaṇḍī, who slays the negativities of Too Much and Too Little and other Thoughts; Who is the Destroyer of the Great Ego, and the Vanquisher of Sinful Eyes, Passion and Anger, and the Seed of Desire; the Energy which tears asunder Self-Conceit and Self-Deprecation, the Grantor of the highest attainment of perfection: may that Goddess who is represented by ninety million divine images, Supreme Lord of the Universe, remain close and protect me.

ॐ अग्निर्ज्योतिर्ज्योतिरग्निः स्वाहा ।
सूर्यो ज्योतिर्ज्योतिः सूर्यः स्वाहा ।
अग्निर्वर्चो ज्योतिर्वर्चः स्वाहा ।
सूर्यो वर्चो ज्योतिर्वर्चः स्वाहा ।
ज्योतिः सूर्यः सूर्यो ज्योतिः स्वाहा ॥

oṁ agnir jyotir jyotir agniḥ svāhā
sūryo jyotir jyotiḥ sūryaḥ svāhā
agnir varco jyotir varcaḥ svāhā
sūryo varco jyotir varcaḥ svāhā
jyotiḥ sūryaḥ sūryo jyotiḥ svāhā

Oṁ The Divine Fire is the Light, and the Light is the Divine Fire; I am One with God! The Light of Wisdom is the Light, and the Light is the Light of Wisdom; I am One with God! The Divine Fire is the offering, and the Light is the Offering; I am One with God! The Light of Wisdom is the Offering, and the Light is the Light of Wisdom; I am One with God!

(Wave light)

ॐ अग्निर्ज्योती रविर्ज्योतिश्चन्द्रो ज्योतिस्तथैव च ।

ज्योतिषामुत्तमो देवि दीपोऽयं प्रतिगृह्यताम् ॥

एष दीपः ॐ ह्रीं श्रीं क्रीं परमेश्वरि कालिके स्वाहा ॥

oṁ agnirjyotī ravirjyotiścandro jyotistathaiva ca
jyotiṣāmuttamo devi dīpo-yaṁ pratigṛhyatām
eṣa dīpaḥ oṁ hrīṁ śrīṁ krīṁ parameśvāri kālike svāhā

Oṁ The Divine Fire is the Light, the Light of Wisdom is the Light, the Light of Devotion is the Light as well. The Light of the Highest Bliss, Oh Goddess, is in the Light which we offer, the Light which we request you to accept. With the offering of Light Oṁ Māyā, Increase, Dissolution, to the Supreme Female Divinity, Kālī, I am One with God!

(Wave incense)

ॐ वनस्पतिरसोत्पन्नो गन्धात्ययी गन्ध उत्तमः ।

आघ्रेयः सर्वदेवानां धूपोऽयं प्रतिगृह्यताम् ॥

एष धूपः ॐ ह्रीं श्रीं क्रीं परमेश्वरि कालिके स्वाहा ॥

oṁ vanaspatirasotpanno gandhātyayī gandha uttamaḥ
āghreyaḥ sarvadevānāṁ dhūpo-yaṁ pratigṛhyatām
eṣa dhūpaḥ oṁ hrīṁ śrīṁ krīṁ parameśvāri kālike svāhā

Oṁ Spirit of the Forest, from you is produced the most excellent of scents. The scent most pleasing to all the Gods, that scent we request you to accept. With the offering of fragrant scent Oṁ Māyā, Increase, Dissolution, to the Supreme Female Divinity, Kālī, I am One with God!

ॐ पयः पृथिव्यां पय ओषधीषु

पयो दिव्यन्तरिक्षे पयो धाः ।

पयःस्वतीः प्रदिशः सन्तु मह्यम् ॥

oṁ payaḥ pṛthivyāṁ paya oṣadhīṣu
payo divyantarikṣe payo dhāḥ
payaḥsvatīḥ pradiśaḥ santu mahyam

Oṁ Earth is a reservoir of nectar, all vegetation is a reservoir of nectar, the divine atmosphere is a reservoir of nectar, and also above. May all perceptions shine forth with the sweet taste of nectar for us.

ॐ अग्निर्देवता वातो देवता सूर्यो देवता चन्द्रमा देवता
वसवो देवता रुद्रो देवता ऽदित्या देवता मरुतो देवता विश्वे
देवा देवता बृहस्पतिर्देवतेन्द्रो देवता वरुणो देवता ॥

oṁ agnirdevatā vāto devatā sūryo devatā candramā devatā vasavo devatā rudro devatā-dityā devatā maruto devatā viśve devā devatā bṛhaspatirdevatendro devatā varuṇo devatā

Oṁ The Divine Fire (Light of Purity) is the shining God, the Wind is the shining God, the Sun (Light of Wisdom) is the shining God, the Moon (Lord of Devotion) is the shining God, the Protectors of the Wealth are the shining Gods, the Relievers of Sufferings are the shining Gods, the Sons of the Light are the shining Gods; the Emancipated seers (Maruts) are the shining Gods, the Universal Shining Gods are the shining Gods, the Guru of the Gods is the shining God, the Ruler of the Gods is the shining God, the Lord of Waters is the shining God.

(With folded hands)

ॐ भूर्भुवः स्वः ।
तत् सवितुर्वरेण्यम् भर्गो देवस्य धीमहि ।
धियो यो नः प्रचोदयात् ॥

oṁ bhūr bhuvaḥ svaḥ
tat savitur vareṇyam bhargo devasya dhīmahi
dhiyo yo naḥ pracodayāt

Oṁ the Infinite Beyond Conception, the gross body, the subtle body and the causal body; we meditate upon that Light of Wisdom which is the Supreme Wealth of the Gods. May it grant to us increase in our meditations.

ॐ भूः

oṁ bhūḥ

Oṁ the gross body

ॐ भुवः

oṁ bhuvaḥ

Oṁ the subtle body

ॐ स्वः

oṁ svaḥ

Oṁ the causal body

ॐ महः

oṁ mahaḥ

Oṁ the great body of existence

ॐ जनः

oṁ janaḥ

Oṁ the body of knowledge

ॐ तपः

oṁ tapaḥ

Oṁ the body of light

ॐ सत्यं

oṁ satyaṁ

Oṁ the body of Truth

ॐ तत् सवितुर्वरेण्यम् भर्गो देवस्य धीमहि ।
धियो यो नः प्रचोदयात् ॥

oṁ tat savitur vareṇyam bhargo devasya dhīmahi
dhiyo yo naḥ pracodayāt

Oṁ we meditate upon that Light of Wisdom which is the Supreme Wealth of the Gods. May it grant to us increase in our meditations.

ॐ आपो ज्योतीरसोमृतं ब्रह्म भूर्भुवस्स्वरोम् ॥

oṁ āpo jyotīrasomṛtaṁ brahma bhūrbhuvassvarom

May the divine waters luminous with the nectar of immortality of Supreme Divinity fill the earth, the atmosphere and the heavens.

(Touch rosary)

ॐ मां माले महामाये सर्वशक्तिस्वरूपिणि ।
चतुर्वर्गस्त्वयि न्यस्तस्तस्मान्मे सिद्धिदा भव ॥

oṁ māṁ māle mahāmāye sarvaśaktisvarūpiṇi
catur vargas tvayi nyastas tasmān me siddhidā bhava

Oṁ My Rosary, The Great Measurement of Consciousness, containing all energy within as your intrinsic nature, give to me the attainment of your Perfection, fulfilling the four objectives of life.

ॐ अविघ्नं कुरु माले त्वं गृह्णामि दक्षिणे करे ।
जपकाले च सिद्ध्यर्थं प्रसीद मम सिद्धये ॥

oṁ avighnaṁ kuru māle tvaṁ gṛhṇāmi dakṣiṇe kare
japakāle ca siddhyarthaṁ prasīda mama siddhaye

Oṁ Rosary, You please remove all obstacles. I hold you in my right hand. At the time of recitation be pleased with me. Allow me to attain the Highest Perfection.

ॐ अक्षमालाधिपतये सुसिद्धिं देहि देहि सर्वमन्त्रार्थसाधिनि
साधय साधय सर्वसिद्धिं परिकल्पय परिकल्पय मे स्वाहा ॥

oṁ akṣa mālā dhipataye susiddhiṁ dehi dehi sarva mantrārtha sādhini sādhaya sādhaya sarva siddhiṁ parikal-paya parikalpaya me svāhā

Oṁ Rosary of rudrākṣa seeds, my Lord, give to me excellent attainment. Give to me, give to me. Illuminate the meanings of all mantras, illuminate, illuminate! Fashion me with all excellent attainments, fashion me! I am One with God!

(Offer flowers)

एते गन्धपुष्पे ॐ गं गणपतये नमः

ete gandhapuṣpe oṁ gaṁ gaṇapataye namaḥ

With these scented flowers Oṁ we bow to the Lord of Wisdom, Lord of the Multitudes.

एते गन्धपुष्पे ॐ आदित्यादिनवग्रहेभ्यो नमः

ete gandhapuṣpe oṁ ādityādi navagrahebhyo namaḥ

With these scented flowers Oṁ we bow to the Sun, the Light of Wisdom, along with the nine planets.

एते गन्धपुष्पे ॐ शिवादिपञ्चदेवताभ्यो नमः

ete gandhapuṣpe oṁ śivādipañcadevatābhyo namaḥ

With these scented flowers Oṁ we bow to Śiva, the Consciousness of Infinite Goodness, along with the five primary deities (Śiva, Śakti, Viṣṇu, Gaṇeśa, Sūrya).

एते गन्धपुष्पे ॐ इन्द्रादिदशदिक्पालेभ्यो नमः

ete gandhapuṣpe oṁ indrādi daśadikpālebhyo namaḥ

With these scented flowers Oṁ we bow to Indra, the Ruler of the Pure, along with the Ten Protectors of the ten directions.

एते गन्धपुष्पे ॐ मत्स्यादिदशावतारेभ्यो नमः

ete gandhapuṣpe oṁ matsyādi daśāvatārebhyo namaḥ

With these scented flowers Oṁ we bow to Viṣṇu, the Fish, along with the Ten Incarnations which He assumed.

एते गन्धपुष्पे ॐ प्रजापतये नमः

ete gandhapuṣpe oṁ prajāpataye namaḥ

With these scented flowers Oṁ we bow to the Lord of All Created Beings.

एते गन्धपुष्पे ॐ नमो नारायणाय नमः

ete gandhapuṣpe oṁ namo nārāyaṇāya namaḥ

With these scented flowers Oṁ we bow to the Perfect Perception of Consciousness.

एते गन्धपुष्पे ॐ सर्वेभ्यो देवेभ्यो नमः

ete gandhapuṣpe oṁ sarvebhyo devebhyo namaḥ

With these scented flowers Oṁ we bow to All the Gods.

एते गन्धपुष्पे ॐ सर्वाभ्यो देवीभ्यो नमः

ete gandhapuṣpe oṁ sarvābhyo devībhyo namaḥ

With these scented flowers Oṁ we bow to All the Goddesses.

एते गन्धपुष्पे ॐ श्री गुरवे नमः

ete gandhapuṣpe oṁ śrī gurave namaḥ

With these scented flowers Oṁ we bow to the Guru.

एते गन्धपुष्पे ॐ ब्राह्मणेभ्यो नमः

ete gandhapuṣpe oṁ brāhmaṇebhyo namaḥ

With these scented flowers Oṁ we bow to All Knowers of Wisdom.

(Tie a piece of string around right middle finger or wrist)

ॐ कुशासने स्थितो ब्रह्मा कुशे चैव जनार्दनः ।
कुशे ह्याकाशवद् विष्णुः कुशासन नमोऽस्तु ते ॥

oṁ kuśāsane sthito brahmā kuśe caiva janārdanaḥ
kuśe hyākāśavad viṣṇuḥ kuśāsana namo-stu te

Brahmā is in the shining light (or kuśa grass), in the shining light resides Janārdana, the Lord of Beings. The Supreme all-pervading Consciousness, Viṣṇu, resides in the shining light. Oh Repository of the shining light, we bow down to you, the seat of kuśa grass.

ācamana

(sip water with each mantra)

ॐ केशवाय नमः स्वाहा

oṁ keśavāya namaḥ svāhā

We bow to the one of beautiful hair.

ॐ माधवाय नमः स्वाहा

oṁ mādhavāya namaḥ svāhā

We bow to the one who is always sweet.

ॐ गोविन्दाय नमः स्वाहा

oṁ govindāya namaḥ svāhā

We bow to He who is one-pointed light.

(sip water with each mantra and wash hands)

ॐ विष्णुः ॐ विष्णुः ॐ विष्णुः

oṁ viṣṇuḥ oṁ viṣṇuḥ oṁ viṣṇuḥ

Oṁ Consciousness, Oṁ Consciousness, Oṁ Consciousness.

ॐ तत् विष्णोः परमं पदम् सदा पश्यन्ति सूरयः ।
दिवीव चक्षुराततम् ॥

oṁ tat viṣṇoḥ paramaṁ padam sadā paśyanti sūrayaḥ
divīva cakṣurā tatam

Oṁ That Consciousness of the highest station, who always sees the Light of Wisdom, give us Divine Eyes.

ॐ तद् विप्र स पिपानोव जुविग्रन्सो सोमिन्द्रते ।
विष्णुः तत् परमं पदम् ॥

oṁ tad vipra sa pipānova juvigranso somindrate viṣṇuḥ tat paramaṁ padam

Oṁ That twice-born teacher who is always thirsty for accepting the nectar of devotion, Oh Consciousness, you are in that highest station.

ॐ अपवित्रः पवित्रो वा सर्वावस्थां गतोऽपि वा ।
यः स्मरेत् पुण्डरीकाक्षं स बाह्याभ्यन्तरः शुचिः ॥

oṁ apavitraḥ pavitro vā sarvāvasthāṁ gato-pi vā yaḥ smaret puṇḍarīkākṣaṁ sa bāhyābhyantaraḥ śuciḥ

Oṁ The Impure and the Pure reside within all objects. Who remembers the lotus-eyed Consciousness is conveyed to radiant beauty.

ॐ सर्वमङ्गलमाङ्गल्यम् वरेण्यम् वरदं शुभं ।
नारायणं नमस्कृत्य सर्वकर्माणि कारयेत् ॥

oṁ sarva maṅgala māṅgalyam vareṇyam varadaṁ śubhaṁ nārāyaṇaṁ namaskṛtya sarvakarmāṇi kārayet

All the Welfare of all Welfare, the highest blessing of Purity and Illumination, with the offering of respect we bow down to the Supreme Consciousness who is the actual performer of all action.

ॐ सूर्य्यश्चमेति मन्त्रस्य ब्रह्मा ऋषिः प्रकृतिश्छन्दः आपो देवता आचमने विनियोगः ॥

oṁ sūryyaścameti mantrasya brahmā ṛṣiḥ prakṛtiśchandaḥ āpo devatā ācamane viniyogaḥ

Oṁ these are the mantras of the Light of Wisdom, the Creative Capacity is the Seer, Nature is the meter, the divine flow of waters is the deity, being applied in washing the hands and rinsing the mouth.

(Draw the following yantra with some drops of water
and/or sandal paste at the front of your seat.
Place a flower on the bindu in the middle.)

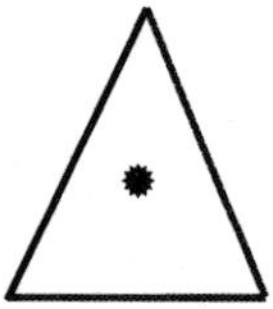

ॐ आसनस्य मन्त्रस्य मेरुपृष्ठ ऋषिः सुतलं छन्दः कूर्म्मो देवता आसनोपवेशने विनियोगः ॐ ॥

oṁ āsanasya mantrasya merupṛṣṭha ṛṣiḥ sutalaṁ chandaḥ kūrmmo devatā āsanopaveśane viniyogaḥ oṁ

Introducing the mantras of the Purification of the seat. The Seer is He whose back is Straight, the meter is of very beautiful form, the tortoise who supports the earth is the deity. These mantras are applied to make the seat free from obstructions.

एते गन्धपुष्पे ॐ ह्रीं आधारशक्तये कमलासनाय नमः ॥

ete gandhapuṣpe oṁ hrīṁ ādhāraśaktaye kamalāsanāya namaḥ

With these scented flowers Oṁ hrīṁ we bow to the Primal Energy situated in this lotus seat.

(Touch seat)

ॐ पृथ्वि त्वया धृता लोका देवि त्वं विष्णुना धृता ।
त्वञ्च धारय मां नित्यं पवित्रं कुरु चासनम् ॥

oṁ pṛthvi tvayā dhṛtā lokā devi tvaṁ viṣṇunā dhṛtā
tvañca dhāraya māṁ nityaṁ pavitraṁ kuru cāsanam

Oṁ Earth! You support the realms of the Goddess. You are supported by the Supreme Consciousness. Also bear me eternally and make pure this seat.

ॐ गुरुभ्यो नमः

oṁ gurubhyo namaḥ

Oṁ I bow to the Guru.

ॐ परमगुरुभ्यो नमः

oṁ paramagurubhyo

Oṁ I bow to the Guru's Guru.

ॐ परापरगुरुभ्यो नमः

oṁ parāparagurubhyo namaḥ

Oṁ I bow to the Gurus of the lineage.

ॐ परमेष्ठिगुरुभ्यो नमः

oṁ parameṣṭhigurubhyo namaḥ

Oṁ I bow to the Supreme Gurus.

ॐ गं गणेशाय नमः

oṁ gaṁ gaṇeśāya namaḥ

Oṁ I bow to the Lord of Wisdom.

ॐ अनन्ताय नमः

oṁ anantāya namaḥ

Oṁ I bow to the Infinite One.

ॐ ह्रीं श्रीं क्रीं परमेश्वरि कालिके स्वाहा

oṁ hrīṁ śrīṁ krīṁ parameśvāri kālike svāhā

Oṁ Māyā, Increase, Dissolution, to the Supreme Female Divinity, Kālī, I am One with God!

ॐ नमः शिवाय

oṁ namaḥ śivāya

Oṁ I bow to the Consciousness of Infinite Goodness.

Clap hands 3 times and snap fingers in the ten directions (N S E W NE SW NW SE UP DOWN) repeating

ॐ ह्रीं श्रीं क्रीं परमेश्वरि कालिके स्वाहा

oṁ hrīṁ śrīṁ krīṁ parameśvāri kālike svāhā

Oṁ Māyā, Increase, Dissolution, to the Supreme Female Divinity, Kālī, I am One with God!

saṅkalpa

(Place flower in left palm, cover with right)

विष्णुः ॐ तत् सत् । ॐ अद्य जम्बूद्वीपे (   ) देशे

(   ) प्रदेशे (   ) नगरे (   ) मन्दिरे (   ) मासे (   ) पक्षे

(   ) तिथौ (   ) गोत्र श्री (   ) कृतैतत् श्रीकालीकामः

पूजाकर्माहं श्रीकालीपूजां करिष्ये ॥

viṣṇuḥ oṁ tat sat oṁ adya jambūdvīpe (Country) deśe (State) pradeśe (City) nagare (Name of house or temple) mandire (month) māse (śukla or kṛṣṇa) pakṣe (name of day) tithau (name of) gotra śrī (your name) kṛtaitat śrī kālī kāmaḥ pūjā karmāhaṁ śrī kālī pūjāṁ kariṣye

The Consciousness Which Pervades All, Oṁ That is Truth. Presently, on the Planet Earth, Country of (Name), State of (Name), City of (Name), in the Temple of (Name), (Name of Month) Month, (Bright or Dark) fort-night, (Name of Day) Day, (Name of Sādhu Family), Śrī (Your Name) is performing the worship for the satisfaction of the Respected Kālī by reciting the Kālī Worship.

ॐ यज्जाग्रतो दूरमुदेति दैवं तदु सुप्तस्य तथैवैति ।

दूरङ्गमं ज्योतिषां ज्योतिरेकं तन्मे मनः शिवसङ्कल्पमस्तु ॥

oṁ yajjāgrato dūramudeti daivaṁ tadu suptasya tathaivaiti dūraṅgamaṁ jyotiṣāṁ jyotirekaṁ tanme manaḥ śiva-saṅkalpamastu

May our waking consciousness replace pain and suffering with divinity as also our awareness when asleep. Far extending be our radiant aura of light, filling our minds with light. May that be the firm determination of the Consciousness of Infinite Goodness.

या गुङ्गूर्या सिनीवाली या राका या सरस्वती ।
ईन्द्राणीमह्व ऊतये वरुणानीं स्वस्तये ॥

yā guṅgūryā sinīvālī yā rākā yā sarasvatī
īndrāṇīmahva ūtaye varuṇānīṁ svastaye

May that Goddess who wears the Moon of Devotion protect the children of Devotion. May that Goddess of All-Pervading Knowledge protect us. May the Energy of the Rule of the Pure rise up. Oh Energy of Equilibrium grant us the highest prosperity.

ॐ स्वस्ति न इन्द्रो वृद्धश्रवाः स्वस्ति नः पूषा विश्ववेदाः ।
स्वस्ति नस्ताक्ष्र्यो अरिष्टनेमिः स्वस्ति नो बृहस्पतिर्दधातु ॥

oṁ svasti na indro vṛddhaśravāḥ svasti naḥ pūṣā viśvavedāḥ
svasti nastārkṣyo ariṣṭanemiḥ svasti no bṛhaspatirdadhātu

The Ultimate Prosperity to us, Oh Rule of the Pure, who perceives all that changes; the Ultimate Prosperity to us, Searchers for Truth, Knowers of the Universe; the Ultimate Prosperity to us, Oh Divine Being of Light, keep us safe; the Ultimate Prosperity to us, Oh Spirit of All-Pervading Delight, grant that to us.

ॐ गणानां त्वा गणपति꣡ँ हवामहे
प्रियाणां त्वा प्रियपति꣡ँ हवामहे
निधीनां त्वा निधिपति꣡ँ हवामहे वसो मम ।
आहमजानि गर्भधमा त्वमजासि गर्भधम् ॥

oṁ gaṇānāṁ tvā gaṇapati guṁ havāmahe
priyāṇāṁ tvā priyapati guṁ havāmahe
nidhīnāṁ tvā nidhipati guṁ havāmahe vaso mama
āhamajāni garbbhadhamā tvamajāsi garbbhadham

We invoke you with offerings, Oh Lord of the Multitudes; we invoke you with offerings, Oh Lord of Love; we invoke you with offerings, Oh

Guardian of the Treasure. Sit within me, giving birth to the realm of the Gods within me; yes, giving birth to the realm of the Gods within me.

ॐ गणानां त्वा गणपति॰ हवामहे
कविं कवीनामुपमश्रवस्तमम् ।
ज्येष्ठराजं ब्रह्मणां ब्रह्मणस्पत
आ नः शृण्वन्नूतिभिः सीद सादनम् ॥

oṁ gaṇānāṁ tvā gaṇapati guṁ havāmahe
kaviṁ kavīnāmupamaśravastamam
jyeṣṭharājaṁ brahmaṇāṁ brahmaṇaspata
ā naḥ śṛṇvannūtibhiḥ sīda sādanam

We invoke you with offerings, Oh Lord of the Multitudes, Seer among Seers, of unspeakable grandeur. Oh Glorious King, Lord of the Knowers of Wisdom, come speedily hearing our supplications and graciously take your seat amidst our assembly.

ॐ अदितिर्द्यौरदितिरन्तरिक्षमदितिर्माता स पिता स पुत्रः ।
विश्वे देवा अदितिः पञ्च जना अदितिर्जातमदितिर्जनित्वम् ॥

oṁ aditir dyauraditirantarikṣamaditirmātā sa pitā sa putraḥ
viśve devā aditiḥ pañca janā aditirjātamaditirjanitvam

The Mother of Enlightenment pervades the heavens; the Mother of Enlightenment pervades the atmosphere; the Mother of Enlightenment pervades Mother and Father and child. All Gods of the Universe are pervaded by the Mother, the five forms of living beings, all Life. The Mother of Enlightenment, She is to be known.

ॐ त्वं स्त्रीस्त्वं पुमानसि त्वं कुमार अत वा कुमारी ।
त्वं जिर्नो दण्डेन वञ्चसि त्वं जातो भवसि विश्वतोमुखः ॥

oṁ tvaṁ strīstvaṁ pumānasi tvaṁ kumāra ata vā kumarī tvaṁ jirno daṇḍena vañcasi tvaṁ jāto bhavasi viśvatomukhaḥ

You are Female, you are Male; you are a young boy, you are a young girl. You are the word of praise by which we are singing; you are all creation existing as the mouth of the universe.

ॐ अम्बेऽम्बिकेऽम्बालिके न मा नयति कश्चन ।
ससस्त्यश्वकः सुभद्रिकां काम्पीलवासिनीम् ॥

oṁ ambe-ambike-mbālike na mā nayati kaścana sasastyaśvakaḥ subhadrikāṁ kāmpīlavāsinīm

Mother of the Perceivable Universe, Mother of the Conceivable Universe, Mother of the Universe of Intuitive Vision, lead me to that True Existence. As excellent crops (or grains) are harvested, so may I be taken to reside with the Infinite Consciousness.

ॐ शान्ता द्यौः शान्तापृथिवी शान्तमिदमुर्वन्तरिक्षम् ।
शान्ता उदन्वतिरापः शान्ताः नः शान्त्वोषधीः ॥

oṁ śāntā dyauḥ śāntā pṛthivī śāntam idamurvantarikṣam śāntā udanvatirāpaḥ śāntāḥ naḥ śāntvoṣadhīḥ

Peace in the heavens, Peace on the earth, Peace upwards and permeating the atmosphere; Peace upwards, over, on all sides and further; Peace to us, Peace to all vegetation;

ॐ शान्तानि पूर्वरूपाणि शान्तं नोऽस्तु कृताकृतम् ।
शान्तं भूतं च भव्यं च सर्वमेव शमस्तु नः ॥

oṁ śāntāni pūrva rūpāṇi śāntaṁ no-stu kṛtākṛtam śāntaṁ bhūtaṁ ca bhavyaṁ ca sarvameva śamastu naḥ

Peace to all that has form, Peace to all causes and effects; Peace to all existence, and to all intensities of reality including all and everything; Peace be to us.

ॐ पृथिवी शान्तिरन्तरिक्षं शान्तिर्द्यौः
शान्तिरापः शान्तिरोषधयः शान्तिः वनस्पतयः शान्तिर्विश्वे मे
देवाः शान्तिः सर्वे मे देवाः शान्तिर्ब्रह्म शान्तिरापः शान्तिः
सर्वं शान्तिरेधि शान्तिः शान्तिः सर्व शान्तिः सा मा शान्तिः
शान्तिभिः ॥

**oṁ pṛthivī śāntir antarikṣaṁ śāntir dyauḥ
śāntir āpaḥ śāntir oṣadhayaḥ śāntiḥ vanaspatayaḥ śāntir
viśve me devāḥ śāntiḥ sarve me devāḥ śāntir brahma
śāntirāpaḥ śāntiḥ sarvaṁ śāntiredhi śāntiḥ śāntiḥ sarva
śāntiḥ sā mā śāntiḥ śāntibhiḥ**

Let the earth be at Peace, the atmosphere be at Peace, the heavens be filled with Peace. Even further may Peace extend, Peace be to waters, Peace to all vegetation, Peace to All Gods of the Universe, Peace to All Gods within us, Peace to Creative Consciousness, Peace be to Brilliant Light, Peace to All, Peace to Everything, Peace, Peace, altogether Peace, equally Peace, by means of Peace.

ताभिः शान्तिभिः सर्वशान्तिभिः समया मोहं यदिह घोरं
यदिह क्रूरं यदिह पापं तच्छान्तं तच्छिवं सर्वमेव समस्तु
नः ॥

**tābhiḥ śāntibhiḥ sarva śāntibhiḥ samayā mohaṁ yadiha
ghoraṁ yadiha krūraṁ yadiha pāpaṁ tacchāntaṁ
tacchivaṁ sarvameva samastu naḥ**

Thus by means of Peace, altogether one with the means of Peace, Ignorance is eliminated, Violence is eradicated, Improper Conduct is eradicated, Confusion (sin) is eradicated, all that is, is at Peace, all that is perceived, each and everything, altogether for us,

ॐ शान्तिः शान्तिः शान्तिः ॥

oṁ śāntiḥ śāntiḥ śāntiḥ

Oṁ Peace, Peace, Peace

ॐ ह्रीं श्रीं क्रीं परमेश्वरि कालिके स्वाहा

oṁ hrīṁ śrīṁ krīṁ parameśvāri kālike svāhā

Oṁ Māyā, Increase, Dissolution, to the Supreme Female Divinity, Kālī, I am One with God!

Oṁ	The Infinite Beyond Conception
Hrīṁ	The Stuff of Consciousness, the substance of awareness, Māyā
Śrīṁ	Increase, also perfect peace in the heart and mind
Krīṁ	Dissolving into Perfection
Parameśvari	Supreme Divinity (female)
Kālike	She who Takes away Darkness
Svāhā	I am One with God!

ॐ कालि कालि महाकालि कालिके पापहारिणी ।

धर्मार्थमोक्षदे देवि नारायणि नमोऽस्तुते ॥

oṁ kāli kāli mahākāli kālike pāpahāriṇī

dharmarthamokṣade devi nārāyaṇi namo-stute

Oṁ Goddess Who Takes Away Darkness, Goddess Who Takes Away Darkness, Great Goddess Who Takes Away Darkness, beloved Goddess Who Takes Away Darkness, Who Takes Away All Sin, Give the way of peace and harmony, the necessities for physical sustenance, and liberation, otherwise known as self-realization, Oh Goddess, Exposer of Consciousness, we bow to you.

gaṇeśa pūjā

worship of gaṇeśa

gaṇeśa gāyatrī

ॐ तत् पुरुषाय विद्महे वक्रतुण्डाय धीमहि ।

तन्नो दन्ती प्रचोदयात् ॥

oṁ tat puruṣāya vidmahe vakratuṇḍāya dhīmahi
tanno dantī pracodayāt

Oṁ we meditate upon that Perfect Consciousness, contemplate the One with a broken tooth. May that One with the Great Tusk grant us increase.

एते गन्धपुष्पे ॐ गं गणपतये नमः

ete gandhapuṣpe oṁ gaṁ gaṇapataye namaḥ

With these scented flowers Oṁ we bow to the Lord of Wisdom, Lord of the Multitudes.

ॐ सुमुखश्चैकदन्तश्च कपिलो गजकर्णकः ।

लम्बोदरश्च विकटो विघ्ननाशो विनायकः ॥

oṁ sumukhaścaika dantaśca kapilo gaja karṇakaḥ
lambodaraśca vikaṭo vighnanāśo vināyakaḥ

He has a beautiful face with only one tooth (or tusk), of red color with elephant ears; with a big belly and a great tooth he destroys all obstacles. He is the Remover of Obstacles.

धूम्रकेतुर्गणाध्यक्षो भालचन्द्रो गजाननः ।

द्वादशैतानि नामानि यः पठेच्छृणुयादपि ॥

dhūmraketurgaṇādhyakṣo bhāla candro gajānanaḥ
dvādaśaitāni nāmāni yaḥ paṭhecchṛṇu yādapi

With a grey banner, the living spirit of the multitudes, having the moon on his forehead, with an elephant's face; whoever will recite or listen to these twelve names

विद्यारम्भे विवाहे च प्रवेशे निर्गमे तथा ।
संग्रामे संकटे चैव विघ्नस्तस्य न जायते ॥

vidyārambhe vivāhe ca praveśe nirgame tathā
saṁgrāme saṁkate caiva vighnastasya na jāyate

at the time of commencing studies, getting married, or upon entering or leaving any place; on a battlefield of war, or in any difficulty, will overcome all obstacles.

शुक्लाम्बरधरं देवं शशिवर्णं चतुर्भुजम् ।
प्रसन्नवदनं ध्यायेत् सर्वविघ्नोपशान्तये ॥

śuklāmbaradharaṁ devaṁ śaśivarṇaṁ caturbhujam
prasannavadanaṁ dhyāyet sarvavighnopaśāntaye

Wearing a white cloth, the God has the color of the moon and four arms. That most pleasing countenance is meditated upon, who gives peace to all difficulties.

अभीप्सितार्थसिद्ध्यर्थं पूजितो यः सुरासुरैः ।
सर्वविघ्नहरस् तस्मै गणाधिपतये नमः ॥

abhīpsitārtha siddhyarthaṁ pūjito yaḥ surā suraiḥ
sarvavighna haras tasmai gaṇādhipataye namaḥ

For gaining the desired objective, or for the attainment of perfection, he is worshiped by the Forces of Union and the Forces of Division alike. He takes away all difficulties, and therefore, we bow down in reverence to the Lord of the Multitudes.

मल्लिकादि सुगन्धीनि मालित्यादीनि वै प्रभो ।
मयाऽहृतानि पूजार्थं पुष्पाणि प्रतिगृह्यताम् ॥

mallikādi sugandhīni mālityādīni vai prabho
mayā-hṛtāni pūjārthaṁ puṣpāṇi pratigṛhyatām

Various flowers such as mallikā and others of excellent scent, are being offered to you, Our Lord. All these flowers have come from the devotion of our hearts for your worship. Be pleased to accept them.

एते गन्धपुष्पे ॐ गं गणपतये नमः

ete gandhapuṣpe oṁ gaṁ gaṇapataye namaḥ

With these scented flowers Oṁ we bow to the Lord of Wisdom, Lord of the Multitudes.

वक्रतुण्ड महाकाय सूर्यकोटिसमप्रभ ।
अविघ्नं कुरु मे देव सर्वकार्येषु सर्वदा ॥

vakratuṇḍa mahākāya sūrya koṭi samaprabha
avighnaṁ kuru me deva sarva kāryeṣu sarvadā

With a broken (or bent) tusk, a great body shining like a million suns, make us free from all obstacles, Oh God. Always remain (with us) in all actions.

एकदन्तं महाकायं लम्बोदरं गजाननम् ।
विघ्ननाशकरं देवं हेरम्बं प्रणमाम्यहम् ॥

ekadantaṁ mahākāyaṁ lambodaraṁ gajānanam
vighnanāśakaraṁ devaṁ herambaṁ praṇamāmyaham

With one tooth, a great body, a big belly and an elephant's face, he is the God who destroys all obstacles to whom we are bowing down with devotion.

puṇyā havācana, svasti vācana

proclamation of merits and eternal blessings

ॐ शान्तिरस्तु

oṁ śāntirastu

Oṁ Peace be unto you.

ॐ पुष्टिरस्तु

oṁ puṣṭirastu

Oṁ Increase or Nourishment be unto you.

ॐ तुष्टिरस्तु

oṁ tuṣṭirastu

Oṁ Satisfaction be unto you.

ॐ वृद्धिरस्तु

oṁ vṛddhirastu

Oṁ Positive Change be unto you.

ॐ अविघ्नमस्तु

oṁ avighnamastu

Oṁ Freedom from Obstacles be unto you.

ॐ आयुष्यमस्तु

oṁ āyuṣyamastu

Oṁ Life be unto you.

ॐ आरोग्यमस्तु

oṁ ārogyamastu

Oṁ Freedom from Disease be unto you.

ॐ शिवमस्तु

oṁ śivamastu

Oṁ Consciousness of Infinite Goodness be unto you.

ॐ शिवकर्माऽस्तु

oṁ śivakarmā-stu

Oṁ Consciousness of Infinite Goodness in all action be unto you.

ॐ कर्मसमृद्धिरस्तु

oṁ karmasamṛddhirastu

Oṁ Progress or Increase in all action be unto you.

ॐ धर्मसमृद्धिरस्तु

oṁ dharmasamṛddhirastu

Oṁ Progress and Increase in all Ways of Truth be unto you.

ॐ वेदसमृद्धिरस्तु

oṁ vedasamṛddhirastu

Oṁ Progress or Increase in all Knowledge be unto you.

ॐ शास्त्रसमृद्धिरस्तु

oṁ śāstrasamṛddhirastu

Oṁ Progress or Increase in Scriptures be unto you.

ॐ धन-धान्यसमृद्धिरस्तु

oṁ dhana-dhānyasamṛddhirastu

Oṁ Progress or Increase in Wealth and Grains be unto you.

ॐ इष्टसम्पदस्तु

oṁ iṣṭasampadastu

Oṁ May your beloved deity be your wealth.

ॐ अरिष्टनिरसनमस्तु

oṁ ariṣṭanirasanamastu

Oṁ May you remain safe and secure, without any fear.

ॐ यत्पापं रोगमशुभमकल्याणं तद्दूरे प्रतिहतमस्तु

oṁ yatpāpaṁ rogamaśubhamakalyāṇaṁ taddūre pratihatamastu

Oṁ May sin, sickness, impurity, and that which is not conducive unto welfare, leave from you.

ॐ ब्रह्म पुण्यमहर्यच्च सृष्ट्युत्पादनकारकम् ।
वेदवृक्षोद्भवं नित्यं तत्पुण्याहं ब्रुवन्तु नः ॥

oṁ brahma puṇyamaharyacca sṛṣṭyutpādanakārakam
vedavṛkṣodbhavaṁ nityaṁ tatpuṇyāhaṁ bruvantu naḥ

The Creative Capacity with the greatest merit, the Cause of the Birth of Creation, eternally has its being in the tree of Wisdom. May His blessing of merit be bestowed upon us.

भो ब्राह्मणाः ! मया क्रियमाणस्य कालीपूजनाख्यस्य कर्मणः पुण्याहं भवन्तो ब्रुवन्तु ॥

bho brāhmaṇāḥ ! mayā kriyamāṇasya kālīpūjanākhyasya karmaṇaḥ puṇyāhaṁ bhavanto bruvantu

Oh Brahmiṇs! My sincere effort is to perform the worship of Kālī. Let these activities yield merit.

ॐ पुण्याहं ॐ पुण्याहं ॐ पुण्याहं ॥

oṁ puṇyāhaṁ oṁ puṇyāhaṁ oṁ puṇyāhaṁ

Oṁ Let these activities yield merit.

ॐ अस्य कर्मणः पुण्याहं भवन्तो ब्रुवन्तु ॥

oṁ asya karmaṇaḥ puṇyāhaṁ bhavanto bruvantu

Oṁ Let these activities yield merit.

ॐ पुण्याहं ॐ पुण्याहं ॐ पुण्याहं ॥

oṁ puṇyāhaṁ oṁ puṇyāhaṁ oṁ puṇyāhaṁ

Oṁ Let these activities yield merit (3 times).

पृथिव्यामुद्धृतायां तु यत्कल्याणं पुरा कृतम् ।
ऋषिभिः सिद्धगन्धर्वैस्तत्कल्याणं ब्रुवन्तु नः ॥

pṛthivyāmuddhṛtāyāṁ tu yatkalyāṇaṁ purā kṛtam
ṛṣibhiḥ siddha gandharvaistatkalyāṇaṁ bruvantu naḥ

With the solidity of the earth, let supreme welfare be. May the Ṛṣis, the attained ones and the celestial singers bestow welfare upon us.

भो ब्राह्मणाः ! मया क्रियमाणस्य कालीपूजनाख्यस्य कर्मणः
कल्याणं भवन्तो ब्रुवन्तु ॥

bho brāhmaṇāḥ ! mayā kriyamāṇasya kālīpūjanākhyasya karmaṇaḥ kalyāṇaṁ bhavanto bruvantu

Oh Brahmiṇs! My sincere effort is to perform the worship of Kālī. Let these activities bestow welfare.

ॐ कल्याणं ॐ कल्याणं ॐ कल्याणं

oṁ kalyāṇaṁ oṁ kalyāṇaṁ oṁ kalyāṇaṁ

Oṁ Let these activities bestow welfare (3 times).

सागरस्य तु या ऋद्धिर्महालक्ष्म्यादिभिः कृता ।
सम्पूर्णा सुप्रभावा च तामृद्धिं प्रब्रुवन्तु नः ॥

sāgarasya tu yā ṛddhirmahālakṣmyādibhiḥ kṛtā
sampūrṇā suprabhāvā ca tāmṛddhiṁ prabruvantu naḥ

May the ocean yield Prosperity, as it did when the Great Goddess of True Wealth and others were produced; fully and completely giving forth excellent luster, may Prosperity be unto us.

भो ब्राह्मणाः ! मया क्रियमाणस्य कालीपूजनाख्यस्य कर्मणः
ऋद्धिं भवन्तो ब्रुवन्तु ॥

bho brāhmaṇāḥ ! mayā kriyamāṇasya kālīpūjanākhyasya karmaṇaḥ ṛddhiṁ bhavanto bruvantu

Oh Brahmiṇs! My sincere effort is to perform the worship of Kālī. Let these activities bestow Prosperity.

ॐ कर्म ऋध्यताम् ॐ कर्म ऋध्यताम् ॐ कर्म ऋध्यताम्

oṁ karma ṛdhyatām oṁ karma ṛdhyatām oṁ karma ṛdhyatām

Oṁ Let these activities bestow Prosperity (3 times).

स्वस्तिरस्तु याविनाशाख्या पुण्यकल्याणवृद्धिदा ।
विनायकप्रिया नित्यं तां च स्वस्तिं ब्रुवन्तु नः ॥

svastirastu yā vināśākhyā puṇya kalyāṇa vṛddhidā
vināyakapriyā nityaṁ tāṁ ca svastiṁ bruvantu naḥ

Let the Eternal Blessings which grant changes of indestructible merit and welfare be with us. May the Lord who removes all obstacles be pleased and grant to us Eternal Blessings.

भो ब्राह्मणाः ! मया क्रियमाणस्य कालीपूजनाख्यस्य कर्मणः
स्वस्तिं भवन्तो ब्रुवन्तु ॥

bho brāhmaṇāḥ ! mayā kriyamāṇasya kālīpūjanākhyasya karmaṇaḥ svastiṁ bhavanto bruvantu

Oh Brahmiṇs! My sincere effort is to perform the worship of Kālī. Let these activities bestow Eternal Blessings.

ॐ आयुष्मते स्वस्ति ॐ आयुष्मते स्वस्ति ॐ आयुष्मते स्वस्ति

oṁ āyuṣmate svasti oṁ āyuṣmate svasti oṁ āyuṣmate svasti

Oṁ May life be filled with Eternal Blessings (3 times).

ॐ स्वस्ति न इन्द्रो वृद्धश्रवाः स्वस्ति नः पूषा विश्ववेदाः ।
स्वस्ति नस्तार्क्ष्यो अरिष्टनेमिः स्वस्ति नो बृहस्पतिर्दधातु ॥

oṁ svasti na indro vṛddhaśravāḥ
svasti naḥ pūṣā viśvavedāḥ
svasti nastārkṣyo ariṣṭanemiḥ svasti no bṛhaspatirdadhātu

The Eternal Blessings to us, Oh Rule of the Pure, who perceives all that changes; the Eternal Blessings to us, Searchers for Truth, Knowers of the Universe; the Eternal Blessings to us, Oh Divine Being of Light, keep us safe; the Eternal Blessings to us, Oh Spirit of All-Pervading Delight, grant that to us.

समुद्रमथनाज्जाता जगदानन्दकारिका ।
हरिप्रिया च माङ्गल्या तां श्रियं च ब्रुवन्तु नः ॥

samudramathnājjātā jagadānandakārikā
haripriyā ca māṅgalyā tāṁ śriyaṁ ca bruvantu naḥ

Who was born from the churning of the ocean, the cause of bliss to the worlds, the beloved of Viṣṇu and Welfare Herself, may Śrī, the Highest Respect, be unto us.

भो ब्राह्मणाः ! मया क्रियमाणस्य कालीपूजनाख्यस्य कर्मणः
श्रीरस्त्विति भवन्तो ब्रुवन्तु ॥

bho brāhmaṇāḥ ! mayā kriyamāṇasya kālīpūjanākhyasya karmaṇaḥ śrīrastviti bhavanto bruvantu

Oh Brahmiṇs! My sincere effort is to perform the worship of Kālī. Let these activities bestow the Highest Respect.

ॐ अस्तु श्रीः ॐ अस्तु श्रीः ॐ अस्तु श्रीः

oṁ astu śrīḥ oṁ astu śrīḥ oṁ astu śrīḥ

Oṁ Let these activities bestow the Highest Respect (3 times).

ॐ श्रीश्च ते लक्ष्मीश्च पत्न्यावहोरात्रे पार्श्वे नक्षत्राणि रूपमश्विनौ व्यात्तम् । इष्णन्निषाणामुं म इषाण सर्वलोकं म इषाण ॥

oṁ śrīśca te lakṣmīśca patnyāvahorātre pārśve nakṣatrāṇi rūpamaśvinau vyāttam
iṣṇanniṣāṇāmuṁ ma iṣāṇa sarvalokaṁ ma iṣāṇa

Oṁ the Highest Respect to you, Goal of all Existence, wife of the full and complete night (the Unknowable One), at whose sides are the stars, and who has the form of the relentless search for Truth. Oh Supreme Divinity, Supreme Divinity, my Supreme Divinity, all existence is my Supreme Divinity.

मृकण्डसूनोरायुर्यद्ध्रुवलोमशयोस्तथा ।
आयुषा तेन संयुक्ता जीवेम शरदः शतम् ॥

mṛkaṇḍasūnorāyuryaddhruvalomaśayostathā
āyuṣā tena saṁyuktā jīvema śaradaḥ śatam

As the son of Mṛkaṇḍa, Mārkaṇḍeya, found imperishable life, may we be united with life and blessed with a hundred autumns.

शतं जीवन्तु भवन्तः

śataṁ jīvantu bhavantaḥ

May a hundred autumns be unto you.

शिवगौरीविवाहे या या श्रीरामे नृपात्मजे ।
धनदस्य गृहे या श्रीरस्माकं साऽस्तु सद्मनि ॥

śiva gaurī vivāhe yā yā śrīrāme nṛpātmaje
dhanadasya gṛhe yā śrīrasmākaṁ sā-stu sadmani

As the imperishable union of Śiva and Gaurī, as the soul of kings manifested in the respected Rāma, so may the Goddess of Respect forever be united with us and always dwell in our house.

ॐ अस्तु श्रीः ॐ अस्तु श्रीः ॐ अस्तु श्रीः

oṁ astu śrīḥ oṁ astu śrīḥ oṁ astu śrīḥ

May Respect be unto you.

प्रजापतिर्लोकपालो धाता ब्रह्मा च देवराट् ।
भगवाञ्छाश्वतो नित्यं नो वै रक्षन्तु सर्वतः ॥

prajāpatirlokapālo dhātā brahmā ca devarāṭ
bhagavāñchāśvato nityaṁ no vai rakṣantu sarvataḥ

The Lord of all beings, Protector of the worlds, Creator, Brahmā, Support of the Gods; may the Supreme Lord be gracious eternally and always protect us.

ॐ भगवान् प्रजापतिः प्रियताम्

oṁ bhagavān prajāpatiḥ priyatām

May the Supreme Lord, Lord of all beings, be pleased.

आयुष्मते स्वस्तिमते यजमानाय दाशुषे ।
श्रिये दत्ताशिषः सन्तु ऋत्विग्भिर्वेदपारगैः ॥

āyuṣmate svastimate yajamānāya dāśuṣe
śriye dattāśiṣaḥ santu ṛtvigbhirvedapāragaiḥ

May life and eternal blessings be unto those who perform this worship and to those who assist. May respect be given to the priests who impart this wisdom.

ॐ स्वस्तिवाचनसमृद्धिरस्तु

oṁ svastivācanasamṛddhirastu

Oṁ May this invocation for eternal blessings find excellent prosperity.

sāmānyārghya

purification of water

Draw the following yantra on the plate or space for worship with sandal paste and/or water. Offer rice on the yantra for each of the four mantras.

ॐ आधारशक्तये नमः

oṁ ādhāra śaktaye namaḥ

Oṁ we bow to the Primal Energy

ॐ कूर्माय नमः

oṁ kūrmmāya namaḥ

Oṁ we bow to the Support of the Earth

ॐ अनन्ताय नमः

oṁ anantāya namaḥ

Oṁ we bow to Infinity

ॐ पृथिव्यै नमः

oṁ pṛthivyai namaḥ

Oṁ we bow to the Earth

Place an empty water pot on the bindu in the center of the yantra when saying Phaṭ.

स्थां स्थीं स्थिरो भव फट्

sthāṁ sthīṁ sthiro bhava phaṭ

Be Still in the Gross Body! Be Still in the Subtle Body! Be Still in the Causal Body! Purify!

Fill the pot with water while chanting the mantra.

ॐ गङ्गे च जमुने चैव गोदावरि सरस्वति ।
नर्मदे सिन्धु कावेरि जलऽस्मिन् सन्निधिं कुरु ॥

oṁ gaṅge ca jamune caiva godāvari sarasvati
narmade sindhu kāveri jale-asmin sannidhiṁ kuru

Oṁ the Ganges, Jamunā, Godāvarī, Sarasvatī, Narmadā, Sindhu, Kāverī, these waters are mingled together.

The Ganges is the Iḍā, Jamunā is the Piṅgalā, the other five rivers are the five senses. The land of the seven rivers is within the body as well as outside.

Offer Tulasī leaves into water

ॐ ऐं ह्रीं क्लीं श्रीं वृन्दावनवासिन्यै स्वाहा

oṁ aiṁ hrīṁ klīṁ śrīṁ vṛndāvanavāsinyai svāhā

Oṁ Wisdom, Māyā, Increase, to She who resides in Vṛndāvana, I am One with God!

Offer 3 flowers into the water pot with the mantras

एते गन्धपुष्पे ॐ अं अर्कमण्डलाय द्वादशकलात्मने नमः

ete gandhapuṣpe oṁ aṁ arkamaṇḍalāya dvādaśakalātmane namaḥ

With these scented flowers Oṁ "A" we bow to the twelve aspects of the realm of the sun. Tapinī, Tāpinī, Dhūmrā, Marīci, Jvālinī, Ruci, Sudhūmrā, Bhoga-dā, Viśvā, Bodhinī, Dhārinī, Kṣamā; Containing heat, Emanating heat, Smoky, Ray-producing, Burning, Lustrous, Purple or Smoky-red, Granting enjoyment, Universal, Which makes known, Productive of Consciousness, Which supports, Which forgives.

एते गन्धपुष्पे ॐ उं सोममण्डलाय षोडशकलात्मने नमः

ete gandhapuṣpe oṁ uṁ somamaṇḍalāya ṣoḍaśakalātmane namaḥ

With these scented flowers Oṁ "U" we bow to the sixteen aspects of the realm of the moon. Amṛtā, Prāṇadā, Puṣā, Tuṣṭi, Puṣṭi, Rati, Dhṛti, Śaśinī, Candrikā, Kānti, Jyotsnā, Śrī, Prīti, Aṅgadā, Pūrṇā, Pūrṇāmṛtā; Nectar, Which sustains life, Which supports, Satisfying, Nourishing, Playful, Constancy, Unfailing, Producer of Joy, Beauty enhanced by love, Light, Grantor of Prosperity, Affectionate, Purifying the body, Complete, Full of Bliss.

एते गन्धपुष्पे ॐ मं वह्निमण्डलाय दशकलात्मने नमः

ete gandhapuṣpe oṁ maṁ vahnimaṇḍalāya daśakalātmane namaḥ

With these scented flowers Oṁ "M" we bow to the ten aspects of the realm of fire: Dhūmrā, Arciḥ, Jvalinī, Śūkṣmā, Jvālinī, Visphuliṅginī, Suśrī, Surūpā, Kapilā, Havya-Kavya-Vahā; Smoky Red, Flaming, Shining, Subtle, Burning, Sparkling, Beautiful, Well-formed, Tawny, The Messenger to Gods and Ancestors.

Wave hands in matsyā, dhenu and
aṅkuśa mudrās while chanting this mantra.

ॐ गङ्गे च जमुने चैव गोदावरि सरस्वति ।
नर्मदे सिन्धु कावेरि जलेऽस्मिन् सन्निधिं कुरु ॥

oṁ gaṅge ca jamune caiva godāvari sarasvati
narmade sindhu kāveri jale-asmin sannidhiṁ kuru

Oṁ the Ganges, Jamunā, Godāvarī, Sarasvatī, Narmadā, Sindhu, Kāverī, these waters are mingled together.

ॐ ह्रीं श्रीं क्रीं परमेश्वरि कालिके स्वाहा

oṁ hrīṁ śrīṁ krīṁ parameśvari kālike svāhā

Oṁ Māyā, Increase, Dissolution, to the Supreme Female Divinity, Kālī, I am One with God!

Sprinkle water over all articles to be offered, then throw some drops of water over your shoulders while repeating the mantra.

अमृताम् कुरु स्वाहा

amṛtām kuru svāhā

Make this immortal nectar! I am One with God!

puṣpa śuddhi

purification of flowers

Wave hands over flowers with prārthanā mudrā while chanting first line and with dhenu mudrā while chanting second line of this mantra.

ॐ पुष्प पुष्प महापुष्प सुपुष्प पुष्पसम्भवे ।
पुष्पचयावकीर्णे च हुं फट् स्वाहा ॥

oṁ puṣpa puṣpa mahāpuṣpa supuṣpa puṣpa sambhave
puṣpa cayāvakīrṇe ca huṁ phaṭ svāhā

Oṁ Flowers, flowers, Oh Great Flowers, excellent flowers; flowers in heaps and scattered about, cut the ego, purify, I am One with God!

kara śuddhi

wipe hands with a damp flower

ॐ ऐं रं अस्त्राय फट्

oṁ aiṁ raṁ astrāya phaṭ

Oṁ Wisdom, the divine fire, with the weapon, Purify !

काली गायत्री

Kālī Gāyatrī

ॐ महाकाल्यै च विद्महे श्मशानवासिन्यै च धीमहि ।

तन्नो काली प्रचोदयात् ॥

oṁ mahākālyai ca vidmahe śmaśāna vāsinyai ca dhīmahi
tanno kālī pracodayāt

Oṁ We meditate upon the Great Goddess Who Takes Away Darkness, contemplate She Who Resides in the Cremation Grounds (the ultimate form into which creation dissolves). May that Goddess grant to us increase.

ध्यानम्

dhyānam

Meditation

करालवदनां घोरां मुक्तकेशीं चतुर्भुजां ।

कालिकां दक्षिणां दिव्यां मुण्डमालाविभूषिताम् ॥

karālavadanāṁ ghorāṁ muktakeśīṁ caturbhujām
kālikāṁ dakṣiṇāṁ divyāṁ muṇḍamālā vibhūṣitām

The sound of her voice is dreadfully fearful. She has loose hair and four arms, She Who Takes Away the Darkness, of Divine Ability (or bearing the divine gift), displaying the garland of heads of impure thoughts.

सद्यश्छिन्नशिरःखड्गवामाधोर्द्ध्वकराम्भुजां ।

अभयां वरदाञ्चैव दक्षिणोर्द्धाधःपाणिकाम् ॥

sadyaśchinnaśiraḥkhaṅga vāmādhorddhva karāmbhujāṁ
abhayāṁ varadañcaiva dakṣiṇorddhādhaḥpāṇikām

In her lower left hand is the recently severed head (of the Ego), in the upper left hand, which is raised, is the sword. With her lower right hand She grants fearlessness, and her upper right She gives blessings.

महामेघप्रभां श्यामां तथा चैव दिगम्बरीं ।

कण्ठावसक्तमुण्डालीगलद्रुधिरचर्च्चितां ॥

mahāmegha prabhāṁ śyāmāṁ tathā caiva digambarīṁ
kaṇṭhāvasaktamuṇḍālīgaladrudhiracarcitāṁ

She shines like a big dark cloud, and She is clothed in space (naked, without any covering). From her neck dangles the garland of heads, dripping the blood of attachment from their severed necks.

कर्णावतंसतानीतशव युग्मभयानकां ।

घोरदंष्ट्रां करालास्यां पीनोन्नतपयोधराम् ॥

karṇāvataṁsatānītaśava yugmabhayānakāṁ
ghoradaṁṣṭrāṁ karālāsyāṁ pīnonnatapayodharām

Her two ears are adorned with ring-shaped ornaments, her body is withered like a corpse. Her large protruding teeth are extremely terrifying to the ego, and her large upraised breasts overflowing.

शवानां करसङ्घातैःकृतकाञ्चीं हसन्मुखीं ।

सृक्कद्वयगलद्रक्तधाराविस्फुरिताननां ॥

śavānāṁ karasaṅghātaiḥkṛtakāñcīṁ hasanmukhīṁ
sṛkkadvayagaladraktadhārāvisphuritānanāṁ

She wears a girdle made from the severed arms of the corpses of impurity that She has slain. Her face is filled with laughter. Pouring forth from the throats She has cut, comes a torrent of blood, the life of all passion, in a glistening river.

घोररावां महारौद्रीं श्मशानालयवासिनीम् ।
बालार्कमण्डलाकारलोचनत्रितयान्वितां ॥

ghorarāvāṁ mahāraudrīṁ śmaśānālayavāsinīm
bālārkamaṇḍalākāralocanatritayānvitāṁ

Extremely frightful and greatly terrifying is this resident of the cremation grounds; this young woman with a figure like an asetic's begging bowl, with three eyes.

दन्तुरां दक्षिणव्यापि मुक्तालम्बिकचोच्चयां ।
शवरूप महादेवहृदयोपरिसंस्थितां ॥

danturāṁ dakṣiṇavyāpi muktālanvikacoccayāṁ
śavarūpa mahādevahṛdayoparisaṁsthitāṁ

Pervading the South, and filling up everywhere, unattached, She is resting with ease on the corpse-like form of Mahādeva, the Great Lord of All, standing upon his heart.

शिवाभिर्घोररवाभिश्चतुर्दिक्षु समन्वितां ।
महाकालेन च समं विपरीतरतातुरां ॥

śivābhirghoraravābhiścaturddikṣu samanvitāṁ
mahākālena ca samaṁ viparītaratāturāṁ

Śivā, the Energy of Infinite Goodness (Kālī) emits a dreadful roar which pervades the four directions, and Mahākāla, the Great Time (Śiva), equally reverses, or sends it back, with the greatest of delight.

सुखप्रसन्नवदनां स्मेराननसरोरुहां ।
एवं संचिन्तयेत् कालीं सर्वकामसमृद्धिदाम् ॥

sukhaprasannavadanāṁ smerānana saroruhāṁ
evaṁ saṁcintayet kālīṁ sarvakāmasamṛddhidām

If one contemplates Kālī, the Remover of Darkness, in this way, with her face of radiant beauty giving pleasure, and its wide expansive smile, one will become prosperous and fulfill all desires.

ॐ क्रीं क्रीं क्रीं हुं हुं ह्रीं ह्रीं दक्षिणे कालिके क्रीं क्रीं क्रीं हुं हुं ह्रीं ह्रीं स्वाहा

oṁ krīṁ krīṁ krīṁ huṁ huṁ hrīṁ hrīṁ dakṣiṇe kālike krīṁ krīṁ krīṁ huṁ huṁ hrīṁ hrīṁ svāhā

The Cause Which Moves the Subtle Body to the Infinite Perfection and Beyond, cut the ego! Cut the ego! Māyā! Māyā! Oh Goddess Who Removes All Darkness, the Cause Which Moves the Subtle Body to the Infinite Perfection and Beyond, cut the ego! Cut the ego! Māyā! Māyā! I am ONE with God!

kalaśa sthāpana

establishment of the pot

touch earth with tattva mudrā

ॐ भूरसि भूमिरस्यदितिरसि विश्वधारा विश्वस्य भुवनस्य धर्त्री ।

पृथिवीं यच्छ पृथिवीं दृंह पृथिवीं मा हिंसीः ॥

oṁ bhūrasi bhūmirasyaditirasi viśvadhārā viśvasya bhuvanasya dhartrī

pṛthivīṁ yaccha pṛthivīṁ dṛṁha pṛthivīṁ mā hiṁsīḥ

You are the object of sensory perception; you are the Goddess who distributes the forms of the earth. You are the Producer of the Universe, the Support of all existing things in the universe. Control (or sustain) the earth, firmly establish the earth, make the earth efficient in its motion.

give rice

ॐ धान्यमसि धिनुहि देवान् धिनुहि यज्ञं ।

धिनुहि यज्ञपतिं धिनुहि मां यज्ञन्यम् ॥

oṁ dhānyamasi dhinuhi devān dhinuhi yajñaṁ dhinuhi yajñapatiṁ dhinuhi māṁ yajñanyam

You are the grains which satisfy and gladden the Gods, gladden the sacrifice, gladden the Lord of Sacrifice. Bring satisfaction to us through sacrifice.

place pot

ॐ आजिघ्र कलशं मह्या त्वा विशन्त्विन्दवः ।
पुनरूर्ज्जा निवर्तस्व सा नः सहस्रं धुक्क्ष्वोरुधारा पयस्वती
पुनर्म्माविशताद्द्रयिः ॥

oṁ ājigghra kalaśaṁ mahyā tvā viśantvindavaḥ punarūrjjā nivartasva sā naḥ sahasraṁ dhukkṣvorudhārā payasvatīḥ punarmmāviśatāddrayiḥ

Cause the effulgent fire of perception to enter into your highly honored container for renewed nourishment. Remaining there, let it increase in thousands, so that upon removal, abounding in spotlessly pure strength, it may come flowing into us.

pour water into pot

ॐ वरुणस्योत्तम्भनमसि वरुणस्य स्कम्भसर्ज्जनी स्थो ।
वरुणस्य ऋतसदन्न्यसि । वरुणस्य ऋतसदनमसि ।
वरुणस्य ऋतसदनमासीद ॥

oṁ varuṇasyottambhanamasi varuṇasya skambhasarjjanī stho varuṇasya ṛtasadannyasi varuṇasya ṛtasadanamasi varuṇasya ṛtasadanamāsīda

You, Waters, are declared the Ultimate of waters established in all creation begotten, abiding in waters as the eternal law of truth; always abiding in waters as the eternal law of truth, and forever abiding in waters as the eternal law of truth.

place wealth or coins

ॐ धन्वना गा धन्वनाजिं जयेम धन्वना तीव्राः समद्रो जयेम ।

धनुः शत्रोरपकामं कृणोति धन्वना सर्वाः प्रदिशो जयेम ॥

oṁ dhanvanā gā dhanvanājiṁ jayema dhanvanā tīvrāḥ samadro jayema

dhanuḥ śatrorapakāmaṁ kṛṇoti dhanvanā sarvāḥ pradiśo jayema

Let wealth, even abundance, be victorious. Let wealth be sufficient as to be victorious over the severe ocean of existence. As a bow to protect us safe from the enemies of desire, let it be victorious to illuminate all.

place fruit

ॐ याः फलिनीर्याऽफलाऽअपुष्पाऽयाश्च पुष्पिणीः ।

बृहस्पतिप्रसूतास्ता नो मुञ्चन्त्वंहसः ॥

oṁ yāḥ phalinīryā-aphalā-apuṣpā-yāśca puṣpiṇīḥ

bṛhaspatiprasūtāstā no muñcantvaṁhasaḥ

That which bears fruit, and that which bears no fruit; that without flowers and that with flowers as well. To we who exist born of the Lord of the Vast, set us FREE! ALL THIS IS GOD!

red powder

ॐ सिन्धोरिव प्राध्वने शूघनासो वातप्रमियः पतयन्ति यह्वाः । घृतस्य धारा अरुषो न वाजी काष्ठा भिन्दन्नर्म्मिभिः पिन्वमानः ॥

oṁ sindhoriva prādhvane śūghanāso vātapramiyaḥ patayanti yahvāḥ

ghṛtasya dhārā aruṣo na vājī kāṣṭhā bhindannarmmibhiḥ pinvamānaḥ

The pious mark of red vermilion symbolizing the ocean of love placed prominently upon the head above the nose bursting forth, allows the vibrance of youth to fly. As the stream of ghee pours into the flames, those spirited flames of the Divine Fire consume the logs of wood increasing the will and self-reliance of the worshiper.

ॐ सिन्दूरमरुणाभासं जपाकुसुमसन्निभम् ।
पूजिताऽसि मया देवि प्रसीद परमेश्वरि ॥
ॐ ह्रीं श्रीं क्रीं परमेश्वरि कालिके स्वाहा सिन्दूरं समर्पयामि

oṁ sindūramaruṇābhāsaṁ japākusumasannibham
pūjitā-si mayā devi prasīda parameśvari
oṁ hrīṁ śrīṁ krīṁ parameśvari kālike svāhā
sindūraṁ samarpayāmi

This red colored powder indicates Love, who drives the chariot of the Light of Wisdom, with which we are worshiping our Lord. Please be pleased, Oh Great Seer of All. With this offering of red colored powder Oṁ Māyā, Increase, Dissolution, to the Supreme Female Divinity, Kālī, I am One with God!

kuṅkum

ॐ कुङ्कुमं कान्तिदं दिव्यं कामिनीकामसम्भवम् ।
कुङ्कुमेनाऽर्चिते देवि प्रसीद परमेश्वरि ॥
ॐ ह्रीं श्रीं क्रीं परमेश्वरि कालिके स्वाहा कुङ्कुमं समर्पयामि

oṁ kuṅkumaṁ kāntidaṁ divyaṁ kāminī kāmasambhavam
kuṅkumenā-rcite devi prasīda parameśvari
oṁ hrīṁ śrīṁ krīṁ parameśvari kālike svāhā kuṅkumaṁ samarpayāmi

You are being adorned with this divine red powder, which is made more beautiful by the love we share with you, and is so pleasing. Oh Lord, when we present this red powder be pleased, Oh Supreme Ruler of All. With this offering of red colored powder Oṁ Māyā, Increase, Dissolution, to the Supreme Female Divinity, Kālī, I am One with God!

sandal paste

ॐ श्रीखण्डचन्दनं दिव्यं गन्धाढ्यं सुमनोहरम् ।
विलेपनं च देवेशि चन्दनं प्रतिगृह्यताम् ॥
ॐ ह्रीं श्रीं क्रीं परमेश्वरि कालिके स्वाहा चन्दनं समर्पयामि

oṁ śrīkhaṇḍacandanaṁ divyaṁ gandhāḍhyaṁ sumano haram
vilepanaṁ ca deveśi candanaṁ pratigṛhyatām
oṁ hrīṁ śrīṁ krīṁ parameśvari kālike svāhā candanaṁ samarpayāmi

You are being adorned with this beautiful divine piece of sandal wood, ground to a paste which is so pleasing. Please accept this offering of sandal paste, Oh Supreme Sovereign of all the Gods. With the offering of sandal paste Oṁ Māyā, Increase, Dissolution, to the Supreme Female Divinity, Kālī, I am One with God!

turmeric

ॐ हरिद्रारञ्जिता देवि सुख-सौभाग्यदायिनि ।
तस्मात्त्वं पूजयाम्यत्र दुःखशान्तिं प्रयच्छ मे ॥
ॐ ह्रीं श्रीं क्रीं परमेश्वरि कालिके स्वाहा हरिद्रां समर्पयामि

oṁ haridrārañjitā devi sukha saubhāgyadāyini
tasmāttvaṁ pūjayāmyatra duḥkha śāntiṁ prayaccha me
oṁ hrīṁ śrīṁ krīṁ parameśvari kālike svāhā haridrāṁ samarpayāmi

Oh Lord, you are being gratified by this turmeric, the giver of comfort and beauty. When you are worshiped like this, then you must bestow upon us the greatest peace. With the offering of turmeri Oṁ Māyā, Increase, Dissolution, to the Supreme Female Divinity, Kālī, I am One with God!

Collect the bath offerings in a bowl

milk bath

ॐ कामधेनुसमुद्भूतं सर्वेषां जीवनं परम् ।
पावनं यज्ञहेतुश्च स्नानार्थं प्रतिगृह्यताम् ॥
ॐ ह्रीं श्रीं क्रीं परमेश्वरि कालिके स्वाहा पयस्नानं समर्पयामि

oṁ kāmadhenu samudbhūtaṁ sarveṣāṁ jīvanaṁ param
pāvanaṁ yajña hetuśca snānārthaṁ pratigṛhyatām
oṁ hrīṁ śrīṁ krīṁ parameśvari kālike svāhā paya snānaṁ samarpayāmi

Coming from the ocean of being, the Fulfiller of all Desires, Grantor of Supreme Bliss to all souls. For the motive of purifying or sanctifying this holy union, we request you to accept this bath. With this offering of milk for your bath Oṁ Māyā, Increase, Dissolution, to the Supreme Female Divinity, Kālī, I am One with God!

yogurt bath

ॐ पयसस्तु समुद्भूतं मधुराम्लं शशिप्रभम् ।
दध्यानितं मया दत्तं स्नानार्थं प्रतिगृह्यताम् ॥
ॐ ह्रीं श्रीं क्रीं परमेश्वरि कालिके स्वाहा दधिस्नानं समर्पयामि

oṁ payasastu samudbhūtaṁ madhurāmlaṁ śaśiprabham
dadhyānitaṁ mayā dattaṁ snānārthaṁ pratigṛhyatām
oṁ hrīṁ śrīṁ krīṁ parameśvari kālike svāhā dadhi snānaṁ samarpayāmi

Derived from milk from the ocean of being, sweet and pleasing like the glow of the moon, let these curds eternally be our ambassador, as we request you to accept this bath. With this offering of yogurt for your bath Oṁ Māyā, Increase, Dissolution, to the Supreme Female Divinity, Kālī, I am One with God!

ghee bath

ॐ नवनीतसमुत्पन्नं सर्वसन्तोषकारकम् ।
घृतं तुभ्यं प्रदास्यामि स्नानार्थं प्रतिगृह्यताम् ॥
ॐ ह्रीं श्रीं क्रीं परमेश्वरि कालिके स्वाहा घृतस्नानं समर्पयामि

oṁ navanīta samutpannaṁ sarvasantoṣakārakam
ghṛtaṁ tubhyaṁ pradāsyāmi snānārthaṁ pratigṛhyatām
oṁ hrīṁ śrīṁ krīṁ parameśvari kālike svāhā ghṛta snānaṁ samarpayāmi

Freshly prepared from the ocean of being, causing all fulfillment, we offer this delightful ghee (clarified butter) and request you to accept this bath. With this offering of ghee for your bath Oṁ Māyā, Increase, Dissolution, to the Supreme Female Divinity, Kālī, I am One with God!

honey bath

ॐ तरुपुष्पसमुद्भूतं सुस्वादु मधुरं मधु ।
तेजोपुष्टिकरं दिव्यं स्नानार्थं प्रतिगृह्यताम् ॥
ॐ ह्रीं श्रीं क्रीं परमेश्वरि कालिके स्वाहा मधुस्नानं समर्पयामि

oṁ tarupuṣpa samudbhūtam susvādu madhuraṁ madhu
tejo puṣṭikaraṁ divyaṁ snānārtham pratigṛhyatām
oṁ hrīṁ śrīṁ krīṁ parameśvari kālike svāhā madhu snānaṁ samarpayāmi

Prepared from flowers of the ocean of being, enjoyable as the sweetest of the sweet, causing the fire of divine nourishment to burn swiftly, we request you to accept this bath. With this offering of honey for your bath Oṁ Māyā, Increase, Dissolution, to the Supreme Female Divinity, Kālī, I am One with God!

sugar bath

ॐ इक्षुसारसमुद्भूता शर्करा पुष्टिकारिका ।
मलापहारिका दिव्या स्नानार्थं प्रतिगृह्यताम् ॥
ॐ ह्रीं श्रीं क्रीं परमेश्वरि कालिके स्वाहा शर्करास्नानं समर्पयामि

oṁ ikṣusāra samudbhūtā śarkarā puṣṭikārikā
malāpahārikā divyā snānārthaṁ pratigṛhyatām
oṁ hrīṁ śrīṁ krīṁ parameśvari kālike svāhā śarkarā snānaṁ samarpayāmi

From the lake of sugar-cane, from the ocean of being, which causes the nourishment of sugar to give divine protection from all impurity, we request you to accept this bath. With this offering of sugar for your bath Oṁ Māyā, Increase, Dissolution, to the Supreme Female Divinity, Kālī, I am One with God!

five nectars bath

ॐ पयो दधि घृतं चैव मधु च शर्करायुतम् ।
पञ्चामृतं मयाऽऽनीतं स्नानार्थं प्रतिगृह्यताम् ॥
ॐ ह्रीं श्रीं क्रीं परमेश्वरि कालिके स्वाहा पञ्चामृतस्नानं समर्पयामि

oṁ payo dadhi ghṛtaṁ caiva madhu ca śarkarāyutam
pañcāmṛtaṁ mayā--nītaṁ snānārthaṁ pratigṛhyatām
oṁ hrīṁ śrīṁ krīṁ parameśvari kālike svāhā pañcāmṛta snānaṁ samarpayāmi

Milk, curd, ghee and then honey and sugar mixed together; these five nectars are our ambassador, as we request you to accept this bath. With this offering of five nectars for your bath Oṁ Māyā, Increase, Dissolution, to the Supreme Female Divinity, Kālī, I am One with God!

scented oil

ॐ नानासुगन्धिद्रव्यं च चन्दनं रजनीयुतम् ।
उद्वर्तनं मया दत्तं स्नानार्थं प्रतिगृह्यताम् ॥
ॐ ह्रीं श्रीं क्रीं परमेश्वरि कालिके स्वाहा उद्वर्तनस्नानं समर्पयामि

oṁ nānāsugandhidravyaṁ ca candanaṁ rajanīyutam
udvartanaṁ mayā dattaṁ snānārthaṁ pratigṛhyatām
oṁ hrīṁ śrīṁ krīṁ parameśvari kālike svāhā udvartana snānaṁ samarpayāmi

Oṁ With various beautifully smelling ingredients, as well as the scent of sandal, we offer you this scented oil, Oh Lord. With this offering of scented oil Oṁ Māyā, Increase, Dissolution, to the Supreme Female Divinity, Kālī, I am One with God!

scent bath

गन्धद्वारां दुराधर्षां नित्यपुष्टां करीषिणीम् ।
ईश्वरीं सर्वभूतानां तामिहोपह्वये श्रियम् ॥
ॐ ह्रीं श्रीं क्रीं परमेश्वरि कालिके स्वाहा गन्धस्नानं समर्पयामि

gandhadvārāṁ durādharṣāṁ nityapuṣṭāṁ karīṣiṇīm
īśvarīṁ sarvabhūtānāṁ tāmihopahvaye śriyam
oṁ hrīṁ śrīṁ krīṁ parameśvari kālike svāhā gandha snānaṁ samarpayāmi

She is the cause of the scent which is the door to religious ecstasy, unconquerable (never-failing), continually nurturing for all time. May we never tire from calling that manifestation of the Highest Respect, the Supreme Goddess of all existence. With this offering of scented bath Oṁ Māyā, Increase, Dissolution, to the Supreme Female Divinity, Kālī, I am One with God!

water bath

ॐ गङ्गे च जमुने चैव गोदावरि सरस्वति ।

नर्मदे सिन्धु कावेरि स्नानार्थं प्रतिगृह्यताम् ॥

ॐ ह्रीं श्रीं क्रीं परमेश्वरि कालिके स्वाहा गङ्गास्नानं

समर्पयामि

oṁ gaṅge ca jamune caiva godāvari sarasvati
narmade sindhu kāveri snānārthaṁ pratigṛhyatām
oṁ hrīṁ śrīṁ krīṁ parameśvari kālike svāhā gaṅgā
snānaṁ samarpayāmi

Please accept the waters from the Gaṅges, the Jamunā, Godāvarī, Sarasvatī, Narmadā, Sindhu and Kāverī, which have been provided for your bath. With this offering of Ganges bath waters Oṁ Māyā, Increase, Dissolution, to the Supreme Female Divinity, Kālī, I am One with God!

cloth

ॐ शीतवातोष्णसंत्राणं लज्जायै रक्षणं परं ।

देहालंकरणं वस्त्रं अथ शान्तिं प्रयच्छ मे ॥

ॐ ह्रीं श्रीं क्रीं परमेश्वरि कालिके स्वाहा वस्त्रं समर्पयामि

oṁ śīta vātoṣṇa saṁ trāṇaṁ lajjāyai rakṣaṇaṁ paraṁ
dehālaṅkaraṇaṁ vastraṁ atha śāntiṁ prayaccha me
oṁ hrīṁ śrīṁ krīṁ parameśvari kālike svāhā vastraṁ
samarpayāmi

To take away the cold and the wind and to fully protect your modesty, we adorn your body with this cloth, and thereby find the greatest Peace. With this offering of wearing apparel Oṁ Māyā, Increase, Dissolution, to the Supreme Female Divinity, Kālī, I am One with God!

sacred thread

ॐ यज्ञोपवीतं परमं पवित्रं प्रजापतेर्यत् सहजं पुरस्तात् ।
आयुष्यमग्रं प्रतिमुञ्च शुभ्रं यज्ञोपवीतं बलमस्तु तेजः ॥

oṁ yajñopavītaṁ paramaṁ pavitraṁ prajāpateryat sahajaṁ purastāt
āyuṣyamagraṁ pratimuñca śubhraṁ yajñopavītaṁ balamastu tejaḥ

Oṁ the sacred thread of the highest purity is given by Prajāpati, the Lord of Creation, for the greatest facility. You bring life and illuminate the greatness of liberation. Oh sacred thread, let your strength be of radiant light.

शमो दमस्तपः शौचं क्षान्तिरार्जवमेव च ।
ज्ञानं विज्ञानमास्तिक्यं ब्रह्मकर्म स्वभावजम् ॥

śamo damastapaḥ śaucaṁ kṣāntirārjavameva ca
jñānaṁ vijñānamāstikyaṁ brahmakarma svabhāvajam

Peacefulness, self-control, austerity, purity of mind and body, patience and forgiveness, sincerity and honesty, wisdom, knowledge, and self-realization, are the natural activities of a Brāhmaṇa.

नवभिस्तन्तुभिर्युक्तं त्रिगुणं देवतामयं ।
उपवीतं मया दत्तं गृहाण त्वं सुरेश्वरि ॥
ॐ ह्रीं श्रीं क्रीं परमेश्वरि कालिके स्वाहा यज्ञोपवीतं समर्पयामि

navamiṣṭantubhiryuktaṁ triguṇaṁ devatā mayaṁ
upavītaṁ mayā dattaṁ gṛhāṇa tvaṁ sureśvari
oṁ hrīṁ śrīṁ krīṁ parameśvari kālike svāhā yajñopavītaṁ samarpayāmi

With nine desirable threads all united together, exemplifying the three guṇas (or three qualities of harmony of our deity), this sacred thread will be our ambassador. Oh Ruler of the Gods, please accept. With this offering of a sacred thread Oṁ Māyā, Increase, Dissolution, to the Supreme Female Divinity, Kālī, I am One with God!

rudrākṣa

त्र्यम्बकं यजामहे सुगन्धिं पुष्टिवर्द्धनम् ।

उर्व्वारुकमिव बन्धनान्मृत्योर्म्मुक्षीयमामृतात् ॥

ॐ ह्रीं श्रीं क्रीं परमेश्वरि कालिके स्वाहा रुद्राक्षं समर्पयामि

tryambakaṁ yajāmahe sugandhiṁ puṣṭivarddhanam
urvvārukamiva bandhanānmṛtyormmukṣīyamāmṛtāt
oṁ hrīṁ śrīṁ krīṁ parameśvari kālike svāhā rudrākṣaṁ samarpayāmi

We adore the Father of the three worlds, of excellent fame, Grantor of Increase. As a cucumber is released from its bondage to the stem, so may we be freed from Death to dwell in immortality. With this offering of rudrākṣa Oṁ Māyā, Increase, Dissolution, to the Supreme Female Divinity, Kālī, I am One with God!

mālā

ॐ मां माले महामाये सर्वशक्तिस्वरूपिणि ।

चतुर्वर्गस्त्वयि न्यस्तस्तस्मान्मे सिद्धिदा भव ॥

ॐ ह्रीं श्रीं क्रीं परमेश्वरि कालिके स्वाहा मालां समर्पयामि

oṁ māṁ māle mahāmāye sarvaśaktisvarūpiṇi
caturvargastvayi nyastastasmānme siddhidā bhava
oṁ hrīṁ śrīṁ krīṁ parameśvari kālike svāhā mālāṁ samarpayāmi

Oṁ My rosary, the Great Limitation of Consciousness, containing all energy within as your intrinsic nature, fulfilling the four desires of men, give us the attainment of your perfection. With this offering of a Mālā Oṁ Māyā, Increase, Dissolution, to the Supreme Female Divinity, Kālī, I am One with God!

rice

अक्षतान् निर्मलान् शुद्धान् मुक्ताफलसमन्वितान् ।
गृहाणेमान महादेवि देहि मे निर्मलां धियम् ॥
ॐ ह्रीं श्रीं क्रीं परमेश्वरि कालिके स्वाहा अक्षतान् समर्पयामि

akṣatān nirmalān śuddhān muktāphalasamanvitān
gṛhāṇemān mahādevi dehi me nirmalāṁ dhiyam
oṁ hrīṁ śrīṁ krīṁ parameśvari kālike svāhā akṣatān samarpayāmi

Oh Great Lord, please accept these grains of rice, spotlessly clean, bestowing the fruit of liberation, and give us a spotlessly clean mind. With the offering of grains of rice Oṁ Māyā, Increase, Dissolution, to the Supreme Female Divinity, Kālī, I am One with God!

flower garland

शङ्ख-पद्मजपुष्पादि शतपत्रैर्विचित्रताम् ।
पुष्पमालां प्रयच्छामि गृहाण त्वं सुरेश्वरि ॥
ॐ ह्रीं श्रीं क्रीं परमेश्वरि कालिके स्वाहा पुष्पमालां समर्पयामि

śaṅkha-padma japuṣpādi śatapatrairvicitratām
puṣpamālāṁ prayacchāmi gṛhāṇa tvaṁ sureśvari
oṁ hrīṁ śrīṁ krīṁ parameśvari kālike svāhā puṣpamālāṁ samarpayāmi

We offer you this garland of flowers with spiraling lotuses, other flowers and leaves. Be pleased to accept it, Oh Ruler of All Gods. With the offering of a garland of flowers Oṁ Māyā, Increase, Dissolution, to the Supreme Female Divinity, Kālī, I am One with God!

flower

मल्लिकादि सुगन्धीनि मालित्यादीनि वै प्रभो ।

मयाऽहृतानि पूजार्थं पुष्पाणि प्रतिगृह्यताम् ॥

ॐ ह्रीं श्रीं क्रीं परमेश्वरि कालिके स्वाहा पुष्पम् समर्पयामि

mallikādi sugandhīni mālityādīni vai prabho
mayā-hṛtāni pūjārthaṁ puṣpāṇi pratigṛhyatām
oṁ hrīṁ śrīṁ krīṁ parameśvari kālike svāhā puṣpam samarpayāmi

Various flowers such as mallikā and others of excellent scent, are being offered to you, Our Lord. All these flowers have come from the devotion of our hearts for your worship. Be pleased to accept them. With the offering of flowers Oṁ Māyā, Increase, Dissolution, to the Supreme Female Divinity, Kālī, I am One with God!

sthirī karaṇa

establishment of stillness

ॐ सर्वतीर्थमयं वारि सर्वदेवसमन्वितम् ।

इमं घटं समागच्छ तिष्ठ देवगणैः सह ॥

oṁ sarvatīrthamayaṁ vāri sarvadevasamanvitam
imaṁ ghaṭaṁ samāgaccha tiṣṭha devagaṇaiḥ saha

All the places of pilgrimage as well as all of the Gods, all are placed within this container. Oh Multitude of Gods, be established within!

lelihānā mudrā

(literally, sticking out, pointing baby finger)

स्थां स्थीं स्थिरो भव विड्वङ्ग आशुर्भव वाज्यर्व्वन् ।

पृथुर्भव शुषदस्त्वमग्नेः पुरीषवाहनः ॥

sthāṁ sthīṁ sthiro bhava viḍvaṅga āśurbhava vājyarvvan
pṛthurbhava śuṣadastvamagneḥ purīṣavāhanaḥ

Be Still in the Gross Body! Be Still in the Subtle Body! Be Still in the Causal Body! Quickly taking in this energy and shining forth as the

Holder of Wealth, Oh Divine Fire, becoming abundant, destroy the current of rubbish from the face of this earth.

prāṇa pratiṣṭhā

establishment of life

ॐ अं आं ह्रीं क्रों यं रं लं वं शं षं सं हों हं सः

oṁ aṁ āṁ hrīṁ kroṁ yaṁ raṁ laṁ vaṁ śaṁ ṣaṁ saṁ hoṁ haṁ saḥ

Oṁ The Infinite Beyond Conception, Creation (the first letter), Consciousness, Māyā, the cause of the movement of the subtle body to perfection and beyond; the path of fulfillment: control, subtle illumination, one with the earth, emancipation, the soul of peace, the soul of delight, the soul of unity (all this is I), perfection, Infinite Consciousness, this is I.

ॐ ह्रीं श्रीं क्रीं परमेश्वरि कालिके स्वाहा प्राणा इह प्राणाः

oṁ hrīṁ śrīṁ krīṁ parameśvari kālike svāhā prāṇā iha prāṇāḥ

Oṁ Māyā, Increase, Dissolution, to the Supreme Female Divinity, Kālī, I am One with God! You are the life of this life!

ॐ अं आं ह्रीं क्रों यं रं लं वं शं षं सं हों हं सः

oṁ aṁ āṁ hrīṁ kroṁ yaṁ raṁ laṁ vaṁ śaṁ ṣaṁ saṁ hoṁ haṁ saḥ

Oṁ The Infinite Beyond Conception, Creation (the first letter), Consciousness, Māyā, the cause of the movement of the subtle body to perfection and beyond; the path of fulfillment: control, subtle illumination, one with the earth, emancipation, the soul of peace, the soul of delight, the soul of unity (all this is I), perfection, Infinite Consciousness, this is I.

ॐ ह्रीं श्रीं क्रीं परमेश्वरि कालिके स्वाहा जीव इह स्थितः

oṁ hrīṁ śrīṁ krīṁ parameśvari kālike svāhā jīva iha sthitaḥ
Oṁ Māyā, Increase, Dissolution, to the Supreme Female Divinity, Kālī, I am One with God! You are situated in this life (or individual consciousness).

ॐ अं आं ह्रीं क्रों यं रं लं वं शं षं सं हों हं सः

oṁ aṁ āṁ hrīṁ kroṁ yaṁ raṁ laṁ vaṁ śaṁ ṣaṁ saṁ hoṁ haṁ saḥ
Oṁ The Infinite Beyond Conception, Creation (the first letter), Consciousness, Māyā, the cause of the movement of the subtle body to perfection and beyond; the path of fulfillment: control, subtle illumination, one with the earth, emancipation, the soul of peace, the soul of delight, the soul of unity (all this is I), perfection, Infinite Consciousness, this is I.

ॐ ह्रीं श्रीं क्रीं परमेश्वरि कालिके स्वाहा सर्वेन्द्रियाणि

oṁ hrīṁ śrīṁ krīṁ parameśvari kālike svāhā sarvendriyāṇi
Oṁ Māyā, Increase, Dissolution, to the Supreme Female Divinity, Kālī, I am One with God! You are all these organs (of action and knowledge).

ॐ अं आं ह्रीं क्रों यं रं लं वं शं षं सं हों हं सः

oṁ aṁ āṁ hrīṁ kroṁ yaṁ raṁ laṁ vaṁ śaṁ ṣaṁ saṁ hoṁ haṁ saḥ
Oṁ The Infinite Beyond Conception, Creation (the first letter), Consciousness, Māyā, the cause of the movement of the subtle body to perfection and beyond; the path of fulfillment: control, subtle illumination, one with the earth, emancipation, the soul of peace, the soul of delight, the soul of unity (all this is I), perfection, Infinite Consciousness, this is I.

ॐ ह्रीं श्रीं क्रीं परमेश्वरि कालिके स्वाहा वाग् मनस्त्
वक्चक्षुः-श्रोत्र-घ्राण-प्राणा इहागत्य सुखं चिरं तिष्ठन्तु स्वाहा

oṁ hrīṁ śrīṁ krīṁ parameśvari kālike svāhā vāg manas-tvakcakṣuḥ śrotra ghrāṇa prāṇā ihāgatya sukhaṁ ciraṁ tiṣṭhantu svāhā

Oṁ Māyā, Increase, Dissolution, to the Supreme Female Divinity, Kālī, I am One with God! You are all these vibrations, mind, sound, eyes, ears, tongue, nose and life force. Bring forth infinite peace and establish it forever, I am One with God!

ॐ क्रीं काल्यै नमः

oṁ krīṁ kālyai namaḥ

I bow to the Goddess Kālī Who Takes Away Darkness.

ॐ क्रां अंगुष्ठाभ्यां नमः

oṁ krāṁ aṅguṣṭhābhyāṁ namaḥ *thumb/forefinger*

oṁ krāṁ in the thumb I bow.

ॐ क्रीं तर्जनीभ्यां स्वाहा

oṁ krīṁ tarjanībhyāṁ svāhā *thumb/forefinger*

oṁ krīṁ in the forefinger, I am One with God!

ॐ क्रूं मध्यमाभ्यां वषट्

oṁ krūṁ madhyamābhyāṁ vaṣaṭ *thumb/middlefinger*

oṁ krūṁ in the middle finger, Purify!

ॐ क्रैं अनामिकाभ्यां हुं

oṁ kraiṁ anāmikābhyāṁ huṁ *thumb/ringfinger*

oṁ kraiṁ in the ring finger, Cut the Ego!

ॐ क्रौं कनिष्ठिकाभ्यां वौषट्

oṁ krauṁ kaniṣṭhikābhyāṁ vauṣaṭ *thumb/littlefinger*

oṁ krauṁ in the little finger, Ultimate Purity!

Roll hand over hand forwards while reciting karatala kara, and backwards while chanting pṛṣṭhābhyāṁ, then clap hands when chanting astrāya phaṭ

ॐ क्रः करतलकरपृष्ठाभ्यां अस्त्राय फट्

oṁ kraḥ karatala kara pṛṣṭhābhyāṁ astrāya phaṭ
oṁ I bow to the Goddess Kālī with the weapon of Virtue.

ॐ क्रीं काल्यै नमः

oṁ krīṁ kālyai namaḥ
I bow to the Goddess Kālī Who Takes Away Darkness.

Holding tattva mudrā, touch heart.

ॐ क्रां हृदयाय नमः

oṁ krāṁ hṛdayāya namaḥ *touch heart*
oṁ krāṁ in the heart, I bow.

Holding tattva mudrā, touch top of head.

ॐ क्रीं शिरसे स्वाहा

oṁ krīṁ śirase svāhā *top of head*
oṁ krīṁ on the top of the head, I am One with God!

Make a fist with thumb extended, touch back of head.

ॐ क्रूं शिखायै वषट्

oṁ krūṁ śikhāyai vaṣaṭ *back of head*
oṁ krūṁ on the back of the head, Purify!

Holding tattva mudrā, cross both arms.

ॐ क्रैं कवचाय हुं

oṁ kraiṁ kavacāya huṁ *cross both arms*
oṁ kraiṁ crossing both arms, Cut the Ego!

Holding tattva mudrā, touch three eyes
at once with three middle fingers.

ॐ क्रौं नेत्रत्रयाय वौषट्

oṁ krauṁ netratrayāya vauṣaṭ *touch three eyes*

oṁ krauṁ in the three eyes, Ultimate Purity!

Roll hand over hand forwards while reciting karatala kara, and backwards while chanting pṛṣṭhābhyāṁ, then clap hands when chanting astrāya phaṭ.

ॐ क्रः करतलकरपृष्ठाभ्यां अस्त्राय फट्

oṁ kraḥ karatala kara pṛṣṭhābhyāṁ astrāya phaṭ

oṁ I bow to the Goddess Kālī with the weapon of Virtue.

ॐ क्रीं काल्यै नमः

oṁ krīṁ kālyai namaḥ

I bow to the Goddess Kālī Who Takes Away Darkness.

head:	ॐ नमः	**oṁ namaḥ**
genital:	स्त्रीं नमः	**strīṁ namaḥ**
anus:	एं नमः	**eṁ namaḥ**
navel:	स्त्रीं नमः	**strīṁ namaḥ**
heart:	ऐं नमः	**aiṁ namaḥ**
throat:	क्लीं नमः	**klīṁ namaḥ**
third eye:	सैं नमः	**saiṁ namaḥ**
right arm:	ॐ नमः	**oṁ namaḥ**
left arm:	श्रीं नमः	**śrīṁ namaḥ**
right foot:	ह्रीं नमः	**hrīṁ namaḥ**

left foot:	क्लीं नमः	**klīṁ namaḥ**
back:	क्रों नमः	**kroṁ namaḥ**

ॐ क्रीं काल्यै नमः

oṁ krīṁ kālyai namaḥ (108 times)
I bow to the Goddess Kālī Who Takes Away Darkness.

Japa
prāṇa pratiṣṭhā sūkta
hymn of the establishment of life

ॐ अस्यै प्राणाः प्रतिष्ठन्तु अस्यै प्राणाः क्षरन्तु च ।
अस्यै देवत्वमर्चायै मामहेति कश्चन ॥

oṁ asyai prāṇāḥ pratiṣṭhantu asyai prāṇāḥ kṣarantu ca
asyai devatvamārcāyai māmaheti kaścana
Thus has the life force been established in you, and thus the life force has flowed into you. Thus to you, God, offering is made, and in this way make us shine.

कलाकला हि देवानां दानवानां कलाकलाः ।
संगृह्य निर्मितो यस्मात् कलशस्तेन कथ्यते ॥

kalākalā hi devānāṁ dānavānāṁ kalākalāḥ
saṁgṛhya nirmito yasmāt kalaśastena kathyate
All the Gods are Fragments of the Cosmic Whole. Also all the asuras are Fragments of the Cosmic Whole. Thus we make a house to contain all these energies.

कलशस्य मुखे विष्णुः कण्ठे रुद्रः समाश्रितः ।
मूले त्वस्य स्थितो ब्रह्मा मध्ये मातृगणाः स्मृताः ॥

kalaśasya mukhe viṣṇuḥ kaṇṭhe rudraḥ samāśritaḥ
mūle tvasya sthito brahmā madhye mātṛgaṇāḥ smṛtāḥ

In the mouth of the pot is Viṣṇu, in the neck resides Rudra. At the base is situated Brahmā, and in the middle we remember the multitude of Mothers.

कुक्षौ तु सागराः सप्त सप्तद्वीपा च मेदिनी ।
अर्जुनी गोमती चैव चन्द्रभागा सरस्वती ॥

kukṣau tu sāgarāḥ sapta saptadvīpā ca medinī
arjunī gomatī caiva candrabhāgā sarasvatī

In the belly are the seven seas and the seven islands of the earth. The rivers Arjunī, Gomatī, Candrabhāgā, Sarasvatī,

कावेरी कृष्णवेणा च गङ्गा चैव महानदी ।
ताप्ती गोदावरी चैव माहेन्द्री नर्मदा तथा ॥

kāverī kṛṣṇaveṇā ca gaṅgā caiva mahānadī
tāptī godāvarī caiva māhendrī narmadā tathā

Kāverī, Kṛṣṇaveṇā and the Gaṅges and other great rivers: the Tāptī, Godāvarī, Māhendrī and Narmadā.

नदाश्च विविधा जाता नद्यः सर्वास्तथापराः ।
पृथिव्यां यानि तीर्थानि कलशस्थानि तानि वै ॥

nadāśca vividhā jātā nadyaḥ sarvāstathāparāḥ
pṛthivyāṁ yāni tīrthāni kalaśasthāni tāni vai

The various rivers and the greatest of beings born, and all the respected places of pilgrimage upon the earth, are established within this pot.

सर्वे समुद्राः सरितस्तीर्थानि जलदा नदाः ।
आयान्तु मम शान्त्यर्थं दुरितक्षयकारकाः ॥

sarve samudrāḥ saritastīrthāni jaladā nadāḥ
āyāntu mama śāntyarthaṁ duritakṣayakārakāḥ

All of the seas, rivers, and waters from all the respected places of pilgrimage have been brought for the peace of that which is bad or wicked.

ऋग्वेदोऽथ यजुर्वेदः सामवेदो ह्यथर्वणः ।
अङ्गैश्च सहिताः सर्वे कलशं तु समाश्रिताः ॥

ṛgvedo-tha yajurvedaḥ sāmavedo hyatharvaṇaḥ
aṅgaiśca sahitāḥ sarve kalaśaṁ tu samāśritāḥ

The Ṛg Veda, the Yajur Veda, Sāma Veda and the Atharva Veda, along with all of their limbs, are assembled together in this pot.

अत्र गायत्री सावित्री शान्तिः पुष्टिकरी तथा ।
आयान्तु मम शान्त्यर्थं दुरितक्षयकारकाः ॥

atra gāyatrī sāvitrī śāntiḥ puṣṭikarī tathā
āyāntu mama śāntyarthaṁ duritakṣayakārakāḥ

Here Gāyatrī, Sāvitrī, Peace and Increase have been brought for the peace of that which is bad or wicked.

देवदानवसंवादे मथ्यमाने महोदधौ ।
उत्पन्नोऽसि तदा कुम्भ विधृतो विष्णुना स्वयम् ॥

deva dānava saṁvāde mathyamāne mahodadhau
utpanno-si tadā kumbha vidhṛto viṣṇunā svayam

The Gods and asuras speaking together are the great givers of churning to the mind. Rise to the top of this pot to separate them from what is actually Viṣṇu, Himself.

त्वत्तोये सर्वतीर्थानि देवाः सर्वे त्वयि स्थिताः ।
त्वयि तिष्ठन्ति भूतानि त्वयि प्राणाः प्रतिष्ठिताः ॥

tvattoye sarvatīrthāni devāḥ sarve tvayi sthitāḥ
tvayi tiṣṭhanti bhūtāni tvayi prāṇāḥ pratiṣṭhitāḥ

Within you are all the pilgrimage places. All the Gods are situated within you. All existence is established within you. All life is established within you.

शिवः स्वयं त्वमेवासि विष्णुस्त्वं च प्रजापतिः ।
आदित्या वसवो रुद्रा विश्वेदेवाः सपैतृकाः ॥

śivaḥ svayaṁ tvamevāsi viṣṇustvaṁ ca prajāpatiḥ
ādityā vasavo rudrā viśvedevāḥ sapaitṛkāḥ

You alone are Śiva; you are Brahmā and Viṣṇu, the sons of Aditi, Finders of the Wealth, Rudra, the Universal Deities and the ancestors.

त्वयि तिष्ठन्ति सर्वेऽपि यतः कामफलप्रदाः ।
त्वत्प्रसादादिमं यज्ञं कर्तुमीहे जलोद्भव ।
सान्निध्यं कुरु मे देव प्रसन्नो भव सर्वदा ॥

tvayi tiṣṭhanti sarve-pi yataḥ kāmaphalapradāḥ
tvatprasādādimaṁ yajñaṁ kartumīhe jalodbhava
sānnidhyaṁ kuru me deva prasanno bhava sarvadā

All and everything has been established in you, from whence you grant the fruits of desires. From you comes the blessed fruit of the sacrifice performed with excellence. May those riches increase. Manifest your presence within us, Lord. Always be pleased.

नमो नमस्ते स्फटिकप्रभाय सुश्वेतहाराय सुमङ्गलाय ।
सुपाशहस्ताय झषासनाय जलाधिनाथाय नमो नमस्ते ॥

namo namaste sphaṭikaprabhāya
suśvetahārāya sumaṅgalāya
supāśahastāya jhaṣāsanāya jalādhināthāya namo namaste

We bow, we bow to He who shines like crystal, to He who emits excellent clarity and excellent welfare. With the net of unity in his hand, who takes the form of a fish, to the Lord of all waters and that which dwells within, we bow, we bow!

पाशपाणे नमस्तुभ्यं पद्मिनीजीवनायक ।
पुण्याहवाचनं यावत् तावत्त्वं सन्निधौ भव ॥

pāśapāṇe namastubhyaṁ padminījīvanāyaka
puṇyāhavācanaṁ yāvat tāvattvaṁ sannidhau bhava

We bow to He with the net of unity in his hand, Seer of the Life of the Lotus One. With this meritorious invocation, please make your presence manifest.

आद्यास्तोत्रम्

ādyā stotram

The Song of the Foremost
(Kālī as the Supreme Divinity)

श‍ृणु वत्स प्रवक्ष्यामि आद्यास्तोत्रम् महाफलं ।
यः पठेत् सततं भक्त्या स एव विष्णुवल्लभः ॥

śṛṇu vatsa pravakṣyāmi ādyā stotram mahāphalaṁ
yaḥ paṭhet satataṁ bhaktyā sa eva viṣṇu vallabhaḥ

Listen, my child, while I elucidate the Song of the Foremost, which grants the great fruit. Who will always recite this with devotion, will have strength comparable to that of Viṣṇu.

मृत्युव्याधिभयं तस्य नास्ति कञ्चित् कलौ युगे ।
अपुत्रो लभते पुत्रं त्रिपक्षं श्रवणं यदि ॥

mṛtyuvyādhibhayaṁ tasya nāsti kiñcit kalau yuge
aputro labhate putraṁ tripakṣaṁ śravaṇaṁ yadi

Neither death nor illness will bring fear, nor anything else of the Kali Yuga. Those without children will attain children, if they listen (to this) three times (a day).

द्वौ मासौ बन्धनान् मुक्तिर्विप्रवक्त्रा श्रुतं यदि ।
मृतवत्सा जीववत्सा षण्मासान् श्रवणं यदि ॥

dvau māsau bandhanān muktirvipravaktrā śrutaṁ yadi
mṛtavatsā jīvavatsā ṣaṇmāsān śravaṇaṁ yadi

If this be heard from the mouth of a twice-born for two months, one will be liberated from bondage. If one will listen thus for six months, he will be liberated from the cycles of birth and death.

नौकायां सङ्कटे युद्धे पठनाज्जयमाप्नुयात् ।
लिखित्वा स्थापनाद् गेहे नाग्निचौरभयं क्वचित् ॥

naukāyāṁ saṅkaṭe yuddhe paṭhanājjayamāpnuyāt
likhitvā sthāpanād gehe nāgnicaurabhayaṁ kvacit

It is a boat to cross the difficulties of war; no one will be able to defeat the person who recites it. And if it is duly written and established in one's house, no fear will come from fire, thieves nor from other causes.

राजस्थाने जयी नित्यं प्रसन्नाः सर्वदेवताः ।
पापानि विलयं यान्ति मृतौ मुक्तिमवाप्नुयात् ॥

rājasthāne jayī nityaṁ prasannāḥ sarvadevatāḥ
pāpāni vilayaṁ yānti mṛtau mukti mavāpnuyāt

In the house of kings one will be eternally invincible, and pleasing to all the Gods. Cleaving asunder the sins of all life, one will be liberated even from death.

ॐ ह्रीं ब्रह्माणी ब्रह्मलोके च वैकुण्ठे सर्वमङ्गला ।
इन्द्राणी अमरावत्यामम्बिका वरुणालये ॥

oṁ hrīṁ brahmāṇī brahmaloke ca vaikuṇṭhe sarvamaṅgalā
indrāṇī amarāvatyāmambikā varuṇālaye

Oṁ Hrīṁ (the totality of Māyā what can be perceived, conceived or intuited) in the Brahma Loka, in the reality of Creative Consciousness, is Brahmāṇī, the Energy of Creative Consciousness; in Vaikuṇṭha, the home of Viṣṇu, is All Welfare. In the Land of the Immortals (the heaven of Indra), is Indrāṇī, the Energy of the Rule of the Pure, and Ambikā, the Divine Mother, in the home of Varuṇa, the Lord of Equilibrium.

यमालये कालरूपा कुबेरभवने शुभा ।
महानन्दाग्निकोणे च वायव्यां मृग वाहिनी ॥

yamālaye kālarūpā kuberabhavane śubhā
mahānandāgni koṇe ca vāyavyāṁ mṛga vāhinī

In the house of Death, is the Dark Form, and with the Lord of Wealth, is the Radiant Luster. In the Southeast, home of Agni, the Divine Fire or Purifying Light of Meditation, is Great Delight, and in the Northwest, the home of Vāyu, She Who rides on the deer.

नैर्ऋत्यां रक्तदन्ता च ऐशान्यां शूलधारिणी ।
पाताले वैष्णवीरूपा सिंहले देवमोहिनी ॥

nairṛtyāṁ raktadantā ca aiśānyāṁ śūladhāriṇī
pātāle vaiṣṇavī rūpā siṁhale devamohinī

In the Southwest is She with Red Teeth, and in the Northeast, She Who Holds the Spear. In the regions of Hell is the form of Vaiṣṇavī, She Who Pervades All, and in Laṅkā, She Who mesmerizes the Gods.

सुरसा च मणिद्वीपे लङ्कायां भद्रकालिका ।
रामेश्वरी सेतुबन्धे विमला पुरुषोत्तमे ॥

surasā ca manidvīpe laṅkāyāṁ bhadrakālikā
rāmeśvarī setubandhe vimalā puruṣottame

In the Island of Jewels is the Mother of the Gods, and in the Island of Laṅkā, Bhadrakālikā, the Excellent One Beyond Time. The Supreme Lord of Rāma is at the bridge, and in the Excellent Fullness (or excellent individual), is Vimala, Pure and Stainless.

विरजा औड्रदेशे च कामाख्या नीलपर्वते ।
कालिका बङ्गदेशे च अयोध्यायां महेश्वरी ॥

virajā auḍradeśe ca kāmākhyā nīlaparvate
kālikā baṅgadeśe ca ayodhyāyāṁ maheśvarī

The Great Warrior is in the country of Audra, and Kāmākhyā is in the Blue Mountains. In the country of Bengal is Kālikā, She Who Takes Away the Darkness, and in Ayodhyā, Maheśvarī, the Great Seer of All.

वाराणस्यामन्नपूर्णा गयाक्षेत्रे गयेश्वरी ।
कुरुक्षेत्रे भद्रकाली व्रजे कात्यायनी परा ॥

vārāṇasyāmannapūrṇā gayākṣetre gayeśvarī
kurukṣetre bhadrakālī vraje kātyāyanī parā

Annapūrnā, She Who is Full of Food, is at Vārāṇasi, and in the fields of Gayā, Gayeśvarī, Supreme Lord of the Abode. In Kurukṣetra, the Field of the Family, is Bhadrakālī, the Excellent One Beyond Time, and in the thunderbolt, the Excellence of Illumination, is the Supreme Ever Pure One.

द्वारकायां महामाया मथुरायां माहेश्वरी ।
क्षुधा त्वं सर्वभूतानां वेला त्वं सागरस्य च ॥

dvārakāyāṁ mahāmāyā mathurāyāṁ māheśvarī
kṣudhā tvaṁ sarvabhūtānāṁ velā tvaṁ sāgarasya ca

In Dvārakā is Mahāmāyā, the Great Limitation of Consciousness, and in Mathurā, the Energy of the Great Seer of All. You are Hunger to all Beings, and you are the flow of the tides to the sea.

नवमी कृष्णपक्षस्य शुक्लस्यैकादशी परा ।
दक्षस्य दुहिता देवी दक्षयज्ञविनाशिनी ॥

navamī kṛṣṇa pakṣasya śuklasyaikādaśī parā
dakṣasya duhitā devī dakṣayajña vināśinī

On the ninth day of the dark fortnight, and on the eleventh day of the bright fortnight, remember the Goddess who is Dakṣa's daughter, the Destroyer of Dakṣa's sacrifice.

रामस्य जानकी त्वं हि रावणध्वंसकारिणी ।
चण्डमुण्डवधे देवी रक्तबीजविनाशिनी ॥

rāmasya jānakī tvaṁ hi rāvaṇadhvaṁsa kāriṇī
caṇḍamuṇḍavadhe devī raktabīja vināśinī

Also you are Rāma's Jānakī (Sītā), the cause of Rāvaṇa's destruction, as well as the Goddess who slays Passion and Meaness, destroyer of the Seed of Desire.

निशुम्भशुम्भमथनी मधुकैटभघातिनी ।
विष्णुभक्तिप्रदा दुर्गा सुखदा मोक्षदा सदा ॥

niśumbha śumbha mathanī madhu kaiṭabha ghātinī
viṣṇu bhakti pradā durgā sukhadā mokṣadā sadā

You are the killer of Self-Conceit and Self-Deprecation, and destroyer of Two Much and Two Little. Oh Durgā, Reliever of all Difficulties, bestow eternal devotion upon this Consciousness; always give comfort and liberation.

इमं आद्या स्तवं पुण्यं यः पठेत् सततं नरः ।
सर्वज्वरभयं न स्यात् सर्वव्याधिविनाशनम् ॥

imaṁ ādyā stavaṁ puṇyaṁ yaḥ paṭhet satataṁ naraḥ
sarvajvarabhayaṁ na syāt sarvavyādhi vināśanam

Whoever will constantly recite this meritorious Song of the Foremost will destroy all affliction, fear and disease.

कोटितीर्थफलञ्चासौ लभते नात्र संशयः ।
जया मे चाग्रतः पातु विजया पातु पृष्ठतः ॥

koṭi tīrtha phalañcāsau labhate nātra saṁśayaḥ
jayā me cāgrataḥ pātu vijayā pātu pṛṣṭhataḥ

The fruits of visiting millions of pilgrimage sites will be attained without a doubt. May Victory protect me in my front, and Conquest protect my rear.

नारायणी शीर्षदेशे सर्वाङ्गे सिंहवाहिनी ।
शिवदूती उग्रचण्डा प्रत्यङ्गे परमेश्वरी ॥

nārāyaṇī śīrṣadeśe sarvāṅge siṁhavāhinī
śivadūtī ugracaṇḍā pratyaṅge parameśvarī

The Great Exposer of Consciousness protect the area of the head, and all the limbs be protected by She Who Rides on the Lion, also known as She for Whom Consciousness is Ambassador, She Who is Terrible to Passion, the Supreme Empress of All and every body;

विशालाक्षी महामाया कौमारी शङ्खिनी शिवा ।
चक्रिणी जयदात्री च रणमत्ता रणप्रिया ॥

viśālākṣī mahāmāyā kaumārī śaṅkhinī śivā
cakriṇī jayadātrī ca raṇamattā raṇapriyā

The Goal of the Infinite, the Great Limitation of Consciousness, the Ever-Pure One, She Who Holds the Conch, the Energy of Infinite Goodness; She Who Holds the Discus, the Grantor of Victory, and She Who is Intoxicated with Delight, She Who is the Lover of Delight;

दुर्गा जयन्ती काली च भद्रकाली महोदरी ।
नारसिंही च वाराही सिद्धिदात्री सुखप्रदा ॥

durgā jayantī kālī ca bhadrakālī mahodarī
nārasiṁhī ca vārāhī siddhidātrī sukhapradā

The Reliever of Difficulties, She Who is Always Victorious, She Who Takes Away Darkness, and the Excellent One Beyond Time, the Wielder of Ignorance; She Who is Half Human and Half Lion, and the Boar of Sacrifice, the Grantor of Perfection, Giver of Comfort;

भयङ्करी महारौद्री महाभयविनाशिनी ॥

bhayaṅkarī mahāraudrī mahābhaya vināśinī

Who Destroys all fear, the Great Terrifying One Who Destroys all Fear.

इति आद्यास्तोत्रम् समाप्तम् ॥

iti ādyā stotram samāptam

And that is the completion of the Song of the Foremost.

viśeṣārghya

establishment of the conch shell offering

Draw the following yantra on the plate or space for worship with sandal paste and/or water. Offer rice on the yantra for each of the four mantras.

ॐ आधारशक्तये नमः

oṁ ādhāraśaktaye namaḥ

Oṁ we bow to the Primal Energy

ॐ कूर्म्माय नमः

oṁ kūrmmāya namaḥ

Oṁ we bow to the Support of the Earth

ॐ अनन्ताय नमः

oṁ anantāya namaḥ

Oṁ we bow to Infinity

ॐ पृथिव्यै नमः

oṁ pṛthivyai namaḥ

Oṁ we bow to the Earth

Place a conch shell on the bindu in the center of the yantra when saying Phaṭ.

स्थां स्थीं स्थिरो भव फट्

sthāṁ sthīṁ sthiro bhava phaṭ

Be Still in the Gross Body! Be Still in the Subtle Body! Be Still in the Causal Body! Purify!

Fill conch shell with water while chanting the mantra.

ॐ गङ्गे च जमुने चैव गोदावरि सरस्वति ।
नर्मदे सिन्धनु कावेरि जलेऽस्मिन् सन्निधिं कुरु ॥

oṁ gaṅge ca jamune caiva godāvari sarasvati
narmade sindhu kāveri jale-asmin sannidhiṁ kuru
Oṁ the Ganges, Jamunā, Godāvarī, Sarasvatī, Narmadā, Sindhu, Kāverī, these waters are mingled together.

Offer Tulasī leaves into water

ॐ ऐं ह्रीं क्लीं श्रीं वृन्दावनवासिन्यै स्वाहा

oṁ aiṁ hrīṁ klīṁ śrīṁ vṛndāvanavāsinyai svāhā
Oṁ Wisdom, Māyā, Increase, to She who resides in Vṛndāvana, I am One with God!

Offer 3 flowers into the water pot with the mantras

एते गन्धपुष्पे ॐ अं अर्कमण्डलाय द्वादशकलात्मने नमः

ete gandhapuṣpe oṁ aṁ arkamaṇḍalāya dvādaśakalātmane namaḥ
With these scented flowers Oṁ "A" we bow to the twelve aspects of the realm of the sun. Tapinī, Tāpinī, Dhūmrā, Marīci, Jvālinī, Ruci, Sudhūmrā, Bhoga-dā, Viśvā, Bodhinī, Dhārinī, Kṣamā; Containing heat, Emanating heat, Smoky, Ray-producing, Burning, Lustrous, Purple or Smoky-red, Granting enjoyment, Universal, Which makes known, Productive of Consciousness, Which supports, Which forgives.

एते गन्धपुष्पे ॐ उं सोममण्डलाय षोडशकलात्मने नमः

ete gandhapuṣpe oṁ uṁ somamaṇḍalāya ṣoḍaśakalātmane namaḥ
With these scented flowers Oṁ "U" we bow to the sixteen aspects of the realm of the moon. Amṛtā, Prāṇadā, Puṣā, Tuṣṭi, Puṣṭi, Rati, Dhṛti, Śaśinī, Caṇḍrikā, Kānti, Jyotsnā, Śrī, Prīti, Aṅgadā, Pūrṇā, Pūrṇāmṛta; Nectar, Which sustains life, Which supports, Satisfying, Nourishing, Playful, Constancy, Unfailing, Producer of Joy, Beauty enhanced by love, Light, Grantor of Prosperity, Affectionate, Purifying the body, Complete, Full of Bliss.

एते गन्धपुष्पे ॐ मं वह्निमण्डलाय दशकलात्मने नमः

ete gandhapuṣpe oṁ maṁ vahnimaṇḍalāya daśakalātmane namaḥ

With these scented flowers Oṁ "M" we bow to the ten aspects of the realm of fire: Dhūmrā, Arciḥ, Jvalinī, Śūkṣmā, Jvālinī, Visphūliṅginī, Suśrī, Surūpā, Kapilā, Havya-Kavya-Vahā; Smoky Red, Flaming, Shining, Subtle, Burning, Sparkling, Beautiful, Well-formed, Tawny, The Messenger to Gods and Ancestors.

एते गन्धपुष्पे हुं

ete gandhapuṣpe huṁ

With these scented flowers huṁ

Wave hands in matsyā, dhenu and
aṅkuśa mudrās while chanting this mantra.

ॐ गङ्गे च जमुने चैव गोदावरि सरस्वति ।
नर्मदे सिन्धु कावेरि जलेऽस्मिन् सन्निधिं कुरु ॥

oṁ gaṅge ca jamune caiva godāvari sarasvati
narmade sindhu kāveri jale-asmin sannidhiṁ kuru

Oṁ the Ganges, Jamunā, Godāvarī, Sarasvatī, Narmadā, Sindhu, Kāverī, these waters are mingled together.

ॐ ह्रीं श्रीं क्रीं परमेश्वरि कालिके स्वाहा

oṁ hrīṁ śrīṁ krīṁ parameśvari kālike svāhā

Oṁ Māyā, Increase, Dissolution, to the Supreme Female Divinity, Kālī, I am One with God!

Sprinkle water over all articles to be offered, then throw some drops of water over your shoulders while repeating the mantra.

अमृतम् कुरु स्वाहा

amritam kuru svāhā

Make this immortal nectar! I am One with God!

pūjā naivedya

offerings of worship

invitation

आगच्छेह महादेवि ! सर्वसम्पत्प्रदायिनि ।
यावद् व्रतं समाप्येत तावत्त्वं सन्निधौ भव ॥
ॐ ह्रीं श्रीं क्रीं परमेश्वरि कालिके स्वाहा आवाहनं समर्पयामि

āgaccheha mahādevi ! sarvasampatpradāyini
yāvad vrataṁ samāpyeta tāvattvaṁ sannidhau bhava
oṁ hrīṁ śrīṁ krīṁ parameśvari kālike svāhā āvāhanaṁ samarpayāmi

Please come here, oh Great Goddess, Giver of all wealth! Please remain sitting still until this vow of worship is complete. With the offering of an invitation Oṁ Māyā, Increase, Dissolution, to the Supreme Female Divinity, Kālī, I am One with God!

seat

अनेकरत्नसंयुक्तं नानामणिगणान्वितम् ।
कार्तस्वरमयं दिव्यमासनं प्रतिगृह्यताम् ॥
ॐ ह्रीं श्रीं क्रीं परमेश्वरि कालिके स्वाहा आसनं समर्पयामि

anekaratna saṁyuktaṁ nānāmaṇi gaṇānvitam
kārtasvaramayaṁ divyamāsanaṁ pratigṛhyatām
oṁ hrīṁ śrīṁ krīṁ parameśvari kālike svāhā āsanaṁ samarpayāmi

United with many gems and a multitude of various jewels, voluntarily accept my offering of a divine seat. With the offering of a seat Oṁ Māyā, Increase, Dissolution, to the Supreme Female Divinity, Kālī, I am One with God!

foot bath

ॐ गङ्गादिसर्वतीर्थेभ्यो मया प्रार्थनयाहृतम् ।

तोयमेतत् सुखस्पर्शं पाद्यार्थं प्रतिगृह्यताम् ॥

ॐ ह्रीं श्रीं क्रीं परमेश्वरि कालिके स्वाहा पाद्यं समर्पयामि

oṁ gaṅgādi sarva tīrthebhyo mayā prārthanayāhṛtam
toyametat sukha sparśaṁ pādyārthaṁ pratigṛhyatām
oṁ hrīṁ śrīṁ krīṁ parameśvari kālike svāhā pādyaṁ samarpayāmi

The Gaṅges and other waters from all the places of pilgrimage are mingled together in this our prayer, that you please accept the comfortable touch of these waters offered to wash your lotus feet. With this offering of foot bath waters Oṁ Māyā, Increase, Dissolution, to the Supreme Female Divinity, Kālī, I am One with God!

water for washing hands and mouth

कर्पूरेण सुगन्धेन सुरभिस्वादु शीतलम् ।

तोयमाचमनीयार्थं देवीदं प्रतिगृह्यताम् ॥

ॐ ह्रीं श्रीं क्रीं परमेश्वरि कालिके स्वाहा आचमनीयं समर्पयामि

karpūreṇa sugandhena surabhisvādu śītalam
toyamācamanīyārthaṁ devīdaṁ pratigṛhyatām
oṁ hrīṁ śrīṁ krīṁ parameśvari kālike svāhā ācamanīyaṁ samarpayāmi

With camphor and excellent scent, cool with excellent taste, this water is being offered for washing, oh Goddess, please accept. With this offering of washing waters Oṁ Māyā, Increase, Dissolution, to the Supreme Female Divinity, Kālī, I am One with God!

arghya - corsage or bouquet

निधीनां सर्वदेवानां त्वमनर्घ्यगुणा ह्यसि ।

सिंहोपरिस्थिते देवि ! गृहाणार्घ्यं नमोऽस्तु ते ॥

ॐ ह्रीं श्रीं क्रीं परमेश्वरि कालिके स्वाहा अर्घ्यं समर्पयामि

nidhīnāṁ sarvadevānāṁ tvamanarghyaguṇā hyasi
siṁhoparisthite devi ! gṛhāṇārghyaṁ namo-stu te
oṁ hrīṁ śrīṁ krīṁ parameśvari kālike svāhā arghyaṁ samarpayāmi

Presented to all the Gods, you, oh Arghya, bring an abundance of pleasure. Oh Goddess who is seated upon the lion, accept this arghya. I bow to you. With this offering of arghya Oṁ Māyā, Increase, Dissolution, to the Supreme Female Divinity, Kālī, I am One with God!

madhuparka - yogurt drink

दधिमधुघृतसमायुक्तं पात्रयुग्मं समन्वितम् ।

मधुपर्कं गृहाण त्वं शुभदा भव शोभने ॥

ॐ ह्रीं श्रीं क्रीं परमेश्वरि कालिके स्वाहा मधुपर्कं समर्पयामि

dadhi madhu ghṛtasamāyuktaṁ pātrayugmaṁ samanvitam
madhuparkaṁ gṛhāṇa tvaṁ śubhadā bhava śobhane
oṁ hrīṁ śrīṁ krīṁ parameśvari kālike svāhā madhuparkaṁ samarpayāmi

Yogurt, honey, ghee mixed together, and blended fine in a vessel; please accept this madhuparka shining with radiant purity. With this offering of madhuparka Oṁ Māyā, Increase, Dissolution, to the Supreme Female Divinity, Kālī, I am One with God!

water bath

ॐ गङ्गे च जमुने चैव गोदावरि सरस्वति ।

नर्मदे सिन्धुकावेरि स्नानार्थं प्रतिगृह्यताम् ॥

ॐ ह्रीं श्रीं क्रीं परमेश्वरि कालिके स्वाहा गङ्गास्नानं समर्पयामि

oṁ gaṅge ca jamune caiva godāvari sarasvati
narmade sindhu kāveri snānārthaṁ pratigṛhyatām
oṁ hrīṁ śrīṁ krīṁ parameśvari kālike svāhā gaṅgā
snānaṁ samarpayāmi

Please accept the waters from the Gaṅges, the Jamunā, Godāvarī, Sarasvatī, Narmadā, Sindhu and Kāverī, which have been provided for your bath. With this offering of Ganges bath waters Oṁ Māyā, Increase, Dissolution, to the Supreme Female Divinity, Kālī, I am One with God!

bracelets

ॐ माणिक्यमुक्ताखण्डयुक्ते सुवर्णकारेण च संस्कृते ये ।
ते किङ्किणीभिः स्वरिते सुवर्णे मयाऽर्पिते देवि गृहाण कङ्कणे ॥
ॐ ह्रीं श्रीं क्रीं परमेश्वरि कालिके स्वाहा कङ्कणे समर्पयामि

oṁ māṇikya muktā khaṇḍayukte
suvarṇakāreṇa ca saṁskṛte ye
te kiṅkiṇībhiḥ svarite suvarṇe
mayā-rpite devi gṛhāṇa kaṅkaṇe
oṁ hrīṁ śrīṁ krīṁ parameśvari kālike svāhā kaṅkaṇe
samarpayāmi

Oṁ United with gems and pearls, excellent gold and the alphabets of Saṁskṛta, this bracelet is yours and radiance I am offering. Oh Goddess, accept this bracelet. With the offering of a bracelet Oṁ Māyā, Increase, Dissolution, to the Supreme Female Divinity, Kālī, I am One with God!

conch ornaments

ॐ शङ्खञ्च विविधं चित्रं बाहूनाञ्च विभूषणम् ।
मया निवेदितं भक्त्या गृहाण परमेश्वरि ॥

ॐ ह्रीं श्रीं क्रीं परमेश्वरि कालिके स्वाहा शङ्खालङ्कारं समर्पयामि

oṁ śaṅkhañca vividhaṁ citraṁ bāhūnāñca vibhūṣaṇam
mayā niveditaṁ bhaktyā gṛhāṇa parameśvari
oṁ hrīṁ śrīṁ krīṁ parameśvari kālike svāhā
śaṅkhālaṅkāraṁ samarpayāmi

I am offering you with devotion ornaments worn upon the arms made of various qualities of conch shell. Please accept, oh Supreme Divinity. With the offering of ornaments made of conch shell Oṁ Māyā, Increase, Dissolution, to the Supreme Female Divinity, Kālī, I am One with God!

ornaments

ॐ दिव्यरत्नसमायुक्ता वह्निभानुसमप्रभाः ।
गात्राणि शोभयिष्यन्ति अलङ्काराः सुरेश्वरि ॥
ॐ ह्रीं श्रीं क्रीं परमेश्वरि कालिके स्वाहा अलङ्कारान् समर्पयामि

oṁ divyaratnasamāyuktā vahnibhānusamaprabhāḥ
gātrāṇi śobhayiṣyanti alaṅkārāḥ sureśvari
oṁ hrīṁ śrīṁ krīṁ parameśvari kālike svāhā alaṅkārān samarpayāmi

Oṁ United with divine jewels which are radiant like fire, and stones which are shining, please accept these ornaments, oh Supreme among the Gods. With the offering of ornaments Oṁ Māyā, Increase, Dissolution, to the Supreme Female Divinity, Kālī, I am One with God!

rice

अक्षतान् निर्मलान् शुद्धान् मुक्ताफलसमन्वितान् ।
गृहाणेमान् महादेवि देहि मे निर्मलां धियम् ॥
ॐ ह्रीं श्रीं क्रीं परमेश्वरि कालिके स्वाहा अक्षतान् समर्पयामि

akṣatān nirmalān śuddhān muktāphalasamanvitān
gṛhāṇemān mahādevi dehi me nirmalāṁ dhiyam
oṁ hrīṁ śrīṁ krīṁ parameśvari kālike svāhā akṣatān samarpayāmi

Oh Great Lord, please accept these grains of rice, spotlessly clean, bestowing the fruit of liberation, and give us a spotlessly clean mind. With the offering of grains of rice Oṁ Māyā, Increase, Dissolution, to the Supreme Female Divinity, Kālī, I am One with God!

food offering

ॐ सत्पात्रं शुद्धसुहविर्व्विविधानेकभक्षणम् ।
निवेदयामि देवेशि सर्वतृप्तिकरं परम् ॥

oṁ satpātraṁ śuddhasuhavirv vividhānekabhakṣaṇam
nivedayāmi deveśi sarvatṛptikaraṁ param

This ever-present platter containing varieties of the purest offerings of food we are presenting to the Lord of Gods to cause all satisfaction most excellent and transcendental.

ॐ अन्नपूर्णे सदा पूर्णे शङ्करप्राणवल्लभे ।
ज्ञानवैराग्यसिद्ध्यर्थं भिक्षां देहि नमोऽस्तु ते ॥

oṁ annapūrṇe sadā pūrṇe śaṅkara prāṇavallabhe
jñānavairāgyasiddhyarthaṁ bhikṣāṁ dehi namo-stu te

Oṁ Goddess who is full, complete and perfect with food and grains, always full, complete and perfect, the strength of the life force of Śiva, the Cause of Peace. For the attainment of perfection in wisdom and renunciation, please give us offerings. We bow down to you.

माता च पार्वती देवी पिता देवो महेश्वरः ।
बान्धवाः शिवभक्ताश्च स्वदेशो भुवनत्रयम् ॥

mātā ca pārvatī devī pitā devo maheśvaraḥ
bāndhavāḥ śivabhaktāśca svadeśo bhuvanatrayam

Our Mother is the Goddess, Pārvatī, and our Father is the Supreme Lord, Maheśvara. The Consciousness of Infinite Goodness, Śiva, Lord of the three worlds, is being extolled by his devotees.

ॐ ह्रीं श्रीं क्रीं परमेश्वरि कालिके स्वाहा भोगनैवेद्यम्
समर्पयामि

oṁ hrīṁ śrīṁ krīṁ parameśvari kālike svāhā bhog-naivedyam samarpayāmi

With this presentation of food Oṁ Māyā, Increase, Dissolution, to the Supreme Female Divinity, Kālī, I am One with God!

drinking water

ॐ समस्तदेवदेवेशि सर्वतृप्तिकरं परम् ।
अखण्डानन्दसम्पूर्णं गृहाण जलमुत्तमम् ॥
ॐ ह्रीं श्रीं क्रीं परमेश्वरि कालिके स्वाहा पानार्थं जलम्
समर्पयामि

oṁ samasta devadeveśi sarvatṛptikaraṁ param
akhaṇḍānanda sampūrṇaṁ gṛhāṇa jalamuttamam
oṁ hrīṁ śrīṁ krīṁ parameśvari kālike svāhā pānārthaṁ jalam samarpayāmi

Lord of All the Gods and the fullness of Infinite Bliss, please accept this excellent drinking water. With this offering of drinking water Oṁ Māyā, Increase, Dissolution, to the Supreme Female Divinity, Kālī, I am One with God!

betel-nuts

पूगीफलं महद्दिव्यं नागवल्ली दलैर्युतम् ।
एलादिचूर्णसंयुक्तं ताम्बूलं प्रतिगृह्यताम् ॥
ॐ ह्रीं श्रीं क्रीं परमेश्वरि कालिके स्वाहा ताम्बूलं समर्पयामि

pūgīphalaṁ mahaddivyaṁ nāgavallī dalairyutam
elādicūrṇasaṁyuktaṁ tāmbūlaṁ pratigṛhyatām
oṁ hrīṁ śrīṁ krīṁ parameśvari kālike svāhā tāmbūlaṁ samarpayāmi

These betel-nuts, which are great and divine, come from vines that creep like a snake. United with cardamom ground to a powder, please accept this offering of mouth freshening betel nuts. With this offering of mouth freshening betel-nuts Oṁ Māyā, Increase, Dissolution, to the Supreme Female Divinity, Kālī, I am One with God!

dakṣiṇā - offering of money

ॐ पूजाफलसमृद्ध्यर्थं तवाग्रे स्वर्णमीश्वरि ।
स्थापितं तेन मे प्रीता पूर्णान् कुरु मनोरथान् ॥

oṁ pūjāphalasmṛddhyarthaṁ tavāgre svarṇamīśvari
sthāpitaṁ tena me prītā pūrṇān kuru manorathān

Oṁ For the purpose of increasing the fruits of worship, Oh Supreme Goddess of all Wealth, we establish this offering of that which is dear to me. Bring to perfection the journey of my mind.

हिरण्यगर्भगर्भस्थं हेमबीजं विभावसोः ।
अनन्तपुण्यफलदमतः शान्तिं प्रयच्छ मे ॥

hiraṅyagarbhagarbhasthaṁ hemabījaṁ vibhāvasoḥ
anantapuṇyaphaladamataḥ śāntiṁ prayaccha me

Oh Golden Womb, in whom all wombs are situated, shining brightly with the golden seed. Give infinite merits as fruits, we are wanting for Peace.

ॐ ह्रीं श्रीं क्रीं परमेश्वरि कालिके स्वाहा दक्षिणां समर्पयामि

oṁ hrīṁ śrīṁ krīṁ parameśvari kālike svāhā dakṣiṇāṁ samarpayāmi

With this offering of wealth Oṁ Māyā, Increase, Dissolution, to the Supreme Female Divinity, Kālī, I am One with God!

umbrella

छत्रं देवि जगद्धात्रि ! घर्मवातप्रणाशनम् ।

गृहाण हे महामाये ! सौभाग्यं सर्वदा कुरु ॥

ॐ ह्रीं श्रीं क्रीं परमेश्वरि कालिके स्वाहा छत्रं समर्पयामि

chatraṁ devi jagaddhātri ! gharma vāta praṇāśanam
gṛhāṇa he mahāmāye ! saubhāgyaṁ sarvadā kuru
oṁ hrīṁ śrīṁ krīṁ parameśvari kālike svāhā chatraṁ samarpayāmi

Oh Goddess, Creator of the Universe! This umbrella will protect you from heat and wind. Please accept it, oh Great Māyā, and remain always beautiful. With this offering of an umbrella Oṁ Māyā, Increase, Dissolution, to the Supreme Female Divinity, Kālī, I am One with God!

fly whisk

चामरं हे महादेवि ! चमरीपुच्छनिर्मितम् ।

गृहीत्वा पापराशीनां खण्डनं सर्वदा कुरु ॥

ॐ ह्रीं श्रीं क्रीं परमेश्वरि कालिके स्वाहा चामरं समर्पयामि

cāmaraṁ he mahādevi ! camarīpucchanirmitam
gṛhītvā pāparāśīnāṁ khaṇḍanaṁ sarvadā kuru
oṁ hrīṁ śrīṁ krīṁ parameśvari kālike svāhā cāmaraṁ samarpayāmi

Oh Great Goddess, this fly whisk is made of yak's tail. Please accept it, and always whisk away all sin. With this offering of a fly whisk Oṁ Māyā, Increase, Dissolution, to the Supreme Female Divinity, Kālī, I am One with God!

fan

बर्हिर्बर्हकृताकारं मध्यदण्डसमन्वितम् ।

गृह्यतां व्यजनं दुर्गे देहस्वेदापनुत्तये ॥

ॐ ह्रीं श्रीं क्रीं परमेश्वरि कालिके स्वाहा तालवृन्तं समर्पयामि

barhirbarhakṛtākāraṁ madhyadaṇḍa samanvitam
gṛhyatāṁ vyajanaṁ durge dehasvedāpanuttaye
oṁ hrīṁ śrīṁ krīṁ parameśvari kālike svāhā tālavṛntaṁ samarpayāmi

It moves back and forth with equanimity and has a stick in the middle. Please accept this fan, oh Kālī, to keep the perspiration from your body. With this offering of a fan Oṁ Māyā, Increase, Dissolution, to the Supreme Female Divinity, Kālī, I am One with God!

mirror

दर्पणं विमलं रम्यं शुद्धबिम्बप्रदायकम् ।
आत्मबिम्बप्रदर्शनार्थर्पयामि महेश्वरि ! ॥
ॐ ह्रीं श्रीं क्रीं परमेश्वरि कालिके स्वाहा दर्पणं समर्पयामि

darpaṇaṁ vimalaṁ ramyaṁ śuddhabimbapradāyakam
ātmabimbapradarśanārtharpayāmi maheśvari !
oṁ hrīṁ śrīṁ krīṁ parameśvari kālike svāhā darpaṇaṁ samarpayāmi

This beautiful mirror will give a pure reflection. In order to reflect my soul, I am offering it to you, oh Great Seer of all. With this offering of a mirror Oṁ Māyā, Increase, Dissolution, to the Supreme Female Divinity, Kālī, I am One with God!

ārātrikam - camphor light

ॐ चन्द्रादित्यौ च धरणी विद्युदग्निस्तथैव च ।
त्वमेव सर्वज्योतीषिं आरात्रिकं प्रतिगृह्यताम् ॥
ॐ ह्रीं श्रीं क्रीं परमेश्वरि कालिके स्वाहा आरात्रिकं समर्पयामि

oṁ candrādityau ca dharaṇī vidyudagnistathaiva ca
tvameva sarvajyotīṣiṁ ārātrikaṁ pratigṛhyatām
oṁ hrīṁ śrīṁ krīṁ parameśvari kālike svāhā ārātrikaṁ samarpayāmi

All knowing as the Moon, the Sun and the Divine Fire, you alone are all light, and this light we request you to accept. With the offering of light Oṁ Māyā, Increase, Dissolution, to the Supreme Female Divinity, Kālī, I am One with God!

flower

मल्लिकादि सुगन्धीनि मालित्यादीनि वै प्रभो ।
मयाऽहृतानि पूजार्थं पुष्पाणि प्रतिगृह्यताम् ॥
ॐ ह्रीं श्रीं क्रीं परमेश्वरि कालिके स्वाहा पुष्पम् समर्पयामि

mallikādi sugandhīni mālityādīni vai prabho
mayā-hṛtāni pūjārthaṁ puṣpāṇi pratigṛhyatām
oṁ hrīṁ śrīṁ krīṁ parameśvari kālike svāhā puṣpam samarpayāmi

Various flowers such as mallikā and others of excellent scent, are being offered to you, Our Lord. All these flowers have come from the devotion of our hearts for your worship. Be pleased to accept them. With the offering of flowers Oṁ Māyā, Increase, Dissolution, to the Supreme Female Divinity, Kālī, I am One with God!

आद्याकालिकादेव्याः शतनामस्तोत्रम्

ādyā kālikādevyāḥ śatanāma stotram

Song of a Hundred Names of Kālī

श्रीसदाशिव उवाच

śrīsadāśiva uvāca

The Respected Eternal Consciousness of Infinite Goodness said:

शृणु देवि जगद्वन्द्ये स्तोत्रमेतदनुत्तमम् ।
पठनात् श्रवणाद्यस्य सर्वसिद्धीश्वरो भवेत् ॥ १ ॥

śṛṇu devi jagadvandye stotrametadanuttamam
paṭhanāt śravaṇādyasya sarvasiddhīśvaro bhavet

Listen, Oh Goddess revered by the world, to this song excellent among all songs, which when recited or listened to, becomes the Supreme Lord of All Attainments. 1

असौभाग्यप्रशमनं सुखसम्पद्विवर्द्धनम् ।
अकालमृत्युहरणं सर्वापद्विनिवारणम् ॥ २ ॥

asaubhāgyapraśamanaṁ sukhasampadvivarddhanam
akālamṛtyuharaṇaṁ sarvāpadvinivāraṇam

It removes bad fortune, bestows comfort and wealth, takes away untimely death, and annihilates all obstacles. 2

श्रीमदाद्याकालिकायाः सुखसान्निध्यकारणम् ।
स्तवस्यास्य प्रसादेन त्रिपुरारिरहं शिवे ॥ ३ ॥

śrīmadādyākālikāyāḥ sukhasānnidhyakāraṇam
stavasyāsya prasādena tripurārirahaṁ śive

The Respected Foremost Goddess, She Who Takes Away the Darkness, is the Cause of the Presence of Happiness. Oh Goddess of Goodness, by the grace of this song of praise, one's being becomes merged into the Supreme Consciousness which dwells in the three places. 3

स्तोत्रस्यास्य ऋषिर्देवि सदाशिव उदाहृतः ।
छन्दोऽनुष्टुब्देवताऽऽद्या कालिका परिकीर्त्तिता ।
धर्मकामार्थमोक्षेषु विनियोगः प्रकीर्त्तितः ॥ ४ ॥

stotrasyāsya ṛṣirdevi sadāśiva udāhṛtaḥ
chando-nuṣṭubdevatā--dyā kālikā parikīrttitā
dharmakāmārthamokṣeṣu viniyogaḥ prakīrttitaḥ

The Seer of this divine song is the Goddess Herself, for the Delight of the Consciousness of Infinite Goodness, the meter is anuṣṭup chanda (32 syllables to the verse), and it is in praise of the Foremost She Who Takes Away the Darkness. For the purpose of attaining perfection in the ideals of perfection, the fulfillment of desires, in procuring the requisite material necessities, and liberation, otherwise known as self-realization, this recitation is being performed. 4

ह्रीं काली श्रीं कराली च क्रीं कल्याणी कलावती ।
कमला कलिदर्पघ्नी कपर्दीशकृपान्विता ॥ ५ ॥

hrīṁ kālī śrīṁ karālī ca krīṁ kalyāṇī kalāvatī
kamalā kalidarpaghnī kapardīśakṛpānvitā

ह्रीं काली

hrīṁ kālī

She Who is All of Māyā, what can be perceived through the senses, conceived in the mind, or known through intuition and beyond; She Who Takes Away the Darkness 1

श्रीं कराली च

śrīṁ karālī ca

She Who Gives Increase of Perfect Respect; She Who is Formidable and 2

क्रीं कल्याणी

krīṁ kalyāṇī

She Who is the Cause of the Dissolution of the subtle body into the causal body; Welfare 3

कलावती

kalāvatī

She Who Manifests All Qualities 4

कमला

kamalā
She Who is the Lotus One 5

कलिदर्पघ्नी

kalidarpaghnī
She Who Destroys the Pride of the Age of Darkness 6

कपर्दीशकृपान्विता

kapardīśakṛpānvitā
She Who Gives Grace to the One of Matted Hair 7

कालिका कालमाता च कालानलसमद्युतिः ।
कपर्दिनी करालास्या करुणामृतसागरा ॥ ६ ॥

kālikā kālamātā ca kālānalasamadyutiḥ
kapardinī karālāsyā karuṇāmṛtasāgarā

कालिका

kālikā
She Who is the Cause of Taking Away the Darkness 8

कालमाता च

kālamātā ca
She Who is the Mother of Time and 9

कालानलसमद्युतिः

kālānalasamadyutiḥ
She Who is as Radiant as the Fires of Time 10

कपर्दिनी

kapardinī
She Who Wears Matted Hair 11

करालास्या

karālāsyā
She Who has a Gaping Mouth 12

करुणामृतसागरा

karuṇāmṛtasāgarā
She Who is the Ocean of the Nectar of Compassion 13

कृपामयी कृपाधारा कृपापारा कृपागमा ।
कृशानुः कपिला कृष्णा कृष्णानन्दविवर्द्धिनी ॥ ७ ॥

kṛpāmayī kṛpādhārā kṛpāpārā kṛpāgamā
kṛśānuḥ kapilā kṛṣṇā kṛṣṇānandavivarddhinī

कृपामयी
kṛpāmayī
She Who is the Manifestation of Grace 14

कृपाधारा
kṛpādhārā
She Who is the Supporter of Grace 15

कृपापारा
kṛpāpārā
She Who is Beyond Grace 16

कृपागमा
kṛpāgamā
She Who Moves in Grace 17

कृशानुः
kṛśānuḥ
She Who is Beyond All Grace 18

कपिला
kapilā
She Who is the Giver of Nourishment (Cow)19

कृष्णा
kṛṣṇā
She Who is Black, Doer of All 20

कृष्णानन्दविवर्द्धिनी
kṛṣṇānandavivarddhinī
She Who is the Distributor of the Bliss of the Doer of All 21

कालरात्रिः कामरूपा कामपाशविमोचनी ।
कादम्बिनी कलाधारा कलिकल्मषनाशिनी ॥ ८ ॥

kālarātriḥ kāmarūpā kāmapāśavimocanī
kādambinī kalādhārā kalikalmaṣanāśinī

कालरात्रिः
kālarātriḥ
She Who is the Dark Night of Overcoming Egotism 22

कामरूपा
kāmarūpā
She Who is the Form of Desire 23

कामपाशविमोचनी
kāmapāśavimocanī
She Who Cuts the Bondage of Desire 24

कादम्बिनी
kādambinī
She Who is like a Dark Cloud 25

कलाधारा
kalādhārā
She Who Supports All Qualities 26

कलिकल्मषनाशिनी
kalikalmaṣanāśinī
She Who Destroys the Evils of the Age of Darkness 27

कुमारीपूजनप्रीता कुमारीपूजकालया ।
कुमारीभोजनानन्दा कुमारीरूपधारिणी ॥ ९ ॥

kumārīpūjanaprītā kumārīpūjakālayā
kumārībhojanānandā kumārīrūpadhāriṇī

कुमारीपूजनप्रीता
kumārīpūjanaprītā
She Who Loves the Worship of the Ever Pure One 28

कुमारीपूजकालया
kumārīpūjakālayā
She Who is the Time of Worship of the Ever Pure One 29

कुमारीभोजनानन्दा
kumārībhojanānandā
She Who is the Bliss of Feeding the Ever Pure One 30

कुमारीरूपधारिणी
kumārīrūpadhāriṇī
She Who Wears the Form of the Ever Pure One 31

कदम्बवनसञ्चारा कदम्बवनवासिनी ।
कदम्बपुष्पसन्तोषा कदम्बपुष्पमालिनी ॥ १० ॥

kadambavanasañcārā kadambavanavāsinī
kadambapuṣpasantoṣā kadambapuṣpamālinī

कदम्बवनसञ्चारा
kadambavanasañcārā
She Who Roams in the Forest of Kadamba trees 32

कदम्बवनवासिनी
kadambavanavāsinī
She Who Dwells in the Forest of Kadamba trees 33

कदम्बपुष्पसन्तोषा
kadambapuṣpasantoṣā
She Who is Satisfied With the Flowers of Kadamba trees 34

कदम्बपुष्पमालिनी
kadambapuṣpamālinī
She Who Wears a Garland of the Flowers of Kadamba trees 35

किशोरी कलकण्ठा च कलनादनिनादिनी ।
कादम्बरीपानरता तथा कादम्बरीप्रिया ॥ ११ ॥

kiśorī kalakaṇṭhā ca kalanādaninādinī
kādambarīpānaratā tathā kādambarīpriyā

किशोरी
kiśorī
She Who is Young 36

कलकण्ठा च
kalakaṇṭhā ca
She Whose Throat is Dark and 37

कलनादनिनादिनी
kalanādaninādinī
She Who is the Disseminator of the Subtle Vibrations of Darkness 38

कादम्बरीपानरता तथा
kādambarīpānaratā tathā
She Who Drinks the Nectar of the Kadamba Fruit then 39

कादम्बरीप्रिया

kādambarīpriyā
She Who Enjoys the Nectar of the Kadamba Fruit 40

कपालपात्रनिरता कङ्कालमाल्यधारिणी ।
कमलासनसन्तुष्टा कमलासनवासिनी ॥ १२ ॥

kapālapātraniratā kaṅkālamālyadhāriṇī
kamalāsanasantuṣṭā kamalāsanavāsinī

कपालपात्रनिरता

kapālapātraniratā
She Who Holds a Bowl Made of Skull 41

कङ्कालमाल्यधारिणी

kaṅkālamālyadhāriṇī
She Who Wears a Garland of Skulls 42

कमलासनसन्तुष्टा

kamalāsanasantuṣṭā
She Who is Pleased to Sit on the Lotus Flower 43

कमलासनवासिनी

kamalāsanavāsinī
She Who Sits on the Seat of the Lotus Flower 44

कमलालयमध्यस्था कमलामोदमोदिनी ।
कलहंसगतिः क्लैब्यनाशिनी कामरूपिणी ॥ १३ ॥

kamalālayamadhyasthā kamalāmodamodinī
kalahaṁsagatiḥ klaibyanāśinī kāmarūpiṇī

कमलालयमध्यस्था

kamalālayamadhyasthā
She Who is Established in the Middle Space of the Lotus 45

कमलामोदमोदिनी

kamalāmodamodinī
She Who is Intoxicated From the Intoxication of the Lotus 46

कलहंसगतिः

kalahaṁsagatiḥ
She Who Moves With the Gait of a Black Swan 47

क्लैब्यनाशिनी

klaibyanāśinī
She Who is the Destroyer of Iniquitiy 48

कामरूपिणी

kāmarūpiṇī
She Who is the Intrinsic Nature of Desire 49

कामरूपकृतावासा कामपीठविलासिनी ।
कमनीया कल्पलता कमनीयविभूषणा ॥ १४ ॥

kāmarūpakṛtāvāsā kāmapīṭhavilāsinī
kamanīyā kalpalatā kamanīyavibhūṣaṇā

कामरूपकृतावासा

kāmarūpakṛtāvāsā
She Whose Desire is the Form of Desires 50

कामपीठविलासिनी

kāmapīṭhavilāsinī
She Who Reposes in the Center of Worship of Desire 51

कमनीया

kamanīyā
She Who is Desired 52

कल्पलता

kalpalatā
She Who is All Desires 53

कमनीयविभूषणा

kamanīyavibhūṣaṇā
She Who is the Manifestation of That Which is Desired 54

कमनीयगुणाराध्या कोमलाङ्गी कृशोदरी ।
कारणामृतसन्तोषा कारणानन्दसिद्धिदा ॥ १५ ॥

kamanīyaguṇārādhyā komalāṅgī kṛśodarī
kāraṇāmṛtasantoṣā kāraṇānandasiddhidā

कमनीयगुणाराध्या

kamanīyaguṇārādhyā

She Who is Pleased with the Quality of Tenderness 55

कोमलाङ्गी

komalāṅgī

She Who Has Tender Limbs 56

कृशोदरी

kṛśodarī

She Who Has a Slender Waist 57

कारणामृतसन्तोषा

kāraṇāmṛtasantoṣā

She Who is the Cause of the Nectar of Satisfaction 58

कारणानन्दसिद्धिदा

kāraṇānandasiddhidā

She Who is the Cause of Giving the Perfect Attainment of Bliss 59

कारणानन्दजापेष्टा कारणार्चनहर्षिता ।
कारणार्णवसम्मग्ना कारणव्रतपालिनी ॥ १६ ॥

kāraṇānandajāpeṣṭā kāraṇārcanaharṣitā
kāraṇārṇavasammagnā kāraṇavratapālinī

कारणानन्दजापेष्टा

kāraṇānandajāpeṣṭā

She Who is the Cause of the Bliss of Recitation 60

कारणार्चनहर्षिता

kāraṇārcanaharṣitā

She Who is the Cause of the Delight From Offering 61

कारणार्णवसम्मग्ना

kāraṇārṇavasammagnā

She Who is the Cause of Moving in Waves or Cycles 62

कारणव्रतपालिनी

kāraṇavratapālinī

She Who is the Cause of Protecting Vows 63

कस्तूरीसौरभामोदा कस्तूरीतिलकोज्ज्वला ।
कस्तूरीपूजनरता कस्तूरीपूजकप्रिया ॥ १७ ॥

kastūrīsaurabhāmodā kastūrītilakojjvalā
kastūrīpūjanaratā kastūrīpūjakapriyā

कस्तूरीसौरभामोदा
kastūrīsaurabhāmodā
She Who Gives the Intoxicating Scent of Musk to the Deer 64

कस्तूरीतिलकोज्ज्वला
kastūrītilakojjvalā
She Who is the Shining Tilak of Musk 65

कस्तूरीपूजनरता
kastūrīpūjanaratā
She Who Rejoices in the Worship With Musk 66

कस्तूरीपूजकप्रिया
kastūrīpūjakapriyā
She Who is the Beloved of the Worship With Musk 67

कस्तूरीदाहजननी कस्तूरीमृगतोषिणी ।
कस्तूरीभोजनप्रीता कर्पूरामोदमोदिता ।
कर्पूरमालाभरणा कर्पूरचन्दनोक्षिता ॥ १८ ॥

kastūrīdāhajananī kastūrīmṛgatoṣiṇī
kastūrībhojanaprītā karpūrāmodamoditā
karpūramālābharaṇā karpūracandanokṣitā

कस्तूरीदाहजननी
kastūrīdāhajananī
She Who is the Mother of the Radiance of Musk 68

कस्तूरीमृगतोषिणी
kastūrīmṛgatoṣiṇī
She Who Delights Deer With Musk 69

कस्तूरीभोजनप्रीता
kastūrībhojanaprītā
She Loves Food Cooked With Musk 70

कर्पूरामोदमोदिता
karpūrāmodamoditā
She Who Becomes Extremely Pleased From the Offering of Camphor 71

कर्पूरमालाभरणा
karpūramālābharaṇā
She Who Displays a Garland covered by Camphor 72

कर्पूरचन्दनोक्षिता
karpūracandanokṣitā
She Who Enjoys Sandalwood Mixed With Camphor 73

कर्पूरकारणाह्लादा कर्पूरामृतपायिनी ।
कर्पूरसागरस्नाता कर्पूरसागरालया ॥ १९ ॥

karpūrakāraṇāhlādā karpūrāmṛtapāyinī
karpūrasāgarasnātā karpūrasāgarālayā

कर्पूरकारणाह्लादा
karpūrakāraṇāhlādā
She Who Gives the Cause of Joy with Camphor 74

कर्पूरामृतपायिनी
karpūrāmṛtapāyinī
She Who Drinks the Nectar with Camphor 75

कर्पूरसागरस्नाता
karpūrasāgarasnātā
She Who Bathes in the Ocean of Camphor 76

कर्पूरसागरालया
karpūrasāgarālayā
She Who Dissolves in the Ocean of Camphor 77

कूर्चबीजजपप्रीता कूर्चजापपरायणा ।
कुलीनकौलिकाराध्या कौलिकप्रियकारिणी ॥ २० ॥

kūrcabījajapaprītā kūrcajāpaparāyaṇā
kulīna kaulikārādhyā kaulikapriyakāriṇī

कूर्चबीजजपप्रीता
kūrcabījajapaprītā
She Who Loves Recitation of the Kūrca Bīja mantra, huṁ 78

कूर्चजापपरायणा
kūrcajāpaparāyaṇā
She Who always recites the Kūrca Bīja mantra, huṁ 79

कुलीन
kulīna
She Who is of Excellent Family 80

कौलिकाराध्या
kaulikārādhyā
She Who is Adored by Practitioners of Kulācāra 81

कौलिकप्रियकारिणी
kaulikapriyakāriṇī
She Who is the Cause of Love to the Practitioners of Kulācāra, the behavior of excellence 82

कुलाचारा कौतुकिनी कुलमार्गप्रदर्शिनी ।
काशीश्वरी कष्टहर्त्री काशीशवरदायिनी ॥ २१ ॥

kulācārā kautukinī kulamārgapradarśinī
kāśīśvarī kaṣṭahartrī kāśīśavaradāyinī

कुलाचारा
kulācārā
She Who is the Behavior of Excellence 83

कौतुकिनी
kautukinī
She Who is the Joyous One 84

कुलमार्गप्रदर्शिनी
kulamārgapradarśinī
She Who Illuminates the Path to Excellence 85

काशीश्वरी
kāśīśvarī
She Who is the Supreme Divinity of Kāśī 86

कष्टहर्त्री
kaṣṭahartrī
She Who Takes Away All Difficulties 87

काशीशवरदायिनी
kāśīśavaradāyinī
She Who Gives Blessings to Śiva, the Lord of Kāśī 88

काशीश्वरकृतामोदा काशीश्वरमनोरमा ॥ २२ ॥

kāśīśvarakṛtāmodā kāśīśvaramanoramā

काशीश्वरकृतामोदा
kāśīśvarakṛtāmodā
She Who Causes the Male Lord to Become Intoxicated 89

काशीश्वरमनोरमा
kāśīśvaramanoramā
She Who is the Beauty of the Lord of Kāśī 90

कलमञ्जीरचरणा क्वणत्काञ्चीविभूषणा ।
काञ्चनाद्रिकृतागारा काञ्चनाचलकौमुदी ॥ २३ ॥
kalamañjīracaraṇā kvaṇatkāñcīvibhūṣaṇā
kāñcanādrikṛtāgārā kāñcanācalakaumudī

कलमञ्जीरचरणा
kalamañjīracaraṇā
She Who Moves Swiftly to Remove Darkness 91

क्वणत्काञ्चीविभूषणा
kvaṇatkāñcīvibhūṣaṇā
She Who has Tinkling Bells at Her Girdle 92

काञ्चनाद्रिकृतागारा
kāñcanādrikṛtāgārā
She Who Dwells in the Mountains of Gold 93

काञ्चनाचलकौमुदी
kāñcanācalakaumudī
She Who Displays Radiant Wealth on the top of Her Cloth 94

कामबीजजपानन्दा कामबीजस्वरूपिणी ।
कुमतिघ्नीकुलीनार्त्तिनाशिनी कुलकामिनी ॥ २४ ॥
kāmabījajapānandā kāmabījasvarūpiṇī
kumatighnīkulīnārttināśinī kulakāminī

कामबीजजपानन्दा
kāmabījajapānandā
She Who is the Bliss of Recitation of the Bīja Mantra of Desire Krīṁ 95

कामबीजस्वरूपिणी
kāmabījasvarūpiṇī
She Who is the Intrinsic Nature of the Bīja Mantra of Desire Krīṁ 96

कुमतिघ्नीकुलीनार्त्तिनाशिनी
kumatighnīkulīnārttināśinī
She Who Destroys the Bad Thoughts of the Worshiper 97

कुलकामिनी
kulakāminī
She Who is the Entire Family of Desires 98

क्रीं ह्रीं श्रीं मन्त्रवर्णेन कालकण्टकघातिनी ।
इत्याद्याकालिकादेव्याः शतनाम प्रकीर्त्तितम् ॥ २५ ॥

krīṁ hrīṁ śrīṁ mantravarṇena kālakaṇṭakaghātinī
ityādyākālikādevyāḥ śatanāma prakīrttitam

क्रीं
krīṁ
She Who Dissolves the Subtle Body into the Causal Body 99

ह्रीं
hrīṁ
She Who is All of Māyā, what can be perceived through the senses, conceived in the mind, or known through intuition and beyond 100

श्रीं
śrīṁ
She Who is the Ultimate Respect, the perfect perception of peace in the mind and peace in the heart 101

These are known as the Hundred Names of the Foremost Goddess, She Who Takes Away the Darkness, that begin with the letter **Ka**. By means of these mantras the fear of time is destroyed and

ककारकूटघटितं कालीरूपस्वरूपकम् ॥ २६ ॥

kakārakūṭaghaṭitaṁ kālīrūpasvarūpakam

one attains union with the intrinsic nature of the form of She Who Takes Away the Darkness, the most excellent Manifested Cause. 26

पूजाकाले पठेद्यस्तु कालिकाकृतमानसः ।
मन्त्रसिद्धिर्भवेदाशु तस्य काली प्रसीदति ॥ २७ ॥

pūjākāle paṭhedyastu kālikākṛtamānasaḥ
mantrasiddhirbhavedāśu tasya kālī prasīdati

If these mantras are recited at the time of worship with the mind fully concentrated upon She Who Takes Away the Darkness, She Who Takes Away the Darkness becomes pleased and bestows the attainment of perfection. 27

बुद्धिं विद्याञ्च लभते गुरोरादेशमात्रतः ।
धनवान् कीर्त्तिमान् भूयाद्दानशीलो दयान्वितः ॥ २८ ॥

buddhiṁ vidyāñca labhate gurorādeśamātrataḥ
dhanavān kīrttimān bhūyāddānaśīlo dayānvitaḥ

By practicing according to the instructions of the Guru, one will gain knowledge and intelligence, wealth, fame, and become a Compassionate Giver. 28

पुत्रपौत्रसुखैश्वर्यैर्मोदते साधको भुवि ॥ २९

putrapautrasukhaiśvaryairmodate sādhako bhuvi

The children and grandchildren of such a spiritual seeker delight in the happiness derived from imperishable qualities. 29

भौमावास्यानिशाभागे मपञ्चकसमन्वितः ।
पूजयित्वा महाकालीमाद्यां त्रिभुवनेश्वरीम् ॥ ३० ॥

bhaumāvāsyāniśābhāge mapañcakasamanvitaḥ
pūjayitvā mahākālīmādyāṁ tribhuvaneśvarīm

Whoever will worship on the Tuesday night of the New Moon, offering the five principles to the Great Foremost She Who Takes Away the Darkness, the Supreme Goddess of the Three Worlds, 30

पठित्वा शतनामानि साक्षात् कालीमयो भवेत् ।
नासाध्यं विद्यते तस्य त्रिषु लोकेषु किञ्चन ॥ ३१ ॥

paṭhitvā śatanāmāni sākṣāt kālīmayo bhavet
nāsādhyaṁ vidyate tasya triṣu lokeṣu kiñcana

and recite these hundred names, actually becomes the manifestation of She Who Takes Away the Darkness, and knows no obstacles from anywhere in the three worlds. 31

विद्यायां वाक्पतिः साक्षात् धने धनपतिर्भवेत् ।
समुद्र इव गाम्भीर्ये बले च पवनोपमः ॥ ३२ ॥

vidyāyāṁ vākpatiḥ sākṣāt dhane dhanapatirbhavet
samudra iva gāmbhīrye bale ca pavanopamaḥ

In knowledge one actually becomes the Lord of Vibrations, and in wealth, the Lord of Wealth; in equipoise like the sea, and in strength like the wind. 32

तिग्मांशुरिव दुष्प्रेक्ष्यः शशिवत् शुभदर्शनः ।
रूपे मूर्त्तिधरः कामो योषितां हृदयङ्गमः ॥ ३३ ॥

tigmāṁśuriva duṣprekṣyaḥ śaśivat śubhadarśanaḥ
rūpe mūrttidharaḥ kāmo yoṣitāṁ hṛdayaṅgamaḥ

One shines with the radiance of the sun, yet displays the cooling rays of the moon. In form one displays the image of the God of Love, capturing the hearts of all. 33

सर्वत्र जयमाप्नोति स्तवस्यास्य प्रसादतः ।
यं यं कामं पुरस्कृत्य स्तोत्रमेतदुदीरयेत् ॥ ३४ ॥

sarvatra jayamāpnoti stavasyāsya prasādataḥ
yaṁ yaṁ kāmaṁ puraskṛtya stotrametadudīrayet

Who sings this song is always victorious. Wherever desires are pursued this song should be loudly sung. 34

तं तं काममवाप्नोति श्रीमदाद्याप्रसादतः ।

रणे राजकुले द्यूते विवादे प्राणसङ्कटे ॥ ३५ ॥

taṁ taṁ kāmamavāpnoti śrīmadādyāprasādataḥ

raṇe rājakule dyūte vivāde prāṇasaṅkaṭe

Wherever desires are fulfilled, it is the Grace of the Respected Foremost. In battle, in wealthy families, in gambling, in any dispute or life threatening circumstance, 35

दस्युग्रस्ते ग्रमदाहे सिंहव्याघ्रावृते तथा ॥ ३६ ॥

dasyugraste gramadāhe siṁhavyāghrāvṛte tathā

in the hands of robbers, a burning village, confronted by lions or tigers; 36

अरण्ये प्रान्तरे दुर्गे ग्रहराजभयेऽपि वा ।

ज्वरदाहे चिरव्याधौ महारोगादिसङ्कुले ॥ ३७ ॥

araṇye prāntare durge graharājabhaye-pi vā

jvaradāhe ciravyādhau mahārogādisaṅkule

in the forest or a lonely desert, in fear of the planets or an angry king; burning with fever, in long periods of infirmity, or in great illnesses that place life in danger; 37

बालग्रहादिरोगे च तथा दुःस्वप्नदर्शने ।

दुस्तरे सलिले वापि पोते वातविपद्गते ॥ ३८ ॥

bālagrahādiroge ca tathā duḥsvapnadarśane

dustare salile vāpi pote vātavipadgate

in the sicknesses of children caused by planetary influences, upon seeing a bad dream, when sinking in boundless waters, or tossed about in a boat by the winds; 38

विचिन्त्य परमां मायामाद्यां कालीं परात्पराम् ।
यः पठेच्छतनामानि दृढभक्तिसमन्वितः ॥ ३९ ॥

vicintya paramāṁ māyāmādyāṁ kālīṁ parātparām
yaḥ paṭhecchatanāmāni dṛḍhabhaktisamanvitaḥ

whoever recites these hundred names with strong devotion will remember the Supreme Measurement of Consciousness, Greater than the Greatest, the Foremost She Who Takes Away the Darkness. 39

सर्वापद्भ्यो विमुच्येत देवि सत्यं न संशयः ।
न पापेभ्यो भयं तस्य न रोगेभ्यो भयं क्वचित् ॥ ४० ॥

sarvāpadbhyo vimucyeta devi satyaṁ na saṁśayaḥ
na pāpebhyo bhayaṁ tasya na rogebhyo bhayaṁ kvacit

Truly, without a doubt, the Goddess will remove all dangers. No fear from sin nor disease nor any other fear will be experienced. 40

सर्वत्र विजयस्तस्य न कुत्रापि पराभवः ।
तस्य दर्शनमात्रेण पलायन्ते विपद्गणाः ॥ ४१ ॥

sarvatra vijayastasya na kutrāpi parābhavaḥ
tasya darśanamātreṇa palāyante vipadgaṇāḥ

For such a one there is always victory, and never defeat. Even at the mere vision of such a person, all difficulties flee. 41

स वक्ता सर्वशास्त्राणां स भोक्ता सर्वसम्पदाम् ।
स कर्त्ता जातिधर्माणां ज्ञातीनां प्रभुरेव सः ॥ ४२ ॥

sa vaktā sarvaśāstrāṇāṁ sa bhoktā sarvasampadām
sa karttā jātidharmāṇāṁ jñātīnāṁ prabhureva saḥ

That person expounds upon all scriptures and always enjoys good fortune. That person performs the highest ideals of living beings and becomes respected as a being of wisdom. 42

वाणी तस्य वसेद्वक्त्रे कमला निश्चला गृहे ।
तन्नाम्ना मानवाः सर्वे प्रणमन्ति ससम्भ्रमाः ॥ ४३ ॥

vāṇī tasya vasedvaktre kamalā niścalā gṛhe
tannāmnā mānavāḥ sarve praṇamanti sasambhramāḥ

The Goddess of Speech dwells in such a person's mouth, and the Goddess of Wealth in that person's home. Men bow with respect at the mention of that person's name. 43

दृष्ट्या तस्य तृणायन्ते ह्यणिमाद्यष्टसिद्धयः ।
आद्याकालीस्वरूपाख्यं शतनाम प्रकीर्तितम् ॥ ४४ ॥

dṛṣṭyā tasya tṛṇāyante hyaṇimādyaṣṭasiddhayaḥ
ādyākālīsvarūpākhyaṁ śatanāma prakīrtitam

Such a person compares the eight occult powers such as making one's self small, etc., with the value of grass. These hundred names are known as the intrinsic nature of the Foremost She Who Takes Away the Darkness. 44

अष्टोत्तरशतावृत्त्या पुरश्चर्याऽस्य गीयते ।
पुरस्क्रियान्वितं स्तोत्रं सर्वाभीष्टफलप्रदम् ॥ ४५ ॥

aṣṭottaraśatāvṛttyā puraścaryā-sya gīyate
puraskriyānvitaṁ stotraṁ sarvābhīṣṭaphalapradam

For the perfection of these mantras in the fire sacrifice, they should be sung one hundred eight times. The full offering of this song yields the fruit of all desires. 45

शतनामस्तुतिमिमामाद्याकालीस्वरूपिणीम् ।
पठेद्वा पाठयेद्वापि शृणुयाच्छ्रावयेदपि ॥ ४६ ॥

śatanāmastutimimāmādyākālīsvarūpiṇīm
paṭhedvā pāṭhayedvāpi śṛṇuyācchrāvayedapi

This hymn of a hundred names is the intrinsic essence of the Foremost She Who Takes Away the Darkness. Whoever will recite it or cause it to be recited, whoever will listen to it or cause it to be heard, 46

सर्वपापविनिर्मुक्तो ब्रह्मसायुज्यमाप्नुयात् ॥ ४७ ॥

sarvapāpavinirmukto brahmasāyujyamāpnuyāt

will be freed from all sin and will attain to union with the Supreme Divinity. 47

ॐ

कालीकवचं

kālī kavacaṁ

The Armor of Kālī

श्रीसदाशिव उवाच

śrīsadāśiva uvāca

The Respected Eternal Consciousness of Infinite Goodness said:

कथितं परमं ब्रह्मप्रकृतेः स्तवनं महत् ।
आद्यायाः श्रीकालिकायाः कवचं शृणु साम्प्रतम् ॥ १ ॥

kathitaṁ paramaṁ brahmaprakṛteḥ stavanaṁ mahat
ādyāyāḥ śrīkālikāyāḥ kavacaṁ śṛṇu sāmpratam

Oh Supremely Divine Nature, you have been told of the great song of the Foremost Respected She Who Takes Away the Darkness. Now listen to Her Armor. 1

त्रैलोक्यविजयस्यास्य कवचस्य ऋषिः शिवः ।
छन्दोऽनुष्टुब्देवता च आद्या काली प्रकीर्त्तिता ॥ २ ॥

trailokyavijayasyāsya kavacasya ṛṣiḥ śivaḥ
chando-nuṣṭubdevatā ca ādyā kālī prakīrttitā

The Seer of this hymn of the Goddess who is Victorious over the three worlds is the Consciousness of Infinite Goodness (Śiva). The meter is anuṣṭup (32 syllables to the verse) and the Foremost She Who Takes Away the Darkness is famous as the Deity. 2

मायाबीजं बीजमिति रमा शक्तिरुदाहृता ।
क्रीं कीलकं काम्यसिद्धौ विनियोगः प्रकीर्त्तितः ॥ ३ ॥

māyābījaṁ bījamiti ramā śaktirudāhṛtā
krīṁ kīlakaṁ kāmyasiddhau viniyogaḥ prakīrttitaḥ

The seed mantra of māyā is the seed. Beauty is the energy which lifts to gladness. Krīṁ is the pin and the perfect attainment and protection of desires is its application for which it is widely known. 3

ह्रीमाद्या मे शिरः पातु श्रीं काली वदनं मम ।
हृदयं क्रीं परा शक्तिः पायात् कण्ठं परात्परा ॥ ४ ॥

hrīmādyā me śiraḥ pātu śrīṁ kālī vadanaṁ mama
hṛdayaṁ krīṁ parā śaktiḥ pāyāt kaṇṭhaṁ parātparā

Hrīṁ, may the Foremost protect my head. Śrīṁ, may She Who Takes Away the Darkness protect in the face. Krīṁ, may the Supreme Energy reside in the heart. May the Greater than the Greatest protect in the throat. 4

नेत्रे पातु जगद्धात्री कर्णौ रक्षतु शङ्करी ।
घ्राणं पातु महामाया रसनां सर्वमङ्गला ॥ ५ ॥

netre pātu jagaddhātrī karṇau rakṣatu śaṅkarī
ghrāṇaṁ pātu mahāmāyā rasanāṁ sarvamaṅgalā

In the eyes may the Creator of the Perceivable Universe protect. In the ears may She Who Manifests Peace. May the Great Limitation of Consciousness protect in the nose. May All Welfare protect the taste. 5

दन्तान् रक्षतु कौमारी कपोलौ कमलालया ।
ओष्ठाधरौ क्षमा रक्षेत् चिबुकं चारुहासिनी ॥ ६ ॥

dantān rakṣatu kaumārī kapolau kamalālayā
oṣṭādharau kṣamā rakṣet cibukaṁ cāruhāsinī

May the Ever Pure One protect the teeth. In the cheeks may She Who Resides in the Lotus protect. In the two lips may Forgiveness protect. May She With the Great Laugh protect the chin. 6

ग्रीवां पायात् कुलेशानी ककुत् पातु कृपामयी ।
द्वौ बाहू बाहुदा रक्षेत् करौ कैवल्यदायिनी ॥ ७ ॥

grīvāṁ pāyāt kuleśānī kakut pātu kṛpāmayī
dvau bāhū bāhudā rakṣet karau kaivalyadāyinī

May the Supreme Ruler of Excellence protect the neck. May the Expression of Grace protect the upper back. May the Giver of Strength protect the two arms. May the Giver of Non-Duality protect the hands. 7

स्कन्धौ कपर्दिनी पातु पृष्ठं त्रैलोक्यतारिणी ।
पार्श्वे पायादपर्णा मे कटिं मे कमठासना ॥ ८ ॥

skandhau kapardinī pātu pṛṣṭhaṁ trailokyatāriṇī
pārśve pāyādaparṇā me kaṭiṁ me kamaṭhāsanā

May the Extremely Fierce One protect the two shoulders. May the Illuminator of the three worlds protect the back. May my sides be protected by the Indivisible One. May She Who Resides in Strength and Capacity protect my waist. 8

नाभौ पातु विशालाक्षी प्रजास्थानं प्रभावती ।
ऊरू रक्षतु कल्याणी पादौ मे पातु पार्वती ॥ ९ ॥

nābhau pātu viśālākṣī prajāsthānaṁ prabhāvatī
ūrū rakṣatu kalyāṇī pādau me pātu pārvatī

May She With the Great Eyes protect in the navel. May She Who Manifests Light protect in the region of the sexual organs. May She Who is All Welfare protect the thighs, and may Parvatī (Daughter of the Mountain) protect my two feet. 9

जयदुर्गाऽवतु प्राणान् सर्वाङ्गं सर्वसिद्धिदा ।
रक्षाहीनंतु यत् स्थानं वर्जितं कवचेन च ॥ १० ॥

jayadurgā-vatu prāṇān sarvāṅgaṁ sarvasiddhidā
rakṣāhīnaṁtu yat sthānaṁ varjitaṁ kavacena ca

May the Victorious Reliever of Difficulties also protect the breath and life-force. May She Who Grants All Attainment protect the whole body. May all places that have not been mentioned in the recitation of this armor be protected (as well). 10

तत् सर्वं मे सदा रक्षेदाद्या काली सनातनी ।
इति ते कथितं दिव्यं त्रैलोक्यविजयाभिधम् ॥ ११ ॥

tat sarvaṁ me sadā rakṣedādyā kālī sanātanī
iti te kathitaṁ divyaṁ trailokyavijayābhidham

May I always be protected by the Foremost Eternal Divine Mother Who Takes Away the Darkness. Hey Divine Ones, this is the explaination of the knowledge which confers victory over the three worlds 11

कवचं कालिकादेव्या आद्यायाः परमाद्भुतम् ॥ १२ ॥

kavacaṁ kālikādevyā ādyāyāḥ paramādbhutam

the supremely magnificent armor of the Eternal Divine Mother, She Who Takes Away the Darkness. 12

पूजाकाले पठेद्यस्तु आद्याधिकृतमानसः ।
सर्वान् कामानवाप्नोति तस्याद्या सुप्रसीदति ।
मन्त्रसिद्धिर्भवेदाशु किङ्कराः क्षुद्रसिद्धयः ॥ १३ ॥

pūjākāle paṭhedyastu ādyādhikṛtamānasaḥ
sarvān kāmānavāpnoti tasyādyā suprasīdati
mantrasiddhirbhavedāśu kiṅkarāḥ kṣudrasiddhayaḥ

One should recite these (mantras) at the time of worship with the mind fully absorbed in the Foremost Goddess. When the Foremost is excellently pleased, She grants the fulfillment of all desires. With the fullest offering comes the most complete attainment of perfection, and with a small offering comes a small attainment. 13

अपुत्रो लभते पुत्रं धनार्थी प्राप्नुयाद्धनम् ।
विद्यार्थी लभते विद्यां कामी कामानवाप्नुयात् ॥ १४ ॥

aputro labhate putraṁ dhanārthī prāpnuyāddhanam
vidyārthī labhate vidyāṁ kāmī kāmānavāpnuyāt

Those without children will gain children. Those who desire wealth, will attain wealth. Those who desire knowledge will attain knowledge. Those who desire desires will attain the fulfillment of desires. 14

सहस्रावृत्तपाठेन वर्मणोऽस्य पुरस्क्रिया ॥
पुरश्चरणसम्पन्नं यथोक्तफलदं भवेत् ॥ १५ ॥

sahasrāvṛttapāṭhena varmaṇo-sya puraskriyā
purścaraṇasampannaṁ yathoktaphaladaṁ bhavet

By reciting a thousand times, one completes the homa offering which will grant the appropriate fruit, and aspires to the attainment of perfection. 15

चन्दनागरुकस्तूरीकुङ्कुमैः रक्तचन्दनैः ।
भूर्जे विलिख्य गुटिकां स्वर्णस्थां धारयेद् यदि ॥ १६ ॥

candanāgarukastūrīkuṅkumaiḥ raktacandanaiḥ
bhūrje vilikhya guṭikāṁ svarṇasthāṁ dhārayed yadi

With sandalwood, wood-apple scent, red vermilion, and red sandal paste one should write the mantra on the bark of the Birch tree or on a plate of gold, and the spiritual seeker should wear it 16

शिखायां दक्षिणे बाहौ कण्ठे वा साधकः कटौ ।
तस्याऽऽद्या कालिका वश्या वाञ्छितार्थं प्रयच्छति ॥ १७ ॥

śikhāyāṁ dakṣiṇe bāhau kaṇṭhe vā sādhakaḥ kaṭau
tasyā--dyā kālikā vaśyā vāñchitārthaṁ prayacchati

on the crown of the head, at the right upper arm, at the throat or on the waist. She Who Takes Away the Darkness yields to such a person and bestows the object of desire. 17

न कुत्रापि भयं तस्य सर्वत्र विजयी कविः ।
अरोगी चिरजीवी स्यात् बलवान् धारणक्षमः ॥ १८ ॥

na kutrāpi bhayaṁ tasya sarvatra vijayī kaviḥ
arogī cirajīvī syāt balavān dhāraṇakṣamaḥ

No where is there the experience of fear and everywhere such a poet is victorious. Such a person becomes free from infirmities, is blessed with immortal life and wields great strength. 18

सर्वविद्यासु निपुणः सर्वशास्त्रार्थतत्त्ववित् ।
वशे तस्य महीपाला भोगमोक्षौ करस्थितौ ॥ १९ ॥

sarvavidyāsu nipuṇaḥ sarvaśāstrārthatattvavit
vaśe tasya mahīpālā bhogamokṣau karasthitau

Such a person becomes accomplished in all branches of knowledge and knows the subtle principles of all scriptures. Such a person yields for the protection of the earth and becomes established in enjoyment and liberation otherwise known as self-realization. 19

कलिकल्मषयुक्तानां निःश्रेयसकरं परम् ॥ २० ॥

kalikalmaṣayuktānāṁ niḥśreyasakaraṁ param

You have been allowed to hear this ultimate knowledge in which the darkness of the age of darkness is destroyed. 20

ॐ

श्रीकालीसहस्रनामस्तोत्रम्

Śrī Kālīsahasranāma Stotram

The Thousand Names of Kālī

श्मशानकालिका काली भद्रकाली कपालिनी ।
गुह्यकाली महाकाली कुरुकुल्लाविरोधिनी ॥ १

śmaśānakālikā kālī bhadrakālī kapālinī
guhyakālī mahākālī kurukullāvirodhinī

श्मशानकालिका

śmaśānakālikā

She Who is the Remover of Darkness from the Cremation Grounds or from Death 1

काली

kālī

She Who is the Remover of Darkness 2

भद्रकाली

bhadrakālī

She Who is the Excellent Remover of Darkness 3

कपालिनी

kapālinī

She Who is the Bearer of the Skulls of Impurity 4

गुह्यकाली

guhyakālī

She Who is the Hidden or Secretive Remover of Darkness 5

महाकाली

mahākālī

She Who is the Great Remover of Darkness 6

कुरुकुल्लाविरोधिनी

kurukullāvirodhinī

She Who Confronts the Forces of Duality 7

कालिका कालरात्रिश्च महाकालनितम्बिनी ।
कालभैरवभार्या च कुलवर्त्मप्रकाशिनी ॥ २

kālikā kālarātriśca mahākālanitambinī
kālabhairavabhāryā ca kulavartmaprakāśinī

कालिका
kālikā
She Who is the Cause of Removing Darkness 8

कालरात्रिश्च
kālarātriśca
She Who is the Dark Night of Egotism and 9

महाकालनितम्बिनी
mahākālanitambinī
She Who is the Eternal Mother of Great Time 10

कालभैरवभार्या च
kālabhairavabhāryā ca
She Who is the Wife of the Fearfulness of Infinite Time and 11

कुलवर्त्मप्रकाशिनी
kulavartmaprakāśinī
She Who Illuminates the Whole World Family 12

कामदा कामिनी काम्या कमनीयस्वभाविनी ।
कस्तूरीरसलिप्ताङ्गी कुञ्जरेश्वरगामिनी ॥ ३

kāmadā kāminī kāmyā kamanīyasvabhāvinī
kastūrīrasaliptāṅgī kuñjareśvaragāminī

कामदा
kāmadā
She Who is the Giver of All Desire 13

कामिनी
kāminī
She Who is the Giver of This Desire 14

कम्या

kāmyā
She Who is Desired 15

कमनीयस्वभाविनी

kamanīyasvabhāvinī
She Who is the Intrinsic Nature of that which is Desired 16

कस्तूरीरसलिप्ताङ्गी

kastūrīrasaliptāṅgī
She Whose Limbs are Anointed with the Juice of Musk 17

कुञ्जरेश्वरगामिनी

kuñjareśvaragāminī
She Who Moves like the Lord of Elephants (Indra's Airāvata) 18

ककारवर्णसर्वाङ्गी कामिनी कामसुन्दरी ।
कामार्ता कामरूपा च कामधेनुः कलावती ॥ ४

kakāravarṇasarvāṅgī kāminī kāmasundarī
kāmārtā kāmarūpā ca kāmadhenuḥ kalāvatī

ककारवर्णसर्वाङ्गी

kakāravarṇasarvāṅgī
She Who is All the Limbs of the Letter "Ka," the Cause 19

कामिनी

kāminī
She Who is This Desire 20

कामसुन्दरी

kāmasundarī
She Who is Beautiful Desire 21

कामार्ता

kāmārtā
She Who is the Object of Desire 22

कामरूपा च

kāmarūpā ca
She Who is the Form of Desire and 23

कामधेनुः

kāmadhenuḥ
She Who is the Cow which Fulfills All Desires 24

कलावती

kalāvatī
She Who is the Repository of All Qualities or Arts 25

कान्ता कामस्वरूपा च कामाख्या कुलपालिनी ।
कुलीना कुलवत्यम्बा दुर्गा दुर्गार्तिनाशिनी ॥ ५

kāntā kāmasvarūpā ca kāmākhyā kulapālinī
kulīnā kulavatyambā durgā durgārtināśinī

कान्ता
kāntā
She Who is Beauty Enhanced by Love 26

कामस्वरूपा च
kāmasvarūpā ca
She Who is the Intrinsic Form of Desire and 27

कामाख्या
kāmākhyā
She Whose name is Desire 28

कुलपालिनी
kulapālinī
She Who Protects Excellence 29

कुलीना
kulīnā
She Who is Excellence 30

कुलवत्यम्बा
kulavatyambā
She Who is the Repository of Excellence 31

दुर्गा
durgā
She Who is the Reliever of Difficulties 32

दुर्गार्तिनाशिनी
durgārtināśinī
She Who is the Destroyer of All Various Difficulties 33

कुमारी कुलजा कृष्णा कृष्णदेहा कृशोदरा ।
कृशांगी कुलिशांगी च क्रींकारी कमला कला ॥ ६

kumārī kulajā kṛṣṇā kṛṣṇadehā kṛśodārā
kṛśāṁgī kuliśāṁgī ca krīṁkārī kamalā kalā

कुमारी
kumārī
She Who is Ever Pure 34

कुलजा
kulajā
She Who Gives Birth to Excellence 35

कृष्णा
kṛṣṇā
She Who Manifests All Action 36

कृष्णदेहा
kṛṣṇadehā
She Who Has a Dark Body 37

कृशोदरा
kṛśodarā
She Who Holds Aloft All Action 38

कृशांगी
kṛśāṁgī
She Who Embodies All Action 39

कुलिशांगी च
kuliśāṁgī ca
She Who is the Embodiment of Excellence and 40

क्रींकारी
krīṁkārī
She Who Causes Dissolution of the Subtle Body into the Causal Body 41

कमला
kamalā
She Who is a Lotus (Lakṣmi) 42

कला
kalā
She Who is Art or All Attributes 43

करालास्या कराली च कुलकान्ताऽपराजिता ।
उग्रा उग्रप्रभा दीप्ता विप्रचित्ता महानना ॥ ७

karālāsyā karālī ca kulakāntā-parājitā
ugrā ugraprabhā dīptā vipracittā mahānanā

करालास्या
karālāsyā
She Who Has a Gaping Mouth 44

कराली च
karālī ca
She Who Dissolves All into Her Being and 45

कुलकान्ताऽपराजिता
kulakāntā-parājitā
She Whose Excellent Beauty is Undefeated 46

उग्रा
ugrā
She Who is Terrible 47

उग्रप्रभा
ugraprabhā
She Whose Light is Terrible 48

दीप्ता
dīptā
She Who is Light 49

विप्रचित्ता
vipracittā
She Whose Objects of Consciousness are Varied 50

महानना
mahānanā
She Who has a Great Face 51

नीलाघना वलाका च मात्रा मुद्रामितासिता ।
ब्राह्मी नारायणी भद्रा सुभद्रा भक्तवत्सला ॥ ८

nīlāghanā valākā ca mātrā mudrāmitāsitā
brāhmī nārāyaṇī bhadrā subhadrā bhaktavatsalā

नीलाघना
nīlāghanā
She Who has the Complexion of a Dark Cloud 52

वलाका च
valākā ca
She Who Exemplifies the Freedom of a Swan and 53

मात्रा
mātrā
She Who is Verse 54

मुद्रामितासिता
mudrāmitāsitā
She Whose Positions of Her Limbs are Extremely Elegant 55

ब्राह्मी
brāhmī
She Who is Creative Energy 56

नारायणी
nārāyaṇī
She Who is the Exposer of Consciousness 57

भद्रा

bhadrā
She Who is Excellent 58

सुभद्रा

subhadrā
She Who is the Excellent of Excellence 59

भक्तवत्सला

bhaktavatsalā
She Who Nourishes All Devotees 60

माहेश्वरी च चामुण्डा वाराही नारसिंहिका ।
वज्राङ्गी वज्रकङ्काली नृमुण्डस्रग्विणी शिवा ॥ ९

māheśvarī ca cāmuṇḍā vārāhī nārasiṁhikā
vajrāṅgī vajrakaṅkālī nṛmuṇḍasragviṇī śivā

माहेश्वरी च

māheśvarī ca
She Who is the Great Seer of All and 61

चामुण्डा

cāmuṇḍā
She Who Moves in the Paradigm of Consciousness 62

वाराही

vārāhī
She Who is the Boar of Sacrifice 63

नारसिंहिका

nārasiṁhikā
She Who is the Ferocious Half Human Half Lion of Courage 64

वज्राङ्गी

vajrāṅgī
She Who has Limbs of Lightning 65

वज्रकङ्काली

vajrakaṅkālī
She Whose Head Shines Like Lightning 66

नृमुण्डस्रग्विणी

nṛmuṇḍasragviṇī
She Who is Adorned by a Garland 67

शिवा

śivā
She Who is the Energy of the Consciousness of Infinite Goodness 68

मालिनी नरमुण्डाली गलत्रुधिरभूषणा ।
रक्तचन्दनसिक्ताङ्गी सिन्दूरारुणमस्तका ॥ १०

mālinī naramuṇḍālī galatrudhirabhūṣaṇā
raktacandanasiktāṅgī sindūrāruṇamastakā

मालिनी
mālinī
She Who Wears a Garland of Skulls 69

नरमुण्डाली
naramuṇḍālī
She Who holds the Head of a man 70

गलत्रुधिरभूषणा
galatrudhirabhūṣaṇā
From the Garland of Skulls around Her Neck Fall Drops of Blood 71

रक्तचन्दनसिक्ताङ्गी
ratkacandanasiktāṅgī
She Whose Limbs are Covered by Red Sandal Paste 72

सिन्दूरारुणमस्तका
sindūrāruṇamastakā
She Whose Forehead is Marked with the Vermilion of Love which Brings the Light of Wisdom 73

घोररूपा घोरदंष्ट्रा घोराघोरतरा शुभा ।
महादंष्ट्रा महामाया सुदन्ती युगदन्तुरा ॥ ११

ghorarūpā ghoradaṁṣṭrā ghorāghoratarā śubhā
mahādaṁṣṭrā mahāmāyā sudantī yugadanturā

घोररूपा
ghorarūpā
She Who is of Fearful Form 74

घोरदंष्ट्रा
ghoradaṁṣṭrā
She Whose Teeth are Fearful 75

घोराघोरतरा
ghorāghoratarā
She Who is Auspiciousness which Takes Beyond Inauspiciousness 76

शुभा
śubhā
She Who is Pure 77

महादंष्ट्रा
mahādaṁṣṭrā
She Who Has Great Teeth 78

महामाया
mahāmāyā
She Who is the Great Definition of Consciousness 79

सुदन्ती
sudantī
She Who Has Excellent Teeth 80

युगदन्तुरा
yugadanturā
She Who is Beyond the Ages of Time 81

सुलोचना विरूपाक्षी विशालाक्षी त्रिलोचना ।
शारदेन्दुप्रसन्नास्या स्फुरत्स्मेराम्बुजेक्षणा ॥ १२

sulocanā virūpākṣī viśālākṣī trilocanā
śāradenduprasannāsyā sphuratsmerāmbujekṣaṇā

सुलोचना
sulocanā
She Who Has Beautiful Eyes 82

विरूपाक्षी
virūpākṣī
She Whose Eyes are of Indescribable Form 83

विशालाक्षी
viśālākṣī
She Who Has Great Eyes 84

त्रिलोचना
trilocanā
She Who Has Three Eyes 85

शारदेन्दुप्रसन्नास्या
śāradenduprasannāsyā
She Who is Pleased as the Autumn Moon 86

स्फुरत्स्मेराम्बुजेक्षणा
sphuratsmerāmbujekṣaṇā
She Whose Purity Shines in Her Lotus Eyes 87

अट्टहासप्रसन्नास्या स्मेरवक्त्रा सुभाषिणी ।
प्रसन्नपद्मवदना स्मितास्या प्रियभाषिणी ॥ १३

aṭṭahāsaprasannāsyā smeravaktrā subhāṣiṇī
prasannapadmavadanā smitāsyā priyabhāṣiṇī

अट्टहासप्रसन्नास्या
aṭṭahāsaprasannāsyā
She Who Has a Great Laugh in Extreme Pleasure 88

स्मेरवक्त्रा
smeravaktrā
She Who Speaks Words of Remembrance 89

सुभाषिणी
subhāṣiṇī
She Who Has Excellent Expression 90

प्रसन्नपद्मवदना
prasannapadmavadanā
She Whose Lotus Lips Smile 91

स्मितास्या
smitāsyā
She Whose Face is Always Happy 92

प्रियभाषिणी
priyabhāṣiṇī
She Who is the Beloved Expression of Love 93

कोटराक्षी कुलश्रेष्ठा महती बहुभाषिणी ।
सुमतिः कुमतिश्चण्डा चण्डमुण्डातिवेगिनी ॥ १४

koṭarākṣī kulaśreṣṭhā mahatī bahubhāṣiṇī
sumatiḥ kumatiścaṇḍā caṇḍamuṇḍātiveginī

कोटराक्षी

koṭarākṣī

She Whose Eyes are Infinite 94

कुलश्रेष्ठा

kulaśreṣṭā

She Who is the Excellent of Excellence or of Excellent Family 95

महती

mahatī

She Who Has a Great Mind 96

बहुभाषिणी

bahubhāṣiṇī

She Who Has Various Expressions 97

सुमतिः

sumatiḥ

She Who Has an Excellent Mind 98

कुमतिः

kumatiḥ

She Who has a Devious Mind 99

चण्डा

caṇḍā

She Who is Passion 100

चण्डमुण्डातिवेगिनी

caṇḍamuṇḍātiveginī

She Who Destroys Passion, Meanness and Other Negativities 101

प्रचण्डचण्डिका चण्डी चण्डिका चण्डवेगिनी ।
सुकेशी मुक्तकेशी च दीर्घकेशी महत्कुचा ॥ १८

pracaṇḍacaṇḍikā caṇḍī caṇḍikā caṇḍaveginī
sukeśī muktakeśī ca dīrghakeśī mahatkucā

प्रचण्डचण्डिका

pracaṇḍacaṇḍikā

She Who is Great Terrible Passion 102

चण्डी

caṇḍī

She Who Tears Apart Thought 103

चण्डिका

caṇḍikā

She Who is the Cause of Tearing Apart All Thought 104

चण्डवेगिनी

caṇḍaveginī

She Who Destroys All Passion 105

सुकेशी
sukeśī
She Who Has Beautiful Hair 106

मुक्तकेशी च
muktakeśī ca
She Who Has Unbound Hair and 107

दीर्घकेशी
dīrghakeśī
She Who Has Long Hair 108

महत्कुचा
mahatkucā
She Who Has Large Breasts 109

प्रेतदेहकर्णपूरा प्रेतपाणिसुमेखला ।
प्रेतासना प्रियप्रेता प्रेतभूमिकृतालया ॥ १६

pretadehakarṇapūrā pretapāṇisumekhalā
pretāsanā priyapretā pretabhūmikṛtālayā

प्रेतदेहकर्णपूरा
pretadehakarṇapūrā
She Who Has the Ears of the Cosmic Body 110

प्रेतपाणिसुमेखला
pretapāṇisumekhalā
She Who Has the Hands and Waist of the Cosmic Body 111

प्रेतासना
pretāsanā
She Who Sits with Disembodied Spirits 112

प्रियप्रेता
priyapretā
She Who is the Beloved of Disembodied Spirits 113

प्रेतभूमिकृतालया
pretabhūmikṛtālayā
She Who is the Land Where Disembodied Spirits Reside 114

श्मशानवासिनी पुण्या पुण्यदा कुलपण्डिता ।
पुण्यालया पुण्यदेहा पुण्यश्लोका च पाविनी ॥ १७

śmaśānavāsinī puṇyā puṇyadā kulapaṇḍitā
puṇyālayā puṇyadehā puṇyaślokā ca pāvinī

श्मशानवासिनी

śmaśānavāsinī
She Who Resides in the Cremation Grounds 115

पुण्या

puṇyā
She Who is Merit 116

पुण्यदा

puṇyadā
She Who is the Giver of Merit 117

कुलपण्डिता

kulapaṇḍitā
She Who is the One of Excellent Knowledge 118

पुण्यालया

puṇyālayā
She Who is the Residence of Merit 119

पुण्यदेहा

puṇyadehā
She Who Embodies Merit 120

पुण्यश्लोका च

puṇyaślokā ca
She Whose Every Utterance is Merit and 121

पाविनी

pāvinī
She Who Blows Like a Fresh Breeze 122

पूता पवित्रा परमा पुरापुण्यविभूषणा ।
पुण्यनाम्नी भीतिहरा वरदा खङ्गपालिनी ॥ १८

pūtā pavitrā paramā purāpuṇyavibhūṣaṇā
puṇyanāmnī bhītiharā varadā khaṅgapālinī

पूता

pūtā
She Who is the Daughter 123

पवित्रा

pavitrā
She Who is Pure 124

परमा

paramā
She Who is Supreme 125

पुरापुण्यविभूषणा

purāpuṇyavibhūṣaṇā
She Who Illuminates the Fullest Merit 126

पुण्यनाम्नी

puṇyanāmnī

She Whose Name is Meritorious 127

भीतिहरा

bhītiharā

She Who Takes away Fear and Doubt 128

वरदा

varadā

She Who is the Grantor of Boons 129

खड्गपालिनी

khaṅgapālinī

She Who Has the Sword of Wisdom in Her Hand 130

नृमुण्डहस्तशस्ता च छिन्नमस्ता सुनासिका ।
दक्षिणा श्यामला श्यामा शान्ता पीनोन्नतस्तनी ॥ १९

nṛmuṇḍahastaśastā ca chinnamastā sunāsikā
dakṣiṇā śyāmalā śyāmā śāntā pīnonnatastanī

नृमुण्डहस्तशस्ता च

nṛmuṇḍahastaśastā ca

She Who Holds the Skull of Impure Thought and 131

छिन्नमस्ता

chinnamastā

She Who holds the Severed Head of Duality 132

सुनासिका

sunāsikā

She Who Has an Excellent Organ of Scent 133

दक्षिणा

dakṣiṇā

She Who Looks to the South; She Who is the Offering Made in Respect for Guidance 134

श्यामला

śyāmalā

She Who has a Dark Complexion 135

श्यामा

śyāmā

She Who is Dark 136

शान्ता

śāntā
She Who is Peace 137

पीनोन्नतस्तनी

pīnonnatastanī
She Who Raises the Trident in Her Hand 138

दिगम्बरा घोररावा सृक्कान्ता रक्तवाहिनी ।
घोररावा शिवासंगी विसंगी मदनातुरा ॥ २०

digambarā ghorarāvā sṛkkāntā raktavāhinī
ghorarāvā śivāsaṁgī visaṁgī madanāturā

दिगम्बरा

digambarā
She Who Wears Space 139

घोररावा

ghorarāvā
She Whose Sound is Terrible 140

सृक्कान्ता

sṛkkāntā
She Whose Beauty Creates 141

रक्तवाहिनी

raktavāhinī
She Who is the Vehicle of Passion 142

घोररावा

ghorarāvā
She Whose Sound is Terrible 143

शिवासंगी

śivāsaṁgī
She Who is with Śiva 144

विसंगी

visaṁgī
She Who is Without Any Other 145

मदनातुरा

madanāturā
She Who is the Ultimate Intoxication 146

मत्ता प्रमत्ता प्रमदा सुधासिन्धुनिवासिनी ।
अतिमत्ता महामत्ता सर्वाकर्षणकारिणी ॥ २१

mattā pramattā pramadā sudhāsindhunivāsinī
atimattā mahāmattā sarvākarṣṇakāriṇī

मत्ता

mattā
She Who is the Great Mind or Thinker 147

प्रमत्ता

pramattā
She Who is the Foremost Mind or Thinker 148

प्रमदा

pramadā
She Who is the Giver of Preeminence 149

सुधासिन्धुनिवासिनी

sudhāsindhunivāsinī
She Who Resides in the Ocean of Purity 150

अतिमत्ता

atimattā
She Who is the Extremely Great Mind 151

महामत्ता

mahāmattā
She Who is the Great Great Mind 152

सर्वाकर्षणकारिणी

sarvākarṣaṇakāriṇī
She Who is the Cause of All Attraction 153

गीतप्रिया वाद्यरता प्रेतनृत्यपरायणा ।
चतुर्भुजा दशभुजा अष्टादशभुजा तथा ॥ २२

gītapriyā vādyaratā pretanṛtyaparāyaṇā
caturbhujā daśabhujā aṣṭādaśabhujā tathā

गीतप्रिया

gītapriyā
She Who is the Beloved of Songs 154

वाद्यरता

vādyaratā
She Who is Extremely Pleased by Music 155

प्रेतनृत्यपरायणा

pretanṛtyaparāyaṇā

She Who is the Eternal Dance of Disembodied Spirits 156

चतुर्भुजा

caturbhujā

She Who Has Four Arms 157

दशभुजा

daśabhujā

She Who Has Ten Arms 158

अष्टादशभुजा तथा

aṣṭādaśabhujā tathā

She Who Has Eighteen Arms also 159

कात्यायनी जगन्माता जगतां परमेश्वरी ।
जगद्बन्धुर्जगद्धात्री जगदानन्दकारिणी ॥ २३

kātyāyanī jaganmātā jagatāṁ parameśvarī
jagadbandhurjagaddhātrī jagadānandakāriṇī

कात्यायनी

kātyāyanī

She Who is Ever Pure 160

जगन्माता

jaganmātā

She Who is the Mother of the Perceivable Universe 161

जगतां परमेश्वरी

jagatāṁ parameśvarī

She Who is the Supreme Ruler of the Perceivable Universe 162

जगद्बन्धुः

jagadbandhuḥ

She Who is the Friend of the Perceivable Universe163

जगद्धात्री

jagaddhātrī

She Who Creates the Perceivable Universe 164

जगदानन्दकारिणी

jagadānandakāriṇī

She Who is the Cause of Bliss in the Perceivable Universe 165

जगज्जीवमयी हैमवती माया महामही ।
नागयज्ञोपवीताङ्गी नागिनी नागशायिनी ॥ २४

jagajjīvamayī haimavatī māyā mahāmahī
nāgayajñopavītāṅgī nāginī nāgaśāyinī

जगज्जीवमयी
jagajjīvamayī
She Who is the Manifestation of All Life in the Universe 166

हैमवती
haimavatī
She Who is Born of Himalayas 167

माया
māyā
She Who is the Great Measurement of Consciousness 168

महामही
mahāmahī
She Who is the Great Expression 169

नागयज्ञोपवीताङ्गी
nāgayajñopavītāṅgī
She Who is the Sacred Thread on the Body of the Snake, the Adornment of Kuṇḍalinī 170

नागिनी
nāginī
She Who is the Snake 171

नागशायिनी
nāgaśāyinī
She Who Rests on Snakes 172

नागकन्या देवकन्या गन्धर्वी किन्नरेश्वरी ।
मोहरात्रिर्महारात्रिर्दारुणा भास्वरासुरी ॥ २५

nāgakanyā devakanyā gandharvī kinnareśvarī
moharātrirmahārātrirdāruṇā bhāsvarāsurī

नागकन्या

nāgakanyā
She Who is the Daughter of the Snake 173

देवकन्या

devakanyā
She Who is the Daughter of the Gods 174

गन्धर्वी

gandharvī
She Who Sings Celestial Divine Tunes 175

किन्नरेश्वरी

kinnareśvarī
She Who is the Supreme Ruler of Heavenly Beings 176

मोहरात्रिः

moharātriḥ
She Who is the Night of Ignorance 177

महारात्रिः

mahārātriḥ
She Who is the Great Night 178

दारुणा

dāruṇā
She Who Supports All 179

भास्वरासुरी

bhāsvarāsurī
She Whose Radiance Destroys Duality 180

विद्याधरी वसुमती यक्षिणी योगिनी जरा ।
राक्षसी डाकिनी वेदमयी वेदविभूषणा ॥ २६

vidyādharī vasumatī yakṣiṇī yoginī jarā
rākṣaśī ḍākinī vedamayī vedavibhūṣaṇā

विद्याधरी

vidyādharī
She Who Grants Great Knowledge 181

वसुमती

vasumatī
She Who Has Wealth 182

यक्षिणी

yakṣiṇī
She Who Gives Wealth 183

योगिनी

yoginī
She Who is Always in Union 184

जरा

jarā

She Who is Old 185

राक्षसी

rākṣasī

She Who is the Mother of All Demons 186

डाकिनी

ḍākinī

She Who is the Female Demonic Being 187

वेदमयी

vedamayī

She Who is the Expression of Wisdom 188

वेदविभूषणा

vedavibhūṣaṇā

She Who Illuminates Wisdom 189

श्रुतिः स्मृतिर्महाविद्या गुह्यविद्या पुरातनी ।
चिन्त्याऽचिन्त्या स्वधा स्वाहा निद्रा तन्द्रा च पार्वती ॥ २७

śrutiḥ smṛtirmahāvidyā guhyavidyā purātanī
cintyā-cintyā svadhā svāhā nidrā tandrā ca pārvatī

श्रुतिः

śrutiḥ

She Who is That Which Has Been Heard 190

स्मृतिः

smṛtiḥ

She Who is That Which is Remembered 191

महाविद्या

mahāvidyā

She Who is Great Knowledge 192

गुह्यविद्या

guhyavidyā

She Who is Hidden Knowledge 193

पुरातनी

purātanī

She Who is the Oldest Manifested Existence 194

चिन्त्या

cintyā

She Who is Thought 195

अचिन्त्या

acintyā
She Who is Unthinkable 196

स्वधा

svadhā
She Who is Oblations of Ancestral Praise 197

स्वाहा

svāhā
She Who is Oblations of I am One with God 198

निद्रा

nidrā
She Who is Sleep 199

तन्द्रा च

tandrā ca
She Who is Partially Awake and 200

पार्वती

pārvatī
She Who is Daughter of the Mountain 201

अपर्णा निश्चला लोला सर्वविद्या तपस्विनी ।
गंगा काशी शची सीता सती सत्यपरायणा ॥ २८

aparṇā niścalā lolā sarvavidyā tapasvinī
gaṁgā kāśī śacī sītā satī satyaparāyaṇā

अपर्णा

aparṇā
She Who is Without Parts 202

निश्चला

niścalā
She Who Cannot Be Divided 203

लोला

lolā
She Who has a Protruding Tongue 204

सर्वविद्या

sarvavidyā
She Who is All Knowledge 205

तपस्विनी

tapasvinī
She Who is the Performer of Purifying Austerities 206

गंगा

gaṁgā
She Who is the Holy River 207

काशी
kāśī
She Who is Benares 208

शची
śacī
She Who is the Wife of Indra 209

सीता
sītā
She Who is the Wife of Rāma 210

सती
satī
She Who is the Wife of Śiva 211

सत्यपरायणा
satyaparāyaṇā
She Who Always Moves in Truth 212

नीतिः सुनीतिः सुरुचिस्तुष्टिः पुष्टिर्धृतिः क्षमा ।
वाणी बुद्धिर्महालक्ष्मीर्लक्ष्मीर्नीलसरस्वती ॥ २९

nītiḥ sunītiḥ surucistuṣṭiḥ puṣṭirdhṛtiḥ kṣamā
vāṇī buddhirmahālakṣmīrlakṣmīrnīlasarasvatī

नीतिः
nītiḥ
She Who is Systematized Knowledge or Method 213

सुनीतिः
sunītiḥ
She Who is Excellent Systematized Knowledge 214

सुरुचिः
surucih
She Who is Excellent Taste 215

तुष्टिः
tuṣṭiḥ
She Who is Satisfaction 216

पुष्टिः
puṣṭiḥ
She Who is Nourishment 217

धृतिः
dhṛtiḥ
She Who is Consistent Solidity 218

क्षमा

kṣamā
She Who is Forgiveness 219

वाणी

vāṇī
She Who is Words 220

बुद्धिः

buddhiḥ
She Who is Intelligence 221

महालक्ष्मीः

mahālakṣmīḥ
She Who is the Great Goal of Existence 222

लक्ष्मीः

lakṣmīḥ
She Who is the Goal 223

नीलसरस्वती

nīlasarasvatī
She Who is the Blue Goddess of Knowledge 224

स्रोतस्वती सरस्वती मातंगी विजया जया ।
नदी सिन्धुः सर्वमयी तारा शून्यनिवासिनी ॥ ३०

srotasvatī sarasvatī mātaṁgī vijayā jayā
nadī sindhuḥ sarvamayī tārā śūnyanivāsinī

स्रोतस्वती

srotasvatī
She Who is the Spirit of All Sound 225

सरस्वती

sarasvatī
She Who is the Personification of One's Own Ocean of Existence 226

मातंगी

mātaṁgī
She Who is the Mother of All Bodies 227

विजया

vijayā
She Who is Conquest 228

जया

jayā
She Who is Victory 229

नदी सिन्धुः

nadī sindhuḥ
She Who is Rivers and Oceans 230

सर्वमयी

sarvamayī

She Who is the Expression of All 231

तारा

tārā

She Who is the Illuminator 232

शून्यनिवासिनी

śūnyanivāsinī

She Who Resides in Silence 233

शुद्धा तरङ्गिणी मेधा लाकिनी बहुरूपिणी ।
स्थूला सूक्ष्मा सूक्ष्मतरा भगवत्यनुरागिणी ॥ ३१

śuddhā taraṅgiṇī medhā lākinī bahurūpiṇī
sthūlā sūkṣmā sūkṣmatarā bhagavatyanurāgiṇī

शुद्धा

śuddhā

She Who is Purity 234

तरङ्गिणी

taraṅgiṇī

She Who Makes Waves 235

मेधा

medhā

She Who is the Intellect of Love 236

लाकिनी

lākinī

She Who is Manifested Energies 237

बहुरूपिणी

bahurūpiṇī

She Who has Many Forms 238

स्थूला

sthūlā

She Who is the Gross Body 239

सूक्ष्मा

sūkṣmā

She Who is Subtle 240

सूक्ष्मतरा

sūkṣmatarā

She Who is the Subtle Wave 241

भगवती

bhagavatī
She Who is the Female Ruler of All 242

अनुरागिणी

anurāgiṇī
She Who is the Feeling of Emotions 243

परमानन्दरूपा च चिदानन्दस्वरूपिणी ।
सर्वानन्दमयी नित्या सर्वानन्दस्वरूपिणी ॥ ३२

paramānandarūpā ca cidānandasvarūpiṇī
sarvānandamayī nityā sarvānandasvarūpiṇī

परमानन्दरूपा च

paramānandarūpā ca
She Who is the Form of Supreme Bliss and 244

चिदानन्दस्वरूपिणी

cidānandasvarūpiṇī
She Who is the Intrinsic Nature of the Bliss of Consciousness 245

सर्वानन्दमयी

sarvānandamayī
She Who is the Expression of All Bliss 246

नित्या

nityā
She Who is Eternal 247

सर्वानन्दस्वरूपिणी

sarvānandasvarūpiṇī
She Who is the Intrinsic Nature of All Bliss 248

शुभदा नन्दिनी स्तुत्या स्तवनीयस्वभाविनी ।
रंकिणी भंकिनी चित्रा विचित्रा चित्ररूपिणी ॥ ३३

śubhadā nandinī stutyā stavanīyasvabhāvinī
raṁkiṇī bhaṁkinī citrā vicitrā citrarūpiṇī

शुभदा
śubhadā
She Who is Giver of Purity 249

नन्दिनी
nandinī
She Who is Blissful 250

स्तुत्या
stutyā
She Who is Praise 251

स्तवनीयस्वभाविनी
stavanīyasvabhāvinī
She Who is the Intrinsic Nature of Songs of Prayer 252

रंकिणी
raṁkiṇī
She Who Manifests Subtlety 253

भंकिनी
bhaṁkinī
She Who is Ferocious 254

चित्रा
citrā
She Who is Artistic 255

विचित्रा
vicitrā
She Who has Various Artistic Capacities 256

चित्ररूपिणी
citrarūpiṇī
She Who is the Form of All Art 257

पद्मा पद्मालया पद्ममुखी पद्मविभूषणा ।
हाकिनी शाकिनी शान्ता राकिणी रुधिरप्रिया ॥ ३४

padmā padmālayā padmamukhī padmavibhūṣaṇā
hākinī śākinī śāntā rākiṇī rudhirapriyā

पद्मा
padmā
She Who is a Lotus 258

पद्मालया
padmālayā
She Who Resides in a Lotus 259

पद्ममुखी
padmamukhī
She Who has Lotus Mouth 260

पद्मविभूषणा
padmavibhūṣaṇā
She Who Shines Like a Lotus 261

हाकिनी
hākinī
She Who is the Energy of the Divine "I" 262

शाकिनी
śākinī
She Who is the Energy of Peace 263

शान्ता
śānta
She Who is Peace 264

राकिणी
rākiṇī
She Who is the Energy of Subtlety 265

रुधिरप्रिया
rudhirapriyā
She Who is the Beloved of Those Who Cry 266

भ्रान्तिर्भवानी रुद्राणी मृडानी शत्रुमर्दिनी ।
उपेन्द्राणी महेन्द्राणी ज्योत्स्ना चन्द्रस्वरूपिणी ॥ ३८

bhrāntirbhavānī rudrāṇī mṛḍānī śatrumardinī
upendrāṇī mahendrāṇī jyotsnā candrasvarūpiṇī

भ्रान्तिः
bhrāntiḥ
She Who is Confusion 267

भवानी
bhavānī
She Who is Manifested Existence 268

रुद्राणी
rudrāṇī
She Who is the Energy that Removes Suffering 269

मृडानी
mṛḍānī
She Who is the Rhythm of Life 270

शत्रुमर्दिनी

śatrumardinī

She Who is the Destroyer of All Enmity 271

उपेन्द्राणी

upendrāṇī

She Who is the Highest Energy of the Ruler of the Pure 272

महेन्द्राणी

mahendrāṇī

She Who is the Great Energy of the Ruler of the Pure 273

ज्योत्स्ना

jyotsnā

She Who Radiates Light 274

चन्द्रस्वरूपिणी

candrasvrūpiṇī

She Who is the Intrinsic Nature of the Moon of Devotion 275

सूर्यात्मिका रुद्रपत्नी रौद्री स्त्री प्रकृतिः पुमान् ।
शक्तिः सूक्तिर्मतिर्माता भुक्तिर्मुक्तिः पतिव्रता ॥ ३६

sūryātmikā rudrapatnī raudrī strī prakṛtiḥ pumān
śaktiḥ sūktirmatirmātā bhuktirmuktiḥ pativratā

सूर्यात्मिका

sūryātmikā

She Who is the Soul of the Light of Wisdom 276

रुद्रपत्नी

rudrapatnī

She Who is the Wife of Rudra, the Reliever of Suffering 277

रौद्री

raudrī

She Who is Fierce 278

स्त्री प्रकृतिः

strī prakṛtiḥ

She Who is the Woman of Nature or the Nature of Women 279

पुमान्

pumān

She Who is Masculine 280

शक्तिः

śaktiḥ

She Who is Energy 281

सूक्तिः
sūktiḥ
She Who is Happiness 282

मति
matiḥ
She Who is the Mind 283

माता
māta
She Who is the Mother 284

भुक्तिः
bhuktiḥ
She Who is Enjoyment 285

मुक्तिः
muktiḥ
She Who is Liberation 286

पतिव्रता
pativratā
She Who Observes the Vow of Devotion to Her Husband 287

सर्वेश्वरी सर्वमाता शर्वाणी हरवल्लभा ।
सर्वज्ञा सिद्धिदा सिद्धा भव्या भाव्या भयापहा ॥ ३७

sarveśvarī sarvamātā śarvāṇī haravallabhā
sarvajñā siddhidā siddhā bhavyā bhāvyā bhayāpahā

सर्वेश्वरी
sarveśvarī
She Who is the Supreme Ruler of All 288

सर्वमाता
sarvamātā
She Who is Mother of All 289

शर्वाणी
śarvāṇī
She Who Dwells in All 290

हरवल्लभा
haravallabhā
She Who is Śiva's Strength 291

सर्वज्ञा
sarvajñā
She Who is Knower of All 292

सिद्धिदा
siddhidā
She Who is Giver of the Attainment of Perfection 293

सिद्धा
siddhā
She Who has Attained Perfection 294

भव्या
bhavyā
She Who is Existence 295

भाव्या
bhāvyā
She Who is All Attitudes 296

भयापहा
bhayāpahā
She Who is Beyond All Fear 297

कर्त्री हर्त्री पालयित्री शर्वरी तामसी दया ।
तमिस्रा तामसी स्थाणुः स्थिरा धीरा तपस्विनी ॥ ३८

kartrī hartrī pālayitrī śarvarī tāmasī dayā
tamisrā tāmasī sthāṇuḥ sthirā dhīrā tapasvinī

कर्त्री
kartrī
She Who Creates 298

हर्त्री
hartrī
She Who Transforms or Destroys 299

पालयित्री
pālayitrī
She Who Protects 300

शर्वरी
śarvarī
She Who Gives Rest 301

तामसी
tāmasī
She Who Manifests Darkness 302

दया
dayā
She Who is Compassionate 303

तमिस्रा
tamisrā
She Who Mixes or Mingles 304

तामसी
tāmasī
She Who Manifests Darkness 305

स्थाणुः
sthāṇuḥ
She Who is Established 306

स्थिरा
sthirā
She Who is Still 307

धीरा
dhīrā
She Who is Stationary 308

तपस्विनी
tapasvinī
She Who Performs Austerities 309

चार्वङ्गी चञ्चला लोलजिह्वा चारुचरित्रिणी ।
त्रपा त्रपावती लज्ज्रा विलज्ज्रा ह्रीः रजोवती ॥ ३९

cārvaṅgī cañcalā lolajihvā cārucaritriṇī
trapā trapāvatī lajjā vilajjā hrīḥ rajovatī

चार्वङ्गी
cārvaṅgī
She Whose Body is in Motion 310

चञ्चला
cañcalā
She Who is Restless 311

लोलजिह्वा
lolajihvā
She Who has a Protruding Tongue 312

चारुचरित्रिणी
cārucaritriṇī
She Whose Character is to Heal 313

त्रपा
trapā
She Who Saves from Fear 314

त्रपावती
trapāvatī
She Whose Spirit Saves from Fear 315

लज्ज्रा
lajjā
She Who is Modesty 316

विलज्ज्रा
vilajjā
She Who is Without Modesty 317

ह्रीः

hrīḥ

She Who is Humble Modesty 318

रजोवती

rajovatī

She Who is the Repository of Rajas Guṇa 319

सरस्वती धर्मनिष्ठा श्रेष्ठा निष्ठुरनादिनी ।
गरिष्ठा दुष्टसंहर्त्री विशिष्टा श्रेयसी घृणा ॥ ४०

sarasvatī dharmaniṣṭhā śreṣṭhā niṣṭhuranādinī
gariṣṭhā duṣṭasaṁhartrī viśiṣṭā śreyasī ghṛṇā

सरस्वती

sarasvatī

She Who is the Personification of One's Own Ocean 320

धर्मनिष्ठा

dharmaniṣṭhā

She Who is the Strict Observance of the Ideals of Perfection 321

श्रेष्ठा

śreṣṭhā

She Who is Ultimate 322

निष्ठुरनादिनी

niṣṭhuranādinī

She Whose Vibration is Extremely Subtle 323

गरिष्ठा

gariṣṭhā

She Who is Always Happy to See Her Devotees 324

दुष्टसंहर्त्री

duṣṭasaṁhartrī

She Who Dissolves All Evil 325

विशिष्टा

viśiṣṭā

She Who is Especially Beloved 326

श्रेयसी

śreyasī

She Who is the Ultimate 327

घृणा

ghṛṇā

She Who is Hatred 328

भीमा भयानका भीमनादिनी भीः प्रभावती ।
वागीश्वरी श्रीर्यमुना यज्ञकर्त्री यजुःप्रिया ॥ ४१

bhīmā bhayānakā bhīmanādinī bhīḥ prabhāvatī
vāgīśvarī śrīryamunā yajñakartrī yajuḥpriyā

भीमा
bhīmā
She Who is Terribly Fierce 329

भयानका
bhayānakā
She Who is Extremely Fearful 330

भीमनादिनी
bhīmanādinī
She Who Has a Fierce Roar 331

भीः
bhīḥ
She Who is Fierce 332

प्रभावती
prabhāvatī
She Who is the Spirit of Illumination 333

वागीश्वरी
vāgīśvarī
She Who is the Supreme Ruler of All Vibrations 334

श्रीः
śrīḥ
She Who is Respect 335

यमुना
yamunā
She Who Manifests Complete Control 336

यज्ञकर्त्री
yajñakartrī
She Who is the Performer of Union or Sacrifice 337

यजुःप्रिया
yajuḥpriyā
She Who is the Beloved of Union or Lover of Yajur Veda 338

ऋक्सामाथर्वनिलया रागिणी शोभनस्वरा ।
कलकण्ठी कम्बुकण्ठी वेणुवीणापरायणा ॥ ४२

ṛksāmātharvanilayā rāgiṇī śobhanasvarā
kalakaṇṭhī kambukaṇṭhī veṇuvīṇāparāyaṇā

ऋक्सामाथर्वनिलया

ṛksāmārthāvanilayā

She Who Resides in the Three Vedas (Ṛg, Yajur, Atharva) 339

रागिणी

rāgiṇī

She Who is All Rhythm 340

शोभनस्वरा

śobhanasvarā

She Who is the Supreme Ruler of Illumination 341

कलकण्ठी

kalakaṇṭhī

She Who Has a Dark Throat 342

कम्बुकण्ठी

kambukaṇṭhī

She Whose Neck has Lines like a Conch Shell 343

वेणुवीणापरायणा

veṇuvīṇāparāyaṇā

She Who is Always Playing the Viṇa Instrument 344

वंशिनी वैष्णवी स्वच्छा धरित्री जगदीश्वरी ।
मधुमती कुण्डलिनी ऋद्धिः सिद्धिः शुचिस्मिता ॥ ४३

vaṁśinī vaiṣṇavī svacchā dharitrī jagadīśvarī
madhumatī kuṇḍalinī ṛddhiḥ siddhiḥ śucismitā

वंशिनी

vaṁśinī

She For Whom All is Family 345

वैष्णवी

vaiṣṇavī

She Who Pervades the Universe 346

स्वच्छा

svacchā

She Who Desires Herself 347

धरित्री

dharitrī

She Who Holds the Three 348

जगदीश्वरी

jagadīśvarī

She Who is the Supreme Ruler of the Perceivable Universe 349

मधुमती

madhumatī

She Who is the Nectar of Honey 350

कुण्डलिनी
kuṇḍalinī
She Who is the Manifestation of Individual Energy 351

ऋद्धिः
ṛddhiḥ
She Who is Prosperity 352

सिद्धिः
siddhiḥ
She Who is the Attainment of Perfection 353

शुचिस्मिता
śucismitā
She Who is the Remembrance of the Pure 354

रम्भोर्वशीरतीरमा रोहिणी रेवती मघा ।
शङ्खिनी चक्रिणी कृष्णा गदिनी पद्मिनी तथा ॥ ४४

rambhorvaśīratīramā rohiṇī revatī maghā
śaṅkhinī cakriṇī kṛṣṇā gadinī padminī tathā

रम्भोर्वशी
rambhorvaśī
She Who is the Apsaras Rambhā and Urvaśī 355

रती रमा
ratī ramā
She Who is Extremely Beautiful 356

रोहिणी
rohiṇī
She Who is the Luminous Light of the Heavens 357

रेवती
revatī
She Who is Abundance 358

मघा
maghā
She Who is Infinite Wealth 359

शङ्खिनी
śaṅkhinī
She Who holds a Conch Shell 360

चक्रिणी
cakriṇī
She Who holds a Discus 361

कृष्णा
kṛṣṇā
She Who is Dark, She Who is the Performer of All Action 362

गदिनी
gadinī
She Who holds a Club 363

पद्मिनी तथा
padminī tathā
She Who is a Lotus then 364

शूलिनी परिघास्त्रा च पाशिनी शार्ङ्गपाणिनी ।
पिनाकधारिणी धूम्रा शरभी वनमालिनी ॥ ४८

śūlinī parighāstrā ca pāśinī śārṅgapāṇinī
pinākadhāriṇī dhūmrā śarabhī vanamālinī

शूलिनी
śūlinī
She Who holds a Spear 365

परिघास्त्रा च
parighāstrā ca
She Who holds the Weapon of Good Actions and 366

पाशिनी
pāśinī
She Who holds the Net 367

शार्ङ्गपाणिनी
śārṅgapāṇinī
She Who Holds the Bow named śārṅga in Her Hand 368

पिनाकधारिणी
pinākadhāriṇī
She Who Holds the Spear 369

धूम्रा
dhūmrā
She Who Obscures Perception 370

शरभी
śarabhī
She Whose Strength is Greater than Lions or Elephants 371

वनमालिनी
vanamālinī
She Who is the Gardener of the Forest 372

रथिनी समरप्रीता वेगिनी रणपण्डिता ।
जटिनी वज्रिणी लीला लावण्याम्बुधिचन्द्रिका ॥ ४६

rathinī samaraprītā veginī raṇapaṇḍitā
jaṭinī vajriṇī līlā lāvaṇyāmbudhicandrikā

रथिनी

rathinī
She Who Conveys All 373

समरप्रीता

samaraprītā
She Who Loves the Battle 374

वेगिनी

veginī
She Who is Swift 375

रणपण्डिता

raṇapaṇḍitā
She Who is Expert in War 376

जटिनी

jaṭinī
She Who Has Disheveled Hair 377

वज्रिणी

vajriṇī
She Who holds the Thunderbolt or Lightning 378

लीला

līlā
She Who is the Divine Drama 379

लावण्याम्बुधिचन्द्रिका

lāvaṇyāmbudhicandrikā
She Whose Beauty Radiates the Light of Knowledge 380

बलिप्रिया सदापूज्या पूर्णा दैत्येन्द्रमथिनी ।
महिषासुरसंहर्त्री कामिनी रक्तदन्तिका ॥ ४७

balipriyā sadāpūjyā pūrṇā daityendramathinī
mahiṣāsurasaṁhartrī kāminī raktadantikā

बलिप्रिया

balipriyā
She Who is the Beloved of Sacrifice 381

सदापूज्या

sadāpūjyā
She Who is Worthy of Worship 382

पूर्णा

pūrṇā
She Who is Full, Complete, Perfect 383

दैत्येन्द्रमथिनी

daityendramathinī
She Who is Welcomed by the Leader of All Asuras 384

महिषासुरसंहर्त्री
mahiṣāsurasaṁhartrī
She Who is Destroyer of the Great Ruler of Duality 385

कामिनी
kāminī
She Who is All Desires 386

रक्तदन्तिका
raktadantikā
She Who Has Red Teeth (also Passion or bloody teeth) 387

रक्तपा रुधिराक्ताङ्गी रक्तखर्परहस्तिनी ।
रक्तप्रिया माँसरुचिरासवासक्तमानसा ॥ ४८

raktapā rudhirāktāṅgī raktakharparahastinī
raktapriyā māṁsaruciräsavāsaktamānasā

रक्तपा
raktapā
She Who Protects Passion 388

रुधिराक्ताङ्गी
rudhirāktāṅgī
She Whose Body is Covered With Passion 389

रक्तखर्परहस्तिनी
raktakharparahastinī
She Who Bears a Cup of Passion in Her Hands 390

रक्तप्रिया
raktapriyā
She Who Loves, or is the Beloved of Passion 391

माँसरुचिरासवासक्तमानसा
māṁsaruciräsavāsaktamānasā
She Who Delights in Eating Meat and Drinking Intoxicating Spirits 392

गलच्छोणितमुण्डाली कण्ठमालाविभूषणा ।
शवासना चितान्तःस्था माहेशी वृषवाहिनी ॥ ४९

galacchoṇitamuṇḍālī kaṇṭhamālāvibhūṣaṇā
śavāsanā citāntaḥsthā māheśī vṛṣavāhinī

गलच्छोणितमुण्डाली

galacchoṇitamuṇḍālī
She Who Wears a Garland of Heads Dripping Blood 393

कण्ठमालाविभूषणा

kaṇṭhamālāvibhūṣaṇā
She Who Wears a Garland Upon Her Neck 394

शवासना

śavāsanā
She Who Sits Upon a Corpse 395

चितान्तःस्था

citāntaḥsthā
She Who is Established in the Ulimate Consciousness 396

माहेशी

māheśī
She Who is the Greatest Seer of All 397

वृषवाहिनी

vṛṣavāhinī
She Who Rides Upon the Bull of Determination 398

व्याघ्रत्वगम्बरा चीनचैलिनी सिंहवाहिनी ।
वामदेवी महादेवी गौरी सर्वज्ञभामिनी ॥ ५०

vyāghratvagambarā cīnacailinī siṁhavāhinī
vāmadevī mahādevī gaurī sarvajñabhāminī

व्याघ्रत्वगम्बरा

vyāghratvagambarā
She Who Wears a Garment of Tiger Skin 399

चीनचैलिनी

cīnacailinī
She Who Moves with the Speed of a Deer 400

सिंहवाहिनी

siṁhavāhinī
She Who Rides Upon a Lion 401

वामदेवी

vāmadevī
She Who is the Beloved Goddess 402

महादेवी

mahādevī
She Who is a Great Goddess 403

गौरी

gaurī
She Who is Rays of Light 404

सर्वज्ञभामिनी

sarvajñabhāminī
She Who Illuminates All Wisdom 405

बालिका तरुणी वृद्धा वृद्धमाता जरातुरा ।
सुभ्रूर्विलासिनी ब्रह्मवादिनी ब्राह्मणी मही ॥ ८१

bālikā taruṇī vṛddhā vṛddhamātā jarāturā
subhrūrvilāsinī brahmavādinī brāhmaṇī mahī

बालिका

bālikā
She Who is a Young Girl 406

तरुणी

taruṇī
She Who is a Middle Aged Lady 407

वृद्धा

vṛddhā
She Who is an Old Lady 408

वृद्धमाता

vṛddhamātā
She Who is the Mother of the Aged 409

जरातुरा

jarāturā
She Who is Beyond Age 410

सुभ्रूः

subhrūḥ
She Who Has an Excellent Forehead 411

विलासिनी

vilāsinī
She Who Resides Within Herself 412

ब्रह्मवादिनी

brahmavādinī
She Who is the Vibration of Supreme Divinity 413

ब्राह्मणी

brāhmaṇī

She Who Creates Divinity 414

मही

mahī

She Who is Earth 415

स्वप्नवती चित्रलेखा लोपामुद्रा सुरेश्वरी ।
अमोघारुन्धती तीक्ष्णा भोगवत्यनुरागिणी ॥ ८२

svapnavatī citralekhā lopāmudrā sureśvarī
amoghārundhatī tīkṣṇā bhogavatyanurāgiṇī

स्वप्नवती

svapnavatī

She Who is the Spirit of Dreams 416

चित्रलेखा

citralekhā

She Who is Various Writings 417

लोपामुद्रा

lopāmudrā

She Who is the Manifestation of that Which is Beyond Manifested Existence 418

सुरेश्वरी

sureśvarī

She Who is the Supreme Ruler of All Divinity 419

अमोघा

amoghā

She Who is Always Rewarding 420

अरुन्धती

arundhatī

She Who is the Purity of Devotion, Epitome of Commitment 421

तीक्ष्णा

tīkṣṇā

She Who is Sharp 422

भोगवती

bhogavatī

She Who is the Spirit of All Enjoyment 423

अनुरागिणी

anurāgiṇī

She Who is the Spirit of All Feeling 424

मन्दाकिनी मन्दहासा ज्वालामुख्यसुरान्तका ।
मानदा मानिनी मान्या माननीया मदातुरा ॥ ८३

mandākinī mandahāsā jvālāmukhyasurāntakā
mānadā māninī mānyā mānanīyā madāturā

मन्दाकिनी
mandākinī
She Who Organizes the Mind to Optimum Efficiency 425

मन्दहासा
mandahāsā
She Whose Mind Always Laughs 426

ज्वालामुखी
jvālāmukhī
She Whose Face Radiates Light 427

असुरान्तका
asurāntakā
She Who is the Cause of the End of the Forces of Duality 428

मानदा
mānadā
She Who is the Giver of Discipline 429

मानिनी
māninī
She Who Creates Discipline 430

मान्या
mānyā
She Who is Discipline 431

माननीया
mānanīyā
She Who is the Supreme Lord of Discipline 432

मदातुरा
madāturā
She Who is Completely Intoxicated 433

मदिरा मेदुरोन्मादा मेध्या साध्या प्रसादिनी ।
सुमध्यानन्तगुणिनी सर्वलोकोत्तमोत्तमा ॥ ८४

madirā meduronmādā medhyā sādhyā prasādinī
sumadhyānantaguṇinī sarvalokottamottamā

मदिरा मेदुरोन्मादा

madirā meduronmādā
She Who is Intoxicated with Divine Spirit 434

मेध्या

medhyā
She Who is Born of Intellect 435

साध्या

sādhyā
She Who is the Performer of All Discipline 436

प्रसादिनी

prasādinī
She Who is the Prasāda or Consecration of Offerings 437

सुमध्यानन्तगुणिनी

sumadhyānantaguṇinī
She Who Resides in the Middle of Infinite Excellent Qualities 438

सर्वलोकोत्तमोत्तमा

sarvalokottamottamā
All the Beings of All the Worlds Consider Her to be Greater than the Greatest 439

जयदा जित्वरा जेत्री जयश्रीर्जयशालिनी ।
शुभदा सुखदा सत्या सभासंक्षोभकारिणी ॥ ८८

jayadā jitvarā jetrī jayaśrīrjayaśālinī
śubhadā sukhadā satyā sabhāsaṁkṣobhakāriṇī

जयदा

jayadā
She Who is the Giver of Victory 440

जित्वरा

jitvarā
She Who Grants the Boon of Victory 441

जेत्री

jetrī
She Who is Victorious Over the Three 442

जयश्रीः

jayaśrīḥ
She Who is Victorious with Respect 443

जयशालिनी

jayaśālinī

She Who is the Repository of Victory 444

शुभदा

śubhadā

She Who is the Giver of Purity 445

सुखदा

sukhadā

She Who is the Giver of Happiness or Comfort 446

सत्या

satyā

She Who is the Manifestation of Truth 447

सभासंक्षोभकारिणी

sabhāsaṁkṣobhakāriṇī

She Who is the Cause of Purity for the Entire Community 448

शिवदूती भूतिमती विभूतिर्भीषणानना ।
कौमारी कुलजा कुन्ती कुलस्त्री कुलपालिका ॥ ८६

śivadūtī bhūtimatī vibhūtirbhīṣaṇānanā
kaumārī kulajā kuntī kulastrī kulapālikā

शिवदूती

śivadūtī

She For Whom Śiva is the Ambassador 449

भूतिमती

bhūtimatī

She Who is the Expression of All Manifested Existence 450

विभूतिः

vibhūtiḥ

She Who is the Expression of the Expressionless Deity 451

भीषणानना

bhīṣaṇānanā

She Whose Face is Free From Fear 452

कौमारी

kaumārī

She Who is the Manifestation of the Ever Pure One 453

कुलजा

kulajā

She Who is the Giver of Birth to the Family 454

कुन्ती

kuntī

She Who Takes Away the Deficiency of Others 455

कुलस्त्री

kulastrī

She Who is the Woman of the Family 456

कुलपालिका

kulapālikā

She Who is the Protector of the Family 457

कीर्त्तिर्यशस्विनी भूषा भूष्ठा भूतपतिप्रिया ।
सगुणा निर्गुणा तृष्णा निष्ठा काष्ठा प्रतिष्ठिता ॥ ८७

kīrttiryaśasvinī bhūṣā bhūṣṭhā bhūtapatipriyā
saguṇā nirguṇā tṛṣṇā niṣṭhā kāṣṭhā pratiṣṭhitā

कीर्त्तिः

kīrttiḥ

She Who is Fame 458

यशस्विनी

yaśasvinī

She Who is Welfare 459

भूषा

bhūṣā

She Who is the Peace of All Beings 460

भूष्ठा

bhūṣṭhā

She Who is the Cause of Peace to All Beings 461

भूतपतिप्रिया

bhūtapatipriyā

She Who is Loved by the Lord of All Disembodied Spirits 462

सगुणा

saguṇā

She Who is With Qualities 463

निर्गुणा

nirguṇā

She Who is Without Qualities 464

तृष्णा

tṛṣṇā

She Who is All Thirst 465

निष्ठा

niṣṭhā

She Who Obeys All the Rules 466

काष्ठा

kāṣṭhā

She Who is the Cause of Desire 467

प्रतिष्ठिता

pratiṣṭhitā

She Who Establishes 468

धनिष्ठा धनदा धान्या वसुधा सुप्रकाशिनी ।
उर्वी गुर्वी गुरुश्रेष्ठा सद्गुणा त्रिगुणात्मिका ॥ ९८

dhaniṣṭhā dhanadā dhānyā vasudhā suprakāśinī
urvī gurvī guruśreṣṭhā sadguṇā triguṇātmikā

धनिष्ठा

dhaniṣṭhā

She Who is the Beloved Wealth 469

धनदा

dhanadā

She Who is the Giver of Wealth 470

धान्या

dhānyā

She Who is Wealthy 471

वसुधा

vasudhā

She Who Supports the Earth 472

सुप्रकाशिनी

suprakāśinī

She Who is Excellent Illumination 473

उर्वी

urvī

She Who is the Supreme Lord of Circumstances 474

गुर्वी

gurvī

She Who is the Supreme Lord of Gurus 475

गुरुश्रेष्ठा

guruśreṣṭhā

She Who is the Ultimate Guru 476

सद्गुणा

sadguṇā
She Who is With Qualities of Truth 477

त्रिगुणात्मिका

triguṇātmikā
She Who is the Manifestation of the Soul of the Three Qualities 478

राज्ञामाज्ञा महाप्रज्ञा सगुणा निर्गुणात्मिका ।
महाकुलीना निष्कामा सकामा कामजीवनी ॥ ८९

rājñāmājñā mahāprajñā saguṇā nirguṇātmikā
mahākulīnā niṣkāmā sakāmā kāmajīvanī

राज्ञामाज्ञा

rājñāmājñā
She Who is the Wisdom of the Order of the King 479

महाप्रज्ञा

mahāprajñā
She Who is the Great Ultimate Wisdom 480

सगुणा

saguṇā
She Who is With Qualities 481

निर्गुणात्मिका

nirguṇātmikā
She Who is the Manifestation of the Soul of the Three Qualities 482

महाकुलीना

mahākulīnā
She Who is the Mother of the Great Family 483

निष्कामा

niṣkāmā
She Who is Without Desire 484

सकामा

sakāmā
She Who is With Desire 485

कामजीवनी

kāmajīvanī
She Who is the Life of Desire 486

कामदेवकला रामाभिरामा शिवनर्तकी ।
चिन्तामणिः कल्पलता जाग्रती दीनवत्सला ॥ ९०

kāmadevakalā rāmābhirāmā śivanartakī
cintāmaṇiḥ kalpalatā jāgratī dīnavatsalā

कामदेवकला
kāmadevakalā
She Who is the Attribute of the Lord of Desire 487

रामाभिरामा
rāmābhirāmā
She Who is the Energy of Perfection in the Subtle Body 488

शिवनर्तकी
śivanartakī
She Who Dances With Śiva 489

चिन्तामणिः
cintāmaṇiḥ
She Who is the Jewel of All Thought 490

कल्पलता
kalpalatā
She Who Clings to Thought 491

जाग्रती
jāgratī
She Who Wakes Up the Universe 492

दीनवत्सला
dīnavatsalā
She Who is the Refuge of the Downtrodden 493

कार्त्तिकी कृतिका कृत्या अयोध्या विषमासमा ।
सुमन्त्रा मन्त्रिणी पूर्णा ह्लादिनी क्लेशनाशिनी ॥ ६१

kārttikī kṛtikā kṛtyā ayodhyā viṣamāsamā
sumantra mantriṇī pūrṇā hlādinī kleśanāśinī

कार्त्तिकी
kārttikī
She Who is the Expression of All That is Done 494

कृतिका
kṛtikā
She Who is the Doer or the Cause of All Doing 495

कृत्या

kṛtyā
She Who is That Which is Done 496

अयोध्या विषमासमा

ayodhyā viṣamāsamā
She Who is the Same as the Place Where There is No War 497

सुमन्त्रा

sumantrā
She Who is the Excellent Mantra Which Takes Away the Mind 498

मन्त्रिणी

mantriṇī
She Who is the Energy of All Mantras 499

पूर्णा

pūrṇā
She Who is Perfect 500

ह्लादिनी

hlādinī
She Who is Always Happy 501

क्लेशनाशिनी

kleśanāśinī
She Who is the Destroyer of All Imperfection 502

त्रैलोक्यजननी ज्येष्ठा मीमांसामन्त्ररूपिणी ।
तडागनिम्नजठरा शुष्कमाँसास्थिमालिनी ॥ ६२

trailokyajananī jyeṣṭhā mīmāṁsāmantrarūpiṇī
taḍāganimnajaṭharā śuṣkamāṁsāsthimālinī

त्रैलोक्यजननी

trailokyajananī
She Who is the Mother of the Three Worlds 503

ज्येष्ठा

jyeṣṭhā
She Who is Oldest 504

मीमांसामन्त्ररूपिणी

mīmāṁsāmantrarūpiṇī
She Who is the Intrinsic Nature of Vedic Knowledge 505

तडागनिम्नजठरा

taḍāganimnajaṭharā
She Who is the Fire of All Digestion 506

शुष्कमाँसास्थिमालिनी

śuṣkamāṁsāsthimālinī

She Who Wears a Garland of Dried Limbs 507

अवन्तीमथुराहृदया त्रैलोक्यपावनक्षमा ।
व्यक्ताव्यक्तात्मिका मूर्तिः शरभी भीमनादिनी ॥ ६३

avantīmathurāhṛdayā trailokyapāvanakṣamā
vyaktāvyaktātmikā mūrtiḥ śarabhī bhīmanādinī

अवन्तीमथुराहृदया

avantīmathurāhṛdayā

She Who is the Heart of Mathurā and Avadha, Birth-places of Kṛṣṇa and Rāma 508

त्रैलोक्यपावनक्षमा

trailokyapāvanakṣamā

She Who Brings the Winds of Forgiveness to the Three Worlds 509

व्यक्ताव्यक्तात्मिका मूर्तिः

vyaktāvyaktātmikā mūrtiḥ

She Who is the Image of the Manifest and Unmanifested Soul 510

शरभी भीमनादिनी

śarabhī bhīmanādinī

She Whose Sound is Extremely Loud 511

क्षेमङ्करी शङ्करी च सर्वसम्मोहकारिणी ।
ऊर्ध्वतेजस्विनी क्लिन्ना महातेजस्विनी तथा ॥ ६४

kṣemaṅkarī śaṅkarī ca sarvasammohakāriṇī
ūrdhvatejasvinī klinnā mahātejasvinī tathā

क्षेमङ्करी

kṣemaṅkarī

She Who is the Welfare of All 512

शङ्करी च

śaṅkarī ca

She Who is the Cause of Peace and 513

सर्वसम्मोहकारिणी
sarvasammohakāriṇī
She Who is the Ignorance of All 514

ऊर्ध्वतेजस्विनी
ūrdhvatejasvinī
She Who is the Rising Light of All 515

क्लिन्ना
klinnā
She Whose Heart is Very Soft 516

महातेजस्विनी तथा
mahātejasvinī tathā
She Who is the Great Light then 517

अद्वैतभोगिनी पूज्या युवती सर्वमङ्गला ।
सर्वप्रियङ्करी भोग्या धरणी पिशिताशना ॥ ६८

advaitabhoginī pūjyā yuvatī sarvamaṅgalā
sarvapriyaṅkarī bhogyā dharaṇī piśitāśanā

अद्वैतभोगिनी
advaitabhoginī
She Who Enjoys Non-Duality 518

पूज्या
pūjyā
She Who is Worthy of Worship 519

युवती
yuvatī
She Who is Young 520

सर्वमङ्गला
sarvamaṅgalā
She Who is All Welfare 521

सर्वप्रियङ्करी
sarvapriyaṅkarī
She Who is the Cause of All Love 522

भोग्या
bhogyā
She Who is Enjoyed 523

धरणी
dharaṇī
She Who Supports All 524

पिशिताशना
piśitāśanā
She Who Sits Upon a Deer 525

भयंकरी पापहरा निष्कलंका वशंकरी ।
आशा तृष्णा चन्द्रकला इन्द्राणी वायुवेगिनी ॥ ६६

bhayaṁkarī pāpaharā niṣkalaṁkā vaśaṁkarī
āśā tṛṣṇā candrakalā indrāṇī vāyuveginī

भयंकरी
bhayaṁkarī
She Who is Fearful 526

पापहरा
pāpaharā
She Who Takes Away All Sins (Confusion) 527

निष्कलंका
niṣkalaṁkā
She Who is Without Fault 528

वशंकरी
vaśaṁkarī
She Who Controls 529

आशा
āśā
She Who is Hope 530

तृष्णा
tṛṣṇā
She Who is Thirst 531

चन्द्रकला
candrakalā
She Who is the Digit of the Moon, Attribute of Devotion 532

इन्द्राणी
indrāṇī
She Who is the Energy of the Ruler of the Pure 533

वायुवेगिनी
vāyuveginī
She Who Moves With the Freedom of Emancipation 534

सहस्रसूर्यसंकाशा चन्द्रकोटिसमप्रभा ।
निशुम्भशुम्भसंहन्त्री रक्तबीजविनाशिनी ॥ ६७

sahasrasūryasaṁkāśā candrakoṭisamaprabhā
niśumbhaśumbhasaṁhantrī raktabījavināśinī

सहस्रसूर्यसंकाशा
sahasrasūryasaṁkāśā
She Whose Illumination is Like a Thousand Suns 535

चन्द्रकोटिसमप्रभा
candrakoṭisamaprabhā
She Whose Illumination is Like Ten Million Moons 536

निशुम्भशुम्भसंहन्त्री
niśumbhaśumbhasaṁhantrī
She Who Dissolves Self-Deprecation and Self-Conceit 537

रक्तबीजविनाशिनी
raktabījavināśinī
She Who is the Destroyer of the Seed of Desire 538

मधुकैटभहन्त्री च महिषासुरघातिनी ।
वह्निमण्डलमध्यस्था सर्वसत्त्वप्रतिष्ठिता ॥ ६८

madhukaiṭabhahantrī ca mahiṣāsuraghātinī
vahnimaṇḍalamadhyasthā sarvasattvapratiṣṭhitā

मधुकैटभहन्त्री च
madhukaiṭabhahantrī ca
She Who Dissolves Too Much and Too Little and 539

महिषासुरघातिनी
mahiṣāsuraghātinī
She Who is the Destroyer of the Great Ego 540

वह्निमण्डलमध्यस्था
vahnimaṇḍalamadhyasthā
She Who is Situated in the Middle of the Circle of Fire 541

सर्वसत्त्वप्रतिष्ठिता
sarvasattvapratiṣṭhitā
She Who Establishes All Truth 542

सर्वाचारवती सर्वदेवकन्याधिदेवता ।
दक्षकन्या दक्षयज्ञनाशिनी दुर्गतारिणी ॥ ६९

sarvācāravatī sarvadevakanyādhidevatā
dakṣakanyā dakṣayajñanāśinī durgatāriṇī

सर्वाचारवती

sarvācāravatī
She Who is the Spirit of All that Does Not Move 543

सर्वदेवकन्याधिदेवता

sarvadevakanyādhidevatā
She Who is the Supreme Goddess of All Divine Females 544

दक्षकन्या

dakṣakanyā
She Who is the Daughter of Ability 545

दक्षयज्ञनाशिनी

dakṣayajñanāśinī
She Who is the Destroyer of the Sacrifice of Ability 546

दुर्गतारिणी

durgatāriṇī
She Who is the Reliever of Difficulties, Who Takes us Across the Ocean of Objects and Relationships 547

इज्या पूज्या विभीर्भूतिः सत्कीर्त्तिर्ब्रह्मरूपिणी ।
रम्भोरूश्चतुराकारा जयन्ती करुणा कुहूः ॥ ७०

ijyā pūjyā vibhīrbhūtiḥ satkīrttirbrahmarūpiṇī
rambhorūścaturākārā jayantī karuṇā kuhūḥ

इज्या

ijyā
She Who is Desired 548

पूज्या

pūjyā
She Who is Worthy of Worship 549

विभीर्भूतिः

vibhīrbhūtiḥ
She Who Manifests the Greatest Fears 550

सत्कीर्त्तिः

satkīrttiḥ
She Who is True Fame 551

ब्रह्मरूपिणी

brahmarūpiṇī
She Who Has the Capacity of Form of Supreme Divinity 552

रम्भोरूः

rambhorūḥ
She Who is the Beautiful One Residing in the Thighs (Urvaśi) 553

चतुराकारा
caturākārā
She Who Manifests the Four of Creation 554

जयन्ती
jayantī
She Who is Victory 555

करुणा
karuṇā
She Who is Compassionate 556

कुहूः
kuhūḥ
She Who is the New Moon 557

मनस्विनी देवमाता यशस्या ब्रह्मचारिणी ।
सिद्धिदा वृद्धिदा वृद्धिः सर्वाद्या सर्वदायिनी ॥ ७१

manasvinī devamātā yaśasyā brahmacāriṇī
siddhidā vṛddhidā vṛddhiḥ sarvādyā sarvadāyinī

मनस्विनी
manasvinī
She Who Reflects Mind 558

देवमाता
devamātā
She Who is Mother of Gods 559

यशस्या
yaśasyā
She Who is Worthy of Welfare 560

ब्रह्मचारिणी
brahmacāriṇī
She Who Moves in the Supreme Consciousness 561

सिद्धिदा
siddhidā
She Who is the Giver of Perfection 562

वृद्धिदा
vṛddhidā
She Who is the Giver of Change or Modification 563

वृद्धिः
vṛddhiḥ
She Who is Change or Modification 564

सर्वाद्या
sarvādyā
She Who is Foremost of All; She Who is Before All 565

सर्वदायिनी
sarvadāyinī
She Who is the Giver of All 566

अगाधरूपिणी ध्येया मूलाधारनिवासिनी ।
आज्ञा प्रज्ञा पूर्णमनाश्चन्द्रमुख्यनुकूलिनी ॥ ७२

agādharūpiṇī dhyeyā mūlādhāranivāsinī
ājñā prajñā pūrṇamanāścandramukhyanukūlinī

अगाधरूपिणी
agādharūpiṇī
She Who is the Intrinsic Nature of That Which Does Not End 567

ध्येया
dhyeyā
She Who is Meditated Upon 568

मूलाधारनिवासिनी
mūlādhāranivāsinī
She Who Resides in the Mūlādhāra Cakra 569

आज्ञा
ājñā
She Who Orders Creation 570

प्रज्ञा
prajñā
She Who is Primordial Wisdom 571

पूर्णमनाः
pūrṇamanāḥ
She Who is of Full and Complete Mind 572

चन्द्रमुख्यनुकूलिनी
candramukhyanukūlinī
She Who is the Complete Collection of the Face of the Moon 573

वावदूका निम्ननाभिः सत्यसन्धा दृढव्रता ।
आन्वीक्षिकी दण्डनीतिस्त्रयी त्रिदिवसुन्दरी ॥ ७३

vāvadūkā nimnanābhiḥ satyasandhā dṛḍhavratā
ānvīkṣikī daṇḍanītistrayī tridivasundarī

वावदूका

vāvadūkā
She Who Charms Everyone with Her Speech 574

निम्ननाभिः

nimnanābhiḥ
She Whose Navel is Indented 575

सत्यसन्धा

satyasandhā
She Who Has Found Truth 576

दृढव्रता

dṛḍhavratā
She Who is Determined in Her Vow 577

आन्वीक्षिकी

ānvīkṣikī
She Who Embodies All Spiritual Knowledge 578

दण्डनीति

daṇḍanīti
She Who is the Punishment by Which Discipline is Prescribed 579

त्रयी

trayī
She Who is Three 580

त्रिदिवसुन्दरी

tridivasundarī
She Who is the Beauty of the Three Divinities 581

ज्वलिनी ज्वालिनी शैलतनया विन्ध्यवासिनी ।
प्रत्यया खेचरी धैर्या तुरीया विमलातुरा ॥ ७४

jvalinī jvālinī śailatanayā vindhyavāsinī
pratyayā khecarī dhairyā turīyā vimalāturā

ज्वलिनी

jvalinī
She Who Burns 582

ज्वालिनी

jvālinī
She Who Causes to Burn 583

शैलतनया

śailatanayā

She Who is the Daughter of the Mountain 584

विन्ध्यवासिनी

vindhyavāsinī

She Who Resides in Mountains of Knowledge that Breed Humility 585

प्रत्यया

pratyayā

She Who Sees All Concepts 586

खेचरी

khecarī

She Whose Spirit Soars 587

धैर्या

dhairyā

She Who is Determination 588

तुरीया

turīyā

She Who is Beyond 589

विमलातुरा

vimalātura

She Who is the Highest Expression of Purity 590

प्रगल्भा वारुणीच्छाया शशिनी विस्फुलिङ्गिनी ।
भक्तिः सिद्धिः सदा प्रीतिः प्राकाम्या महिमाणिमा ॥ ७८

pragalbhā vāruṇīcchāyā śaśinī visphuliṅginī
bhaktiḥ siddhiḥ sadā prītiḥ prākāmyā mahimāṇimā

प्रगल्भा

pragalbhā

She Who is Confident 591

वारुणीच्छाया

vāruṇīcchāyā

She Who is the Reflection of the Cause of Equilibrium 592

शशिनी

śaśinī

She Who is the Radiance of the Moon 593

विस्फुलिङ्गिनी

visphuliṅginī

She Who has Subtle Radiance 594

भक्तिः

bhaktiḥ
She Who is Devotion 595

सिद्धिः

siddhiḥ
She Who is Perfection 596

सदाप्रीतिः

sadāprītiḥ
She Who is Always Beloved 597

प्राकाम्या

prākāmyā
She Who is the Foremost of All Desires 598

महिमाणिमा

mahimāṇimā
She Who is the Mother Who is the Jewel of the Earth 599

इच्छासिद्धिर्वशित्वा च ईशित्वोर्ध्वनिवासिनी ।
लघिमा चैव गायत्री सावित्री भुवनेश्वरी ॥ ७६

icchāsiddhirvaśitvā ca īśitvordhvanivāsinī
laghimā caiva gāyatrī sāvitrī bhuvaneśvarī

इच्छासिद्धिः

icchāsiddhiḥ
She Who is the Perfection of All Desires 600

वशित्वा च

vaśitvā ca
She Who is the Supreme Controller and 601

ईशित्वोर्ध्वनिवासिनी

īśitvordhvanivāsinī
She Who Resides Above All that is Desired 602

लघिमा चैव

laghimā caiva
She Who is Extremely Small and again 603

गायत्री

gāyatrī
She Who is the Wisdom of the Three 604

सावित्री

sāvitrī
She Who is the Illuminator of the Three 605

भुवनेश्वरी
bhuvaneśvarī
She Who is the Supreme Ruler of Manifested Existence 606

मनोहरा चिता दिव्या देव्युदारा मनोरमा ।
पिङ्गला कपिला जिह्वा रसज्ञा रसिका रमा ॥ ७७

manoharā citā divyā devyudārā manoramā
piṅgalā kapilā jihvā rasajñā rasikā ramā

मनोहरा
manoharā
She Who Takes Away Thoughts 607

चिता
citā
She Who is Consciousness 608

दिव्या
divyā
She Who is Divine 609

देव्युदारा
devyudārā
She Who Holds Aloft All Goddesses 610

मनोरमा
manoramā
She Who Exemplifies Beauty of the Mind 611

पिङ्गला
piṅgalā
She Who is a Subtle Avenue by Which Energy Flows 612

कपिला
kapilā
She Who is Like a Cow, a Giver of Pure Nourishment 613

जिह्वारसज्ञा
jihvārasajñā
She Who Has the Nectar of Wisdom on Her Tongue 614

रसिका
rasikā
She Who is All Nectar 615

रमा
ramā
She Who is Beauty 616

सुषुम्नेडायोगवती गान्धारी नरकान्तका ।
पाञ्चाली रुक्मिणी राधा राध्या भामा च राधिका ॥ ७८

suṣumneḍāyogavatī gāndhārī narakāntakā
pāñcālī rukmiṇī rādhā rādhyā bhāmā ca rādhikā

सुषुम्नेडायोगवती

suṣumneḍāyogavatī
She Who is the Spirit of Union Within the Suṣumna 617

गान्धारी

gāndhārī
She Who Wears an Excellent Scent 618

नरकान्तका

narakāntakā
She Who is the End of All Hell 619

पाञ्चाली

pāñcālī
She Who Belongs to the Five (Draupadī Married to the five Paṇdava Brothers, or all fives) 620

रुक्मिणी

rukmiṇī
She Who is the Jewel of All Circumstances, The Wife of Kṛṣṇa 621

राधा

rādhā
She Who is the Beloved of Kṛṣṇa; She Who Supports Consciousness in the Subtle Body 622

राध्या

rādhyā
She Who Causes Consciousness in the Subtle Body 623

भामा च

bhāmā ca
She Who is the Mother of Illumination and 624

राधिका

rādhikā
She Who is the Beloved of Kṛṣṇa; She Who is the Cause of Illumination of Consciousness in the Subtle Body 625

अमृता तुलसी वृन्दा कैटभी कपटेश्वरी ।
उग्रचण्डेश्वरी वीरजननी वीरसुन्दरी ॥ ७९

amṛtā tulasī vṛndā kaiṭabhī kapaṭeśvarī
ugracaṇḍeśvarī vīrajananī vīrasundarī

अमृता
amṛtā
She Who is the Nectar of Immortality 626

तुलसी
tulasī
She Who is the Basil Plant 627

वृन्दा
vṛndā
She Who is the Giver of Change 628

कैटभी
kaiṭabhī
She Who Constricts 629

कपटेश्वरी
kapaṭeśvarī
She Who is the Supreme Ruler of All Fraudulent Beings 630

उग्रचण्डेश्वरी
ugracaṇḍeśvarī
She Who is the Ruler of Fearful Passion 631

वीरजननी
vīrajananī
She Who is the Mother of All Heroes and Warriors 632

वीरसुन्दरी
vīrasundarī
She Who is the Beautiful of All Warriors 633

उग्रतारा यशोदाख्या देवकी देवमानिता ।
निरंजना चिता देवी क्रोधिनी कुलदीपिका ॥ ८०

ugratārā yaśodākhyā devakī devamānitā
niraṁjanā citā devī krodhinī kuladīpikā

उग्रतारा

ugratārā
She Whose Illumination is Fearful 634

यशोदाख्या

yaśodākhyā
She Who is the Light in the Eyes of Yaśoda 635

देवकी

devakī
She Who is the Mother of Kṛṣṇa; She Who Causes Divinity to Manifest 636

देवमानिता

devamānitā
She Who is Obeyed by the Gods 637

निरंजना चिता

niraṁjanā citā
She Who is Formless Consciousness 638

देवी

devī
She Who is the Goddess 639

क्रोधिनी

krodhinī
She Who is Angry 640

कुलदीपिका

kuladīpikā
She Who is the Light of Excellence 641

कुलवागीश्वरी ज्वाला मातृका द्रावणी द्रवा ।
योगेश्वरी महामारी भ्रामरी विन्दुरूपिणी ॥ ८१

kulavāgīśvarī jvālā mātṛkā drāvaṇī dravā
yogeśvarī mahāmārī bhrāmarī bindurūpiṇī

कुलवागीश्वरी

kulavāgīśvarī
She Who is the Supreme Ruler of Vibrations of Excellence 642

ज्वाला

jvālā
She Who Radiates 643

मातृका

mātṛkā

She Who is the Mother in the Form of Letters 644

द्रावणी

drāvaṇī

She Who Manifests What You Value 645

द्रवा

dravā

She Who is What You Value 646

योगेश्वरी

yogeśvarī

She Who is the Supreme Ruler of Union 647

महामारी

mahāmārī

She Who is the Great Destroyer 648

भ्रामरी

bhrāmarī

She Who Comes in the Form of a Bee 649

बिन्दुरूपिणी

bindurūpiṇī

She Who is the Intrinsic Nature of the Form of Knowledge 650

दूती प्राणेश्वरी गुप्ता बहुला डामरी प्रभा ।
कुब्जिका ज्ञानिनी ज्येष्ठा भुशुण्डी प्रकटाकृतिः ॥ ८२

dūtī prāṇeśvarī guptā bahulā ḍāmarī prabhā
kubjikā jñāninī jyeṣṭhā bhuśuṇḍī prakaṭākṛtiḥ

दूती

dūtī

She Who is Ambassador 651

प्राणेश्वरी

prāṇeśvarī

She Who is the Supreme Ruler of Life 652

गुप्ता

guptā

She Who is Hidden 653

बहुला

bahulā

She Who is Everywhere 654

डामरी

ḍāmarī

She Who Plays the ḍamaru Drum 655

प्रभा

prabhā

She Who is Radiant Light 656

कुब्जिका

kubjikā

She Who is Hunchbacked or Crippled 657

ज्ञानिनी

jñāninī

She Who Manifests Wisdom 658

ज्येष्ठा

jyeṣṭhā

She Who is Oldest 659

भुशुण्डी

bhuśuṇḍī

She Who Holds the Sling 660

प्रकटाकृतिः

prakaṭākṛtiḥ

She Who Manifests Without Doing 661

द्राविणी गोपिनी माया कामबीजेश्वरी प्रिया ।
शाकम्भरी कोकनदा सुशीला च तिलोत्तमा ॥ ८३

drāviṇī gopinī māyā kāmabījeśvarī priyā
śākambharī kokanadā suśīlā ca tilottamā

द्राविणी

drāviṇī

She Who Manifests Wealth 662

गोपिनी

gopinī

She Who is Secretive 663

माया

māyā

She Who is the Supreme Measurement of Consciousness 664

कामबीजेश्वरी

kāmabījeśvarī

She Who is the Supreme Ruler of the Seed of Desire 665

प्रिया

priyā

She Who is the Beloved 666

शाकम्भरी

śākambharī

She Who Nourishes With Vegetables 667

कोकनदा

kokanadā

She Who Engenders the Seed 668

सुशीला च

suśīlā ca

She Who is Consistently Excellent (like a stone fixed in excellence) and 669

तिलोत्तमा

tilottamā

She Who is Excellently Pure 670

अमेयविक्रमाक्रूरा सम्पच्छीलातिविक्रमा ।
स्वस्तिहव्यवहा प्रीतिरूष्मा धूम्रार्चिरङ्गदा ॥ ८४

ameyavikramākrūrā sampacchīlātivikramā
svastihavyavahā prītirūṣmā dhūmrārciraṅgadā

अमेयविक्रमाक्रूरा

ameyavikramākrūrā

She Who Manifests Unsurpassed Grace 671

सम्पच्छीलातिविक्रमा

sampacchīlātivikramā

She Who is Spinning in the Attachment for the Loss of Wealth 672

स्वस्तिहव्यवहा

svastihavyavahā

She Who is the Conveyance for the Offering of Blessings 673

प्रीति

prīti

She Who is the Beloved 674

ऊष्मा

ūṣmā
She Who is the Mother of Circumstances 675

धूम्रार्चिरङ्गदा

dhūmrārciraṅgadā
She Who Makes the Body Free From Sin 676

तपिनी तापिनी विश्वा भोगदा भोगधारिणी ।
त्रिखण्डा बोधिनी वश्या सकला विश्वरूपिणी ॥ ८९

tapinī tāpinī viśvā bhogadā bhogadhāriṇī
trikhaṇḍā bodhinī vaśyā sakalā viśvarūpiṇī

तपिनी

tapinī
She Who is Heat and Light 677

तापिनी

tāpinī
She Who is the Cause of Heat and Light 678

विश्वा

visvā
She Who is the Universe 679

भोगदा

bhogadā
She Who is the Giver of Enjoyment 680

भोगधारिणी

bhogadhāriṇī
She Who is the Supporter of Enjoyment 681

त्रिखण्डा

trikhaṇḍā
She Who Has Three Parts 682

बोधिनी

bodhinī
She Who Manifests Wisdom 683

वश्या

vaśyā
She Who is Controlled 684

सकला

sakalā
She Who is All 685

विश्वरूपिणी

viśvarūpiṇī
She Who is the Intrinsic Nature of the Universe 686

बीजरूपा महामुद्रा वशिनी योगरूपिणी ।
अनङ्गकुसुमाऽनङ्गमेखलाऽनङ्गरूपिणी ॥ ८६

bījarūpā mahāmudrā vaśinī yogarūpiṇī
anaṅgakusumā-naṅgamekhalā-naṅgarūpiṇī

बीजरूपा
bījarūpā
She Who is the Form of the Seed 687

महामुद्रा
mahāmudrā
She Who is the Great Configuration of the Cosmos 688

वशिनी
vaśinī
She Who Controls 689

योगरूपिणी
yogarūpiṇī
She Who is the Intrinsic Nature of Union 690

अनङ्गकुसुमा
anaṅgakusumā
She Who is the Flower of Infinity 691

अनङ्गमेखला
anaṅgamekhalā
She Who Wears the Girdle of Infinity 692

अनङ्गरूपिणी
anaṅgarūpiṇī
She Who is the Intrinsic Nature of Infinity 693

अनङ्गमदनाऽनङ्गरेखाऽनङ्गाङ्कुशेश्वरी ।
अनङ्गमालिनी कामेश्वरी सर्वार्थसाधिका ॥ ८७

anaṅgamadanā-naṅgarekhā-naṅgāṅkuśeśvarī
anaṅgamālinī kāmeśvarī sarvārthasādhikā

अनङ्गमदना

anaṅgamadanā

She Who is the Intoxication of Infinity 694

अनङ्गरेखा

anaṅgarekhā

She Who is the Limit of Infinity 695

अनङ्गाङ्कुशेश्वरी

anaṅgāṅkuśeśvarī

She Who is the Supreme Ruler of the Goad of Infinity 696

अनङ्गमालिनी

anaṅgamālinī

She Who is the Gardener Who Cultivates Infinity 697

कामेश्वरी

kāmeśvarī

She Who is the Supreme Ruler of All Desire 698

सर्वार्थसाधिका

sarvārthasādhikā

She Who Performs Discipline for all Objectives 699

सर्वतंत्रमयी मोदिन्यरुणानङ्गरूपिणी ।
वज्रेश्वरी च जननी सर्वदुःखाक्षयंकरी ॥ ८८

sarvataṁtramayī modinyaruṇānaṅgarūpiṇī
vajreśvarī ca jananī sarvaduḥkhākṣayaṁkarī

सर्वतंत्रमयी

sarvataṁtramayī

She Who is the Expression of All Applications of Spiritual Knowledge 700

मोदिन्यरुणानङ्गरूपिणी

modinyaruṇānaṅgarūpiṇī

She Who is the Intrinsic Nature of the Intoxicating Light of Infinite Love 701

वज्रेश्वरी च

vajreśvarī ca

She Who is the Supreme Ruler of Lightning and 702

जननी

jananī

She Who is Mother 703

सर्वदुःखक्षयंकरी

sarvaduḥkhakṣayaṁkarī
She Who Dissolves All Pain into the Infinite 704

षडङ्गयुवती योगयुक्ता ज्वालांशुमालिनी ।
दुराशया दुराधर्षा दुर्ज्ञेया दुर्गरूपिणी ॥ ८९

ṣaḍaṅgayuvatī yogayuktā jvālāṁśumālinī
durāśayā durādharṣā durjñeyā durgarūpiṇī

षडङ्गयुवती

ṣaḍaṅgayuvatī
She Who is a Young Lady with Six Limbs 705

योगयुक्ता

yogayuktā
She Who is United in Union 706

ज्वालांशुमालिनी

jvālāṁśumālinī
She Who is the Cultivator of Radiance 707

दुराशया

durāśayā
She Who Resides in the Distance 708

दुराधर्षा

durādharṣā
She Who is a Difficult Ideal to Attain 709

दुर्ज्ञेया

durjñeyā
She Who Gives Knowledge that is Difficult to Attain 710

दुर्गरूपिणी

durgarūpiṇī
She Who is the Intrinsic Nature of the Reliever of Difficulties 711

दुरन्ता दुष्कृतिहरा दुर्ध्येया दुरतिक्रमा ।
हंसेश्वरी त्रिकोणस्था शाकम्भर्यनुकम्पिनी ॥ ९०

durantā duṣkṛtiharā durdhyeyā duratikramā
haṁseśvarī trikoṇasthā śākambharyanukampinī

दुरन्ता
durantā
She Who is the End of Distance 712

दुष्कृतिहरा
duṣkṛtiharā
She Who Takes Away Evil Action 713

दुर्ध्येया
durdhyeyā
She Who is Knowledge that is Difficult to Attain 714

दुरतिक्रमा
duratikramā
She Who is the Mother of All Difficult Action 715

हंसेश्वरी
haṁseśvarī
She Who is the Supreme Ruler of Laughter 716

त्रिकोणस्था
trikoṇasthā
She Who Resides in a Triangle (Kāmakalā, All the Threes) 717

शाकम्भर्यनुकम्पिनी
śākambharyanukampinī
She Who is the Feeling of Nourishment from Vegetables and Produce of the Earth 718

त्रिकोणनिलया नित्या परमामृतरंजिता ।
महाविद्येश्वरी श्वेता भेरुण्डा कुलसुन्दरी ॥ ९१

trikoṇanilayā nityā paramāmṛtaraṁjitā
mahāvidyeśvarī śvetā bheruṇḍā kulasundarī

त्रिकोणनिलया
trikoṇanilayā
She Who Resides Beyond the Triangle 719

नित्या
nityā
She Who is Eternal 720

परमामृतरंजिता

paramāmṛtaraṁjitā

She Who is the Enjoyment of the Supreme Nectar of Immortality 721

महाविद्येश्वरी

mahāvidyeśvarī

She Who is the Supreme Ruler of the Great Knowledge 722

श्वेता

śvetā

She Who is White or Pure 723

भेरुण्डा

bheruṇḍā

She Who is Formidable 724

कुलसुन्दरी

kulasundarī

She Who is the Beauty of Excellence 725

त्वरिता भक्तिसंयुक्ता भक्तिवश्या सनातनी ।
भक्तानन्दमयी भक्तभाविता भक्तशङ्करी ॥ ९२

tvaritā bhaktisaṁyuktā bhaktivaśyā sanātanī
bhaktānandamayī bhaktabhāvitā bhaktaśaṅkarī

त्वरिता

tvaritā

She Who is Quick 726

भक्तिसंयुक्ता

bhaktisaṁyuktā

She Who is Completely United in Devotion 727

भक्तिवश्या

bhaktivaśyā

She Who is Under the Control of Devotion 728

सनातनी

sanātanī

She Who is Eternal 729

भक्तानन्दमयी

bhaktānandamayī

She Who is the Manifestation of the Bliss of Devotion 730

भक्तभाविता

bhaktabhāvitā

She Who is the Attitude of Devotion 731

भक्तशङ्करी

bhaktaśaṅkarī

She Who is the Cause of the Peace of Devotion 732

सर्वसौन्दर्यनिलया सर्वसौभाग्यशालिनी ।
सर्वसम्भोगभवनी सर्वसौख्यानुरूपिणी ॥ ९३

sarvasaundaryanilayā sarvasaubhāgyaśālinī
sarvasambhogabhavanī sarvasaukhyānurūpiṇī

सर्वसौन्दर्यनिलया

sarvasaundaryanilayā

She Who is the Repository of all Beauty 733

सर्वसौभाग्यशालिनी

sarvasaubhāgyaśālinī

She Who is the Repository of all Good Fortune 734

सर्वसम्भोगभवनी

sarvasambhogabhavanī

She Who is the Mother of All Enjoyment 735

सर्वसौख्यानुरूपिणी

sarvasaukhyānurūpiṇī

She Who is the Intrinsic Nature of the Feeling of All Comfort 736

कुमारीपूजनरता कुमारीव्रतचारिणी ।
कुमारी भक्तिसुखिनी कुमारीरूपधारिणी ॥ ९४

kumārīpūjanaratā kumārīvratacāriṇī
kumārī bhaktisukhinī kumārīrūpadhāriṇī

कुमारीपूजनरता

kumārīpūjanaratā

She Who Enjoys the Worship of the Ever Pure One 737

कुमारीव्रतचारिणी

kumārīvratacāriṇī

She Who Continues the Performance of the Vow of Worship for the Ever Pure One 738

कुमारी
kumārī
She Who is the Ever Pure One 739

भक्तिसुखिनी
bhaktisukhinī
She Who Gives the Pleasure of Devotion 740

कुमारीरूपधारिणी
kumārīrūpadhāriṇī
She Who Wears the Form of the Ever Pure One 741

कुमारीपूजकप्रीता कुमारीप्रीतिदप्रिया ।
कुमारीसेवकासंगा कुमारीसेवकालया ॥ ९८

kumārīpūjakaprītā kumārīprītidapriyā
kumārīsevakāsaṁgā kumārīsevakālayā

कुमारीपूजकप्रीता
kumārīpūjakaprītā
She Who Loves the Worship of the Ever Pure One 742

कुमारीप्रीतिदप्रिया
kumārīprītidapriyā
She Who is the Beloved of the Beloved of the Ever Pure One 743

कुमारीसेवकासंगा
kumārīsevakāsaṁgā
She Who is United in the Service of the Ever Pure One 744

कुमारीसेवकालया
kumārīsevakālayā
She Who Resides Within Those Who Serve the Ever Pure One 745

आनन्दभैरवी बालभैरवी बटुभैरवी ।
श्मशानभैरवी कालभैरवी पुरभैरवी ॥ ९९

ānandabhairavī bālabhairavī baṭubhairavī
śmaśānabhairavī kālabhairavī purabhairavī

आनन्दभैरवी

ānandabhairavī
She Who is the Bliss Beyond All Fear 746

बालभैरवी

bālabhairavī
She Who is the Strength Beyond All Fear 747

बटुभैरवी

baṭubhairavī
She Who is Youth Beyond All Fear 748

श्मशानभैरवी

śmaśānabhairavī
She Who is in the Cremation Ground Where All Fear Ends 749

कालभैरवी

kālabhairavī
She Who is Time Beyond All Fear 750

पुरभैरवी

purabhairavī
She Who is Completely Beyond All Fear 751

महाभैरवपत्नी च परमानन्दभैरवी ।
सुरानन्दभैरवी च उन्मत्तानन्दभैरवी ॥ ९७

mahābhairavapatnī ca paramānandabhairavī
surānandabhairavī ca unmattānandabhairavī

महाभैरवपत्नी च

mahābhairavapatnī ca
She Who is the Spouse of the Great One Beyond All Fear and 752

परमानन्दभैरवी

paramānandabhairavī
She Who is the Supreme Bliss Beyond All Fear 753

सुरानन्दभैरवी च

surānandabhairavī ca
She Who is Divine Bliss Beyond All Fear and 754

उन्मत्तानन्दभैरवी

unmattānandabhairavī
She Who is Bliss Beyond All Fear 755

मुक्त्यानन्दभैरवी च तथा तरुणभैरवी ।
ज्ञानानन्दभैरवी च अमृतानन्दभैरवी ॥ ९८

muktyānandabhairavī ca tathā taruṇabhairavī
jñānānandabhairavī ca amṛtānandabhairavī

मुक्त्यानन्दभैरवी च तथा
muktyānandabhairavī ca tathā
She Who is the Bliss of Liberation Beyond All Fear and then 756

तरुणभैरवी
taruṇabhairavī
She Who is the Energy that Pulls Beyond Fear 757

ज्ञानानन्दभैरवी च
jñānānandabhairavī ca
She Who is the Bliss of Wisdom Beyond All Fear and 758

अमृतानन्दभैरवी
amṛtānandabhairavī
She Who is the Nectar of Immortality Beyond All Fear 759

महाभयंकरी तीव्रा तीव्रवेगा तरस्विनी ।
त्रिपुरा परमेशानी सुन्दरी पुरसुन्दरी ॥ ९९

mahābhayaṁkarī tīvrā tīvravegā tarasvinī
tripurā parameśānī sundarī purasundarī

महाभयंकरी
mahābhayaṁkarī
She Who is Greatly Fearful 760

तीव्रा
tīvrā
She Who is Very Swift 761

तीव्रवेगा
tīvravegā
She Who Moves Swiftly 762

तरस्विनी
tarasvinī
She Who Takes Across 763

त्रिपुरा
tripurā
She Who is the Resident of the Three Cities 764

परमेशानी
parameśānī
She Who is the Supreme Ruler of All 765

सुन्दरी
sundarī
She Who is the Beautiful One 766

पुरसुन्दरी
purasundarī
She Who is Completely Beautiful 767

त्रिपुरेश्वरी पञ्चदशी पञ्चमी पुरवासिनी ।
महासप्तदशी चैव षोडशी त्रिपुरेश्वरी ॥ १००

tripureśvarī pañcadaśī pañcamī puravāsinī
mahāsaptadaśī caiva ṣoḍaśī tripureśvarī

त्रिपुरेश्वरी
tripureśvarī
She Who is the Supreme Ruler of the Three Cities 768

पञ्चदशी
pañcadaśī
She Who is the Fifteen Lettered One 769

पञ्चमी
pañcamī
She Who is the Fifth 770

पुरवासिनी
puravāsinī
She Who is the Resident of the City 771

महासप्तदशी चैव
mahāsaptadaśī caiva
She Who is the Great Seventeen and again 772

षोडशी
ṣoḍaśī
She Who is the Sixteen 773

त्रिपुरेश्वरी
tripureśvarī
She Who is the Supreme Ruler of the Three Cities 774

महांकुशस्वरूपा च महाचक्रेश्वरी तथा ।
नवचक्रेश्वरी चक्रेश्वरी त्रिपुरमालिनी ॥ १०१

mahāṁkuśasvarūpā ca mahācakreśvarī tathā
navacakreśvarī cakreśvarī tripuramālinī

महांकुशस्वरूपा च
mahāṁkuśasvarūpā ca
She Who is the Intrinsic Nature of the Great Goad and 775

महाचक्रेश्वरी तथा
mahācakreśvarī tathā
She Who is the Supreme Ruler of the Great Centers of Energy then 776

नवचक्रेश्वरी
navacakreśvarī
She Who is the Supreme Ruler of the Nine Centers of Energy 777

चक्रेश्वरी
cakreśvarī
She Who is the Supreme Ruler of the Centers of Energy 778

त्रिपुरमालिनी
tripuramālinī
She Who is the Gardener of the Three Cities 779

राजचक्रेश्वरी वीरा महात्रिपुरसुन्दरी ।
सिन्दूरपूररुचिरा श्रीमत्त्रिपुरसुन्दरी ॥ १०२

rājacakreśvarī vīrā mahātripurasundarī
sindūrapūrarucirā śrīmattripurasundarī

राजचक्रेश्वरी
rājacakreśvarī
She Who is the Supreme Ruler of the King of all Centers of Energy 780

वीरा
vīrā
She Who is the Female Hero 781

महात्रिपुरसुन्दरी
mahātripurasundarī
She Who is the Great Beautiful One of the Three Cities 782

सिन्दूरपूररुचिरा
sindūrapūraruciरā
She Who is Completely Delighted with the Red Spot of Vermilion 783

श्रीमत्त्रिपुरसुन्दरी
śrīmattripurasundarī
She Who is the Respected Beautiful One of the Three Cities 784

सर्वाङ्गसुन्दरी रक्ता रक्तवस्त्रोत्तरीयका ।
यवा यावकसिन्दूररक्तचन्दनधारिणी ॥ १०३

sarvāṅgasundarī raktā raktavastrottarīyakā
yavā yāvakasindūraraktacandanadhāriṇī

सर्वाङ्गसुन्दरी
sarvāṅgasundarī
She Whose All Limbs are Beautiful 785

रक्ता
raktā
She Who is Passion 786

रक्तवस्त्रोत्तरीयका
raktavastrottarīyakā
She Who is Clothed in a Red Garment 787

यवा
yavā
She Who is Young 788

यावकसिन्दूररक्तचन्दनधारिणी
yāvakasindūraraktacandanadhāriṇī
She Who Wears Vermilion and Red Sandal Paste 789

यवायावकसिन्दूररक्तचन्दनरूपधृक् ।
चमरी वाचकुटिलनिर्मलश्यामकेशिनी ॥ १०४

yavāyāvakasindūraraktacandanarūpadhṛk
camarī vācakuṭilanirmalaśyāmakeśinī

यवायावकसिन्दूररक्तचन्दनरूपधृक्
yavāyāvakasindūraraktacandanarūpadhṛk
She Whose Youthful Countenance is Constantly Adorned with Red Vermilion and Red Sandal paste 790

चमरी
camarī
She Who is Inconstant 791

वाचकुटिलनिर्मलश्यामकेशिनी
vācakuṭilanirmalaśyāmakeśinī
She Who is Spoken of as One Who Has Pure Dark Wavy Hair 792

वज्रमौक्तिकरत्नाद्यकिरीटमुकुटोज्ज्वला ।
रत्नकुण्डलसंयुक्तस्फुरद्गण्डमनोरमा ॥ १०५
vajramauktikaratnādyakirīṭamukuṭojjvalā
ratnakuṇḍalasaṁyuktasphuradgaṇḍamanoramā

वज्रमौक्तिकरत्नाद्यकिरीटमुकुटोज्ज्वला
vajramauktikaratnādyakirīṭamukuṭojjvalā
She in Whose Crown the Pearls and Jewels are Shining Like Lightning 793

रत्नकुण्डलसंयुक्तस्फुरद्गण्डमनोरमा
ratnakuṇḍalasaṁyuktasphuradgaṇḍamanoramā
She Who Disseminates a Beautiful Scent is Wearing a Necklace of Radiantly Shining Jewels Which are United Together 794

कुञ्जरेश्वरकुम्भोत्थमुक्तारञ्जितनासिका ।
मुक्ताविद्रुममाणिक्यहाराढ्यस्तनमण्डला ॥ १०६

kuñjareśvarakumbhotthamuktārañjitanāsikā
muktāvidrūmamāṇikyahārāḍhyastanamaṇḍalā

कुञ्जरेश्वरकुम्भोत्थमुक्तारञ्जितनासिका
kuñjareśvarakumbhotthamuktārañjitanāsikā
She Who Wears an Extremely Beautiful Nose Ring which is made from the Supreme Lord of All Jewels and Pearls 795

मुक्ताविद्रुममाणिक्यहाराढ्यस्तनमण्डला
muktāvidrumamāṇikyahārāḍhyastanamaṇḍalā
She Who Wears a Necklace of Exquisitely Beautiful Pearls and Jewels in the Region of Her Breast 796

सूर्यकान्तेन्दुकान्ताढ्यस्पर्शाश्मकण्ठभूषणा ।
बीजपूरस्फुरद्बीजदन्तपंक्तिरनुत्तमा ॥ १०७
sūryakāntendukāntāḍhyasparśāśmakaṇṭhabhūṣaṇā
bījapūrasphuradbījadantapaṁktiranuttamā

सूर्यकान्तेन्दुकान्ताढ्यस्पर्शाश्मकण्ठभूषणा
sūryakāntendukāntāḍhyasparśāmakaṇṭhabhūṣaṇā
She Whose Throat is Shining by the Ultimate Touch of the Sun and the Moon 797

बीजपूरस्फुरद्बीजदन्तपंक्तिरनुत्तमा
bījapūrasphuradbījadantapaṁktiranuttamā
She Whose fifteen Excellent Teeth are Completely Shining with Bīja Mantras 798

कामकोदण्डकाभुग्नभ्रूयुगाक्षिप्रवर्तिनी ।
मातङ्गकुम्भवक्षोजा लसत्कोकनदेक्षणा ॥ १०८

kāmakodaṇḍakābhugnabhrūyugākṣipravartinī
mātaṅgakumbhavakṣojā lasatkokanadekṣaṇā

कामकोदण्डकाभुग्नभ्रूयुगाक्षिप्रवर्तिनी
kāmakodaṇḍakābhugnabhrūyugākṣipravartinī
She Whose Eye in the middle of Her Forehead Disciplines Desire 799

मातङ्गकुम्भवक्षोजा
mātaṅgakumbhavakṣojā
She Whose Breasts Give Nourishment to Existence 800

लसत्कोकनदेक्षणा
lasatkokanadekṣaṇā
She Who Especially Loves the Red Lotus Flower 801

मनोज्ञशष्कुलीकर्णा हंसीगतिविडम्बिनी ।
पद्मरागांगदद्योतद्दोश्चतुष्कप्रकाशिनी ॥ १०९

manojñaśaṣkulīkarṇā haṁsīgativiḍambinī
padmarāgāṁgadadyotaddoścatuṣkaprakāśinī

मनोज्ञशष्कुलीकर्णा
manojñaśaṣkulīkarṇā
She Who Knows the Entire Path from the Ear to the Mind 802

हंसीगतिविडम्बिनी
haṁsīgativiḍambinī
She Who is the Mother of the Swan's Motion 803

पद्मरागांगदद्योतद्दोश्चतुष्कप्रकाशिनी
padmarāgāṁgadadyotaddoścatuṣkaprakāśinī
She Whose Lotus-like Body is the Illuminator of the Four Vedas 804

नानामणिपरिस्फूर्यच्छुद्धकाञ्चनकंकणा ।
नागेन्द्रदन्तनिर्माणवलयाञ्चितपाणिका ॥ ११०

nānāmaṇiparisphūryacchuddhakāñcanakaṁkaṇā
nāgendradantanirmāṇavalayāñcitapāṇikā

नानामणिपरिस्फूर्यच्छुद्धकाञ्चनकंकणा
nānāmaṇiparisphūryacchuddhakāñcanakaṁkaṇā
She Who Wears Bracelets Shining with Various Gems and Jewels 805

नागेन्द्रदन्तनिर्माणवलयाञ्चितपाणिका
nāgendradantanirmāṇavalayāñcitapāṇikā
She Whose Fingers of Her Hands Bear Rings made of Ivory and other Gems 806

अंगुरीयकचित्रांगी विचित्रक्षुद्रघण्टिका ।
पट्टाम्बरपरीधाना कलमञ्जीररञ्जिनी ॥ १११

aṁgurīyakacitrāṁgī vicitrakṣudraghaṇṭikā
paṭṭāmbaraparīdhānā kalamañjīrarañjinī

अंगुरीयकचित्रांगी
aṁgurīyakacitrāṁgī
She Who Wears Rings on Various Parts of Her Body 807

विचित्रक्षुद्रघण्टिका
vicitrakṣudraghaṇṭikā
She Who Holds an Unusually Small Bell 808

पट्टाम्बरपरीधाना
paṭṭāmbaraparīdhānā
She Who Wears Shiny Silk Cloth 809

कलमञ्जीररञ्जिनी
kalamañjīrarañjinī
She Who Enjoys the Tinkling of Cymbals to Accompany Devotional Chanting 810

कर्पूरागुरुकस्तूरीकुंकुमद्रवलेपिता ।
विचित्ररत्नपृथिवीकल्पशाखातलस्थिता ॥ ११२

karpūrāgurukastūrīkuṁkumadravalepitā
vicitraratnapṛthivīkalpaśākhātalasthitā

कर्पूरागुरुकस्तूरीकुंकुमद्रवलेपिता
karpūrāgurukastūrīkuṁkumadravalepitā
She Who Wears Unguents of Camphor, Woodapple, and Musk, mixed in Red Paste 811

विचित्ररत्नपृथिवीकल्पशाखातलस्थिता
vicitraratnapṛthivīkalpaśākhātalasthitā
She Who is Situated on the Earth Covered with Various Jewels at the Foot of the Tree of All Fulfillment 812

रत्नद्वीपस्फुरद्रत्नसिंहासननिवासिनी ।
षट्चक्रभेदनकरी परमानन्दरूपिणी ॥ ११३

ratnadvīpasphuradratnasiṁhāsananivāsinī
ṣaṭcakrabhedanakarī paramānandarūpiṇī

रत्नद्वीपस्फुरद्रत्नसिंहासननिवासिनी
ratnadvīpasphuradratnasiṁhāsananivāsinī
She Who Sits Upon a Seat of Jewels From the Purity of the Island of Jewels 813

षट्चक्रभेदनकरी
ṣaṭcakrabhedanakarī
She Who Pierces the Six Centers of Energy 814

परमानन्दरूपिणी
paramānandarūpiṇī
She Who is the Intrinsic Nature of the Supreme Bliss 815

सहस्रदलपद्मान्तश्चन्द्रमण्डलवर्तिनी ।
ब्रह्मरूपशिवक्रोडनानासुखविलासिनी ॥ ११४

sahasradalapadmāntaścandramaṇḍalavartinī
brahmarūpaśivakroḍanānāsukhavilāsinī

सहस्रदलपद्मान्तश्चन्द्रमण्डलवर्तिनी

sahasradalapadmāntaścandramaṇḍalavartinī
She Who Resides in the Regions of the Moon at the Apex of the Thousand Petaled Lotus 816

ब्रह्मरूपशिवक्रोडनानासुखविलासिनी

brahmarūpaśivakroḍanānāsukhavilāsinī
She Who Resides in the Form of Supreme Divinity, in the Anger of Śiva, and in Various Forms of Pleasure 817

हरविष्णुविरञ्चीन्द्रग्रहनायकसेविता ।
आत्मयोनिर्ब्रह्मयोनिर्जगद्योनिरयोनिजा ॥ ११८

haraviṣṇuvirañcīndragrahanāyakasevitā
ātmayonirbrahmayonirjagadyonirayonijā

हरविष्णुविरञ्चीन्द्रग्रहनायकसेविता

haraviṣṇuvirañcīndragrahanāyakasevitā
She Who is Served by Śiva, Viṣṇu, Brahma, Indra and the Leaders of the Planets 818

आत्मयोनिः

ātmayoniḥ
She Who is the Womb of the Soul 819

ब्रह्मयोनिः

brahmayoniḥ
She Who is the Womb of Supreme Divinity 820

जगद्योनिः

jagadyoniḥ
She Who is the Womb of Perceivable Universe 821

अयोनिजा

ayonijā
She Who Does Not Take Birth from any Womb 822

भगरूपा भगस्थात्री भगिनीभगधारिणी ।
भगात्मिका भगाधाररूपिणी भगशालिनी ॥ ११६

bhagarūpā bhagasthātrī bhaginībhagadhāriṇī
bhagātmikā bhagādhārarūpiṇī bhagaśālinī

भगरूपा
bhagarūpā
She Who is the Form of Wealth 823

भगस्थात्री
bhagasthātrī
She Who Resides Within Wealth 824

भगिनीभगधारिणी
bhaginībhagadhāriṇī
She Who Upholds Wealth and is the Wealth 825

भगात्मिका
bhagātmikā
She Who is the Capacity for the the Support of Wealth 826

भगाधाररूपिणी
bhagādhārarūpiṇī
She Who is the Intrinsic Nature of the Manifestation of Wealth 827

भगशालिनी
bhagaśālinī
She Who Reposes in Wealth 828

लिङ्गाभिधायिनी लिङ्गप्रियालिङ्गनिवासिनी ।
लिङ्गस्था लिङ्गिनी लिङ्गरूपिणी लिङ्गसुन्दरी ॥ ११७

liṅgābhidhāyinī liṅgapriyāliṅganivāsinī
liṅgasthā liṅginī liṅgarūpiṇī liṅgasundarī

लिङ्गाभिधायिनी
liṅgābhidhāyinī
She Who is a Progenitor of the Subtle Body 829

लिङ्गप्रिया
liṅgapriyā
She Who is the Beloved of the Subtle Body 830

लिङ्गनिवासिनी

liṅganivāsinī
She Who Resides Within the Subtle Body 831

लिङ्गस्था

liṅgasthā
She Who is Situated in the Subtle Body 832

लिङ्गिनी

liṅginī
She Who is the Capacity of the Subtle Body 833

लिङ्गरूपिणी

liṅgarūpiṇī
She Who is the Intrinsic Nature of the Subtle Body 834

लिङ्गसुन्दरी

liṅgasundarī
She Who is the Beautiful One in the Subtle Body 835

लिङ्गगीतिमहाप्रीतिर्भगगीतिर्महासुखा ।
लिङ्गनामसदानन्दा भगनामसदारतिः ॥ ११८

liṅgagītimahāprītirbhagagītirmahāsukhā
liṅganāmasadānandā bhaganāmasadāratiḥ

लिङ्गगीतिमहाप्रीतिः

liṅgagītimahāprītiḥ
She Who is Greatly Enamored of the Songs of Subtlety 836

भगगीतिर्महासुखा

bhagagītirmahāsukhā
She Who Derives great Pleasure from the Wealth of Song 837

लिङ्गनामसदानन्दा

liṅganāmasadānandā
She Who Always Takes Delight in the Subtle Name 838

भगनामसदारतिः

bhaganāmasadāratiḥ
She Who is Always Inspired by the Name Which Bears Wealth 839

भगनामसदानन्दा लिङ्गनामसदारतिः ।
लिङ्गमालाकण्ठभूषा भगमालाविभूषणा ॥ ११९

bhaganāmasadānandā liṅganāmasadāratiḥ
liṅgamālākaṇṭhabhūṣā bhagamālāvibhūṣaṇā

भगनामसदानन्दा
bhaganāmasadānandā
She Who is Always in Bliss with the Names Which Bear Wealth 840

लिङ्गनामसदारतिः
liṅganāmasadāratiḥ
She Who is Always Inspired by the Names of Subtlety 841

लिङ्गमालाकण्ठभूषा
liṅgamālākaṇṭhabhūṣā
She At Whose Throat Shines Forth the Garland of Subtlety 842

भगमालाविभूषणा
bhagamālāvibhūṣaṇā
She Who Shines Forth with the Garland of Wealth 843

भगलिंगामृतप्रीता भगलिंगामृतात्मिका ।
भगलिंगार्चनप्रीता भगलिङ्गस्वरूपिणी ॥ १२०

bhagaliṅgāmṛtaprītā bhagaliṅgāmṛtātmikā
bhagaliṅgārcanaprītā bhagaliṅgaśvarūpiṇī

भगलिंगामृतप्रीता
bhagaliṅgāmṛtaprītā
She Who is Beloved of the Subtle Nectar of Wealth 844

भगलिंगामृतात्मिका
bhagaliṅgāmṛtātmikā
She Who is the Capacity of the Subtle Nectar of Wealth to Manifest 845

भगलिंगार्चनप्रीता
bhagaliṅgārcanaprītā
She Who is the Beloved of the Offering of Subtle Wealth 846

भगलिङ्गस्वरूपिणी
bhagaliṅgaśvarūpiṇī
She Who is the Intrinsic Nature of SubtleWealth 847

भगलिङ्गस्वरूपा च भगलिङ्गसुखावहा ।
स्वयम्भूकुसुमप्रीता स्वयम्भूकुसुमार्चिता ॥ १२१

bhagaliṅgasvarūpā ca bhagaliṅgasukhāvahā
svayambhūkusumaprītā svayambhūkusumārcitā

भगलिङ्गस्वरूपा च
bhagaliṅgasvarūpā ca
She Who is the Essence of Subtle Wealth and 848

भगलिङ्गसुखावहा
bhagaliṅgasukhāvahā
She Who is the Conveyance of the Pleasure of Subtle Wealth 849

स्वयम्भूकुसुमप्रीता
svayambhūkusumaprītā
She Who is the Beloved of the Flower Which is Born of Itself 850

स्वयम्भूकुसुमार्चिता
svayambhūkusumārcitā
She Who is the Offering of the Flower Which is Born of Itself 851

स्वयम्भूकुसुमप्राणा स्वयम्भूकुसुमोत्थिता ।
स्वयम्भूकुसुमस्नाता स्वयम्भूपुष्पतर्पिता ॥ १२२

svayambhūkusumaprāṇā svayambhūkusumotthitā
svayambhūkusumasnātā svayambhūpuṣpatarpitā

स्वयम्भूकुसुमप्राणा
svayambhūkusumaprāṇā
She Who is the Life Force of the Flower Which is Born of Itself 852

स्वयम्भूकुसुमोत्थिता
svayambhūkusumotthitā
She Who Raises Aloft the Flower Which is Born of Itself 853

स्वयम्भूकुसुमस्नाता
svayambhūkusumasnātā
She Who is Bathed by the Flower Which is Born of Itself 854

स्वयम्भूपुष्पतर्पिता
svayambhūpuṣpatarpitā
She Who is the Offering to Ancestors of the Flower Which is Born of Itself 855

स्वयम्भूपुष्पघटिता स्वयम्भूपुष्पधारिणी ।
स्वयम्भूपुष्पतिलका स्वयम्भूपुष्पचर्चिता ॥ १२३

svayambhūpuṣpaghaṭitā svayambhūpuṣpadhāriṇī
svayambhūpuṣpatilakā svayambhūpuṣpacarcitā

स्वयम्भूपुष्पघटिता
svayambhūpuṣpaghaṭitā
She Who is the Refuge of the Flower Which is Born of Itself 856

स्वयम्भूपुष्पधारिणी
svayambhūpuṣpadhāriṇī
She Who Upholds or Supports the Flower Which is Born of Itself 857

स्वयम्भूपुष्पतिलका
svayambhūpuṣpatilakā
She Who Wears a Tilak Made of the Flower Which is Born of Itself 858

स्वयम्भूपुष्पचर्चिता
svayambhūpuṣpacarcitā
She Who Offers the Flower Which is Born of Itself 859

स्वयम्भूपुष्पनिरता स्वयम्भूकुसुमग्रहा ।
स्वयम्भूपुष्पयज्ञांगा स्वयम्भूकुसुमात्मिका ॥ १२४

svayambhūpuṣpaniratā svayambhūkusumagrahā
svayambhūpuṣpayajñāṁgā svayambhūkusumātmikā

स्वयम्भूपुष्पनिरता
svayambhūpuṣpaniratā
She Who is Absorbed in the Essence of the Flower Which is Born of Itself 860

स्वयम्भूकुसुमग्रहा
svayambhūkusumagrahā
She Who is Beyond the Worlds of the Flower Which is Born of Itself 861

स्वयम्भूपुष्पयज्ञांगा

svayambhūpuṣpayajñāṁgā

She Who Offers in Sacrifice to Her Own Self the Flower Which is Born of Itself 862

स्वयम्भूकुसुमात्मिका

svayambhūkusumātmikā

She Who is the Capacity of the Soul to Manifest the Flower Which is Born of Itself 863

स्वयम्भूपुष्परचिता स्वयम्भूकुसुमप्रिया ।
स्वयम्भूकुसुमादानलालसोन्मत्तमानसा ॥ १२८

svayambhūpuṣparacitā svayambhūkusumapriyā
svayambhūkusumādānalālasonmattamānasā

स्वयम्भूपुष्परचिता

svayambhūpuṣparacitā

She Who is the Expression of the Flower Which is Born by Itself 864

स्वयम्भूकुसुमप्रिया

svayambhūkusumapriyā

She Who is the Beloved of the Flower Which is Born by Itself 865

स्वयम्भूकुसुमादानलालसोन्मत्तमानसा

svayambhūkusumādānalālasonmattamānasā

She Whose Mind is Intoxicated with Desire for the Flower Which is Born by Itself 866

स्वयम्भूकुसुमानन्दलहरीस्निग्धदेहिनी ।
स्वयम्भूकुसुमधारा स्वयम्भूकुसुमाकुला ॥ १२६

svayambhūkusumānandalaharīsnigdhadehinī
svayambhūkusumadhārā svayambhūkusumākulā

स्वयम्भूकुसुमानन्दलहरीस्निग्धदेहिनी

svayambhūkusumānandalaharīsnigdhadehinī

She Whose Friendly Body Experiences Waves of Bliss from the Flower Which is Born by Itself 867

स्वयम्भूकुसुमधारा
svayambhūkusumadhārā
She Who Supports the Flower Which is Born by Itself 868

स्वयम्भूकुसुमाकुला
svayambhūkusumākulā
She Who is the Family of the Flower Which is Born by Itself 869

स्वयम्भूपुष्पनिलया स्वयम्भूपुष्पवासिनी ।
स्वयम्भूकुसुमस्निग्धा स्वयम्भूकुसुमोत्सुका ॥ १२७

svayambhūpuṣpanilayā svayambhūpuṣpavāsinī
svayambhūkusumasnigdhā svayambhūkusumotsukā

स्वयम्भूपुष्पनिलया
svayambhūpuṣpanilayā
She Who Resides in the Flower Which is Born by Itself 870

स्वयम्भूपुष्पवासिनी
svayambhūpuṣpavāsinī
She Who Sits on the Flower Which is Born by Itself 871

स्वयम्भूकुसुमस्निग्धा
svayambhūkusumasnigdhā
She Who is the Friend of the Flower Which is Born by Itself 872

स्वयम्भूकुसुमोत्सुका
svayambhūkusumotsukā
She Who is the Supreme Pleasure of the Flower Which is Born by Itself 873

स्वयम्भूपुष्पकारिणी स्वयम्भूपुष्पपालिका ।
स्वयम्भूकुसुमध्याना स्वयमभूकुसुमप्रभा ॥ १२८

svayambhūpuṣpakāriṇī svayambhūpuṣpapālikā
svayambhūkusumadhyānā svayambhūkusumaprabhā

स्वयम्भूपुष्पकारिणी
svayambhūpuṣpakāriṇī
She Who is the Cause of the Flower Which is Born by Itself 874

स्वयम्भूपुष्पपालिका
svayambhūpuṣpapālikā
She Who is the Protector of the Flower Which is Born by Itself 875

स्वयम्भूकुसुमध्याना
svayambhūkusumadhyānā
She Who is the Student or Meditator on the Flower Which is Born by Itself 876

स्वयमभूकुसुमप्रभा
svayambhūkusumaprabhā
She Who is the Radiance of the Flower Which is Born by Itself 877

स्वयम्भूकुसुमज्ञाना स्वयम्भूपुष्पभोगिणी ।
स्वयम्भूकुसुमानन्दा स्वयम्भूपुष्पवर्षिणी ॥ १२९

svayambhūkusumajñānā svayambhūpuṣpabhogiṇī
svayambhūkusumānandā svayambhūpuṣpavarṣiṇī

स्वयम्भूकुसुमज्ञाना
svayambhūkusumajñānā
She Who is the Wisdom of the Flower Which is Born by Itself 878

स्वयम्भूपुष्पभोगिणी
svayambhūpuṣpabhogiṇī
She Who is the Enjoyer of the Flower Which is Born by Itself 879

स्वयम्भूकुसुमानन्दा
svayambhūkusumānandā
She Who is the Bliss of the Flower Which is Born by Itself 880

स्वयम्भूपुष्पवर्षिणी
svayambhūpuṣpavarṣiṇī
She Who Causes the Rain of the Flower Which is Born by Itself 881

स्वयम्भूकुसुमोत्साहा स्वयम्भूपुष्पपुष्पिणी ।
स्वयम्भूकुसुमोत्संगा स्वयम्भूपुष्परूपिणी ॥ १३०

svayambhūkusumotsāhā svayambhūpuṣpapuṣpiṇī
svayambhūkusumotsaṁgā svayambhūpuṣparūpiṇī

स्वयम्भूकुसुमोत्साहा
svayambhūkusumotsāhā
She Who is the Enthusiasm of the Flower Which is Born by Itself 882

स्वयम्भूपुष्पपुष्पिणी
svayambhūpuṣpapuṣpiṇī
She Who is the Flower of the Flower Which is Born by Itself 883

स्वयम्भूकुसुमोत्संगा
svayambhūkusumotsaṁgā
She Who is Always With the Flower Which is Born by Itself 884

स्वयम्भूपुष्परूपिणी
svayambhūpuṣparūpiṇī
She Who is the Intrinsic Nature of the Flower Which is Born by Itself 885

स्वयम्भूकुसुमोन्मादा स्वयम्भूपुष्पसुन्दरी ।
स्वयम्भूकुसुमाराध्या स्वयम्भूकुसुमोद्भवा ॥ १३१

svayambhūkusumonmādā svayambhūpuṣpasundarī
svayambhūkusumārādhyā svayambhūkusumodbhavā

स्वयम्भूकुसुमोन्मादा
svayambhūkusumonmādā
She Who is the Intoxication of the Flower Which is Born by Itself 886

स्वयम्भूपुष्पसुन्दरी
svayambhūpuṣpasundarī
She Who is the Beauty of the Flower Which is Born by Itself 887

स्वयम्भूकुसुमाराध्या
svayambhūkusumārādhyā
She Who is Delighted by the Flower Which is Born by Itself 888

स्वयम्भूकुसुमोद्भवा
svayambhūkusumodbhavā
She Who Gives Birth to the Flower Which is Born by Itself 889

स्वयम्भूकुसुमव्यग्रा स्वयम्भूपुष्पवर्णिता ।
स्वयम्भूपूजकप्रज्ञा स्वयम्भूहोतृमातृका ॥ १३२

svayambhūkusumavyagrā svayambhūpuṣpavarṇitā
svayambhūpūjakaprajñā svayambhūhotṛmātṛkā

स्वयम्भूकुसुमव्यग्रा
svayambhūkusumavyagrā
She Who Distinguishes the Flower Which is Born by Itself 890

स्वयम्भूपुष्पवर्णिता
svayambhūpuṣpavarṇitā
She Who Expresses the Flower Which is Born by Itself 891

स्वयम्भूपूजकप्रज्ञा
svayambhūpūjakaprajñā
She Who is the Supreme Wisdom of Worship of that Which is Born by Itself 892

स्वयम्भूहोतृमातृका
svayambhūhotṛmātṛkā
She Who is the Mother of the Supreme Wisdom of Sacrifical Worship of that Which is Born by Itself 893

स्वयम्भूदातृरक्षित्री स्वयम्भूभक्तभाविका ।
स्वयम्भूकुसुमप्रज्ञा स्वयम्भूपूजकप्रिया ॥ १३३

svayambhūdātṛrakṣitrī svayambhūbhaktabhāvikā
svayambhūkusumaprajñā svayambhūpūjakapriyā

स्वयम्भूदातृरक्षित्री
svayambhūdātṛrakṣitrī
She Who Protects the Bestower of that Which is Born by Itself 894

स्वयम्भूभक्तभाविका
svayambhūbhaktabhāvikā
She Who Intuitively Understands the Attitude of Devotion of that Which is Born by Itself 895

स्वयम्भूकुसुमप्रज्ञा
svayambhūkusumaprajñā
She Who is the Wisdom of the Flower Which is Born by Itself 896

स्वयम्भूपूजकप्रिया
svayambhūpūjakapriyā
She Who is the Beloved of the Worship of that Which is Born by Itself 897

स्वयम्भूवन्दकाधारा स्वयम्भूनिन्दकान्तका ।
स्वयम्भूप्रदसर्वस्वा स्वयम्भूप्रदरूपिणी ॥ १३४

svayambhūvandakādhārā svayambhūnindakāntakā
svayambhūpradasarvasvā svayambhūpradarūpiṇī

स्वयम्भूवन्दकाधारा
svayambhūvandakādhārā
She Who Supports the Cause of Worship of that Which is Born by Itself 898

स्वयम्भूनिन्दकान्तका
svayambhūnindakāntakā
She Who is the Cause of the End of that Which is Born by Itself 899

स्वयम्भूप्रदसर्वस्वा
svayambhūpradasarvasvā
She Who is the Bestower of all that Which is Born by Itself 900

स्वयम्भूप्रदरूपिणी
svayambhūpradarūpiṇī
She Who is the Intrinsic Nature of the Bestower of that Which is Born by Itself 901

स्वयम्भूप्रदसस्मेरा स्वयम्भर्द्धशरीरिणी ।
सर्वकाल्लोद्भवप्रीता सर्वकाल्लोद्भवात्मिका ॥ १३५

svayambhūpradasasmerā svayambharddhaśarīriṇī
sarvakālodbhavaprītā sarvakālodbhavātmīkā

स्वयम्भूप्रदसस्मेरा
svayambhūpradasasmerā
She Who is the Remembrance of the Bestower of that Which is Born of Itself 902

स्वयम्भर्द्धशरीरिणी
svayambharddhaśarīriṇī
She Who is the Half Body of that Which is Born by Itself 903

सर्वकालोद्भवप्रीता
sarvakālodbhavaprītā
She Who is the Beloved Who Gives Birth to All Time 904

सर्वकालोद्भवात्मिका
sarvakālodbhavātmikā
She Who Has the Capacity of the Expression of the Soul Which Gives Birth to All Time 905

सर्वकालोद्भवोद्भावा सर्वकालोद्भवोद्भवा ।
कुण्डपुष्पसदाप्रीतिर्गोलपुष्पसदागतिः ॥ १३६

sarvakālodbhavodbhāvā sarvakālodbhavodbhavā
kuṇḍapuṣpasadāprītirgolapuṣpasadāgatiḥ

सर्वकालोद्भवोद्भावा
sarvakālodbhavodbhāvā
She Who is the Attitude of All Time 906

सर्वकालोद्भवोद्भवा
sarvakālodbhavodbhavā
She Who Gives Birth to Time 907

कुण्डपुष्पसदाप्रीतिः
kuṇḍapuṣpasadāprītiḥ
She Who is the Beloved of All the Flowers in the Receptacle 908

गोलपुष्पसदागतिः
golapuṣpasadāgatiḥ
She Who Always Moves with the Flowers of Light 909

कुण्डगोलोद्भवप्रीता कुण्डगोलोद्भवात्मिका ।
शुक्रधारा शुक्ररूपा शुक्रसिन्धुनिवासिनी ॥ १३७

kuṇḍagolodbhavaprītā kuṇḍagolodbhavātmikā
śukradhārā śukrarūpā śukrasindhunivāsinī

कुण्डगोलोद्भवप्रीता
kuṇḍagolodbhavaprītā
She Who is the Beloved of the Light in the Receptacle 910

कुण्डगोलोद्भवात्मिका
kuṇḍagolodbhavātmikā
She Who has the Capacity of the Soul to Express the Light in the Receptacle 911

शुक्रधारा
śukradhārā
She Who is the Supporter of Purity 912

शुक्ररूपा
śukrarūpā
She Who is the Form of Purity 913

शुक्रसिन्धुनिवासिनी
śukrasindhunivāsinī
She Who Resides Within the Ocean of Purity 914

शुक्रालया शुक्रभोगा शुक्रपूजासदारतिः ।
रक्ताशया रक्तभोगा रक्तपूजासदारतिः ॥ १३८

śukrālayā śukrabhogā śukrapūjāsadāratiḥ
raktāśayā raktabhogā raktapūjāsadāratiḥ

शुक्रालया
śukrālayā
She Who has Indestructible Purity 915

शुक्रभोगा
śukrabhogā
She Who is the Enjoyer of Purity 916

शुक्रपूजासदारतिः
śukrapūjāsadāratiḥ
She Who is Delighted by Worship with Purity 917

रक्ताशया
raktāśayā
She Who Rests in Passion 918

रक्तभोगा
raktabhogā
She Who is the Enjoyer of Passion 919

रक्तपूजासदारतिः
raktapūjāsadāratiḥ
She Who is Constantly Delighted by Worship with Passion 920

रक्तपूजारक्तहोमा रक्तस्था रक्तवत्सला ।
रक्तवर्णा रक्तदेहा रक्तपूजकपुत्रिणी ॥ १३९

raktapūjāraktahomā raktasthā raktavatsalā
raktavarṇā ratkadehā raktapūjakaputriṇī

रक्तपूजा
raktapūjā
She Who is Worshiped with Passion 921

रक्तहोमा
raktahomā
She Who is Offered Sacrificial Offerings With Passion 922

रक्तस्था
raktasthā
She Who is Situated in Passion 923

रक्तवत्सला
raktavatsalā
She Who Takes Refuge in Passion 924

रक्तवर्णा
raktavarṇā
She Who is the Description of Passion 925

रक्तदेहा
raktadehā
She Who has the Body of Passion 926

रक्तपूजकपुत्रिणी
raktapūjakaputriṇī
She Who is the Daughter Born From Worship With Passion 927

रक्तद्युती रक्तस्पृहा देवी च रक्तसुन्दरी ।
रक्ताभिधेया रक्तार्हा रक्तकन्दरवन्दिता ॥ १४०

raktadyutī raktaspṛhā devī ca raktasundarī
raktābhidheyā raktārhā raktakandaravanditā

रक्तद्युती
raktadyutī
She Who is the Dignity of Passion 928

रक्तस्पृहा
raktaspṛhā
She Who is the Touch of Passion 929

देवी च
devī ca
She Who is the Goddess and 930

रक्तसुन्दरी
raktasundarī
She Who is Beautiful Passion 931

रक्ताभिधेया
raktābhidheyā
She Who Knows Passion 932

रक्तार्हा
raktārhā
She Who is Worthy of Passion 933

रक्तकन्दरवन्दिता
raktakandaravanditā
She Who is Celebrated as the Passion of the God of Love 934

महारक्ता रक्तभवा रक्तसृष्टिविधायिनी ।
रक्तस्नाता रक्तसिक्ता रक्तसेव्यातिरक्तिनी ॥ १४१

mahāraktā raktabhavā raktasṛṣṭividhāyinī
raktasnātā raktasiktā raktasevyātiraktinī

महारक्ता
mahāraktā
She Who is Great Passion 935

रक्तभवा
raktabhavā
She Who Exists in Passion 936

रक्तसृष्टिविधायिनी
raktasṛṣṭividhāyinī
She Who Gives the Creation of Passion 937

रक्तस्नाता
raktasnātā
She Who Bathes in Passion 938

रक्तसिक्ता
raktasiktā
She Who is Soaked in Passion 939

रक्तसेव्यातिरक्तिनी
raktasevyātiraktinī
She Who Becomes Extremely Passionate with the Selfless Service of Passion 940

रक्तानन्दकरी रक्तसदानन्दविधायिनी ।
रक्ताशया रक्तपूर्णा रक्तसेव्या मनोरमा ॥ १४२

raktānandakarī raktasadānandavidhāyinī
raktāśayā raktapūrṇā raktasevyā manoramā

रक्तानन्दकरी
raktānandakarī
She Who Manifests the Bliss of Passion 941

रक्तसदानन्दविधायिनी
raktasadānandavidhāyinī
She Who Always Gives the Bliss of Passion 942

रक्ताशया
raktāśayā
She Who Rests Within Passion 943

रक्तपूर्णा
raktapūrṇā
She Who Gives Full, Complete and Perfect Passion 944

रक्तसेव्या
raktasevyā
She Who is Served by Passion 945

मनोरमा
manoramā
She Who is Beautiful 946

रक्तपूजकसर्वस्वा रक्तनिन्दकनाशिनी ।
रक्तात्मिका रक्तरूपा रक्ताकर्षणकारिणी ॥ १४३

raktapūjakasarvasvā raktanindakanāśinī
raktātmikā raktarūpā raktākarṣaṇakāriṇī

रक्तपूजकसर्वस्वा
raktapūjakasarvasvā
She Who is Worshiped in All With Passion 947

रक्तनिन्दकनाशिनी
raktanindakanāśinī
She Who Destroys the Criticism of Passion 948

रक्तात्मिका

raktātmikā

She Who is the Soul's Capacity for the Expression of Passion 949

रक्तरूपा

raktarūpā

She Who is a Form of Passion 950

रक्ताकर्षणकारिणी

raktākarṣaṇakāriṇī

She Who is the Cause of the Attraction of Passion 951

रक्तोत्साहा च रक्ताढ्या रक्तपानपरायणा ।
शोणितानन्दजननी कल्लोलस्निग्धरूपिणी ॥ १४४

raktotsāhā ca raktāḍhyā raktapānaparāyaṇā
śoṇitānandajananī kallolasnigdharūpiṇī

रक्तोत्साहा च

raktotsāhā ca

She Who is the Enthusiasm of Passion and 952

रक्ताढ्या

raktāḍhyā

She Who Rides Upon Passion 953

रक्तपानपरायणा

raktapānaparāyaṇā

She Who Drinks With Passion 954

शोणितानन्दजननी

śoṇitānandajananī

She Who is the Mother of the Bliss of the Female Seed of Life 955

कल्लोलस्निग्धरूपिणी

kallolasnigdharūpiṇī

She Who is the Intrinsic Nature of Attachment to the Family 956

साधकान्तर्गता देवी पायिनी पापनाशिनी ।
साधकानां सुखकरी साधकारिविनाशिनी ॥ १४५

sādhakāntargatā devī pāyinī pāpanāśinī
sādhakānāṁ sukhakarī sādhakārivināśinī

साधकान्तर्गता देवी
sādhakāntargatā devī
She Who is the Goddess Who Goes Inside Sādhus 957

पायिनी
pāyinī
She Who is Pure Nourishment 958

पापनाशिनी
pāpanāśinī
She Who is the Destroyer of All Sin (Confusion) 959

साधकानां सुखकरी
sādhakānāṁ sukhakarī
She Who is the Giver of Delight to All Sādhus 960

साधकारिविनाशिनी
sādhakārivināśinī
She Who Destroys the Impurity of All Sādhus 961

साधकानां हृदिस्थात्री साधकानन्दकारिणी ।
साधकानाञ्च जननी साधकप्रियकारिणी ॥ १४६

sādhakānāṁ hṛdisthātrī sādhakānandakāriṇī
sādhakānāñca jananī sādhakapriyakāriṇī

साधकानां हृदिस्थात्री
sādhakānāṁ hṛdisthātrī
She Who is Situated in the Heart of All Sādhus 962

साधकानन्दकारिणी
sādhakānandakāriṇī
She Who is the Cause of the Bliss of All Sādhus 963

साधकानाञ्च जननी
sādhakānāñca jananī
She Who is the Mother of the Bliss of All Sādhus 964

साधकप्रियकारिणी
sādhakapriyakāriṇī
She Who is the Cause of the Love of Sādhus 965

साधकप्रचुरानन्दसम्पत्तिसुखदायिनी ।
शुक्रपूज्या शुक्रहोमसन्तुष्टा शुक्रवत्सला ॥ १४७

sādhakapracurānandasampatti sukhadāyinī
śukrapūjyā śukrahomasantuṣṭā śukravatsalā

साधकप्रचुरानन्दसम्पत्तिसुखदायिनी
sādhakapracurānandasampatti sukhadāyinī
She Who Gives the Wealth of Delight and Extreme Bliss to Sādhus 966

शुक्रपूज्या
śukrapūjyā
She Who is Worshiped by Purity 967

शुक्रहोमसन्तुष्टा
śukrahomasantuṣṭā
She Who is Satisfied With Sacrificial Offerings of Purity 968

शुक्रवत्सला
śukravatsalā
She Who Takes Refuge in Purity 969

शुक्रमूर्तिः शुक्रदेहा शुक्रपूजकपुत्रिणी ।
शुक्रस्था शुक्रिणी शुक्रसंस्पृहा शुक्रसुन्दरी ॥ १४८

śukramūrtiḥ śukradehā śukrapūjakaputriṇī
śukrasthā śukriṇī śukrasaṁspṛhā śukrasundarī

शुक्रमूर्तिः
śukramūrtiḥ
She Who is the Image of Purity 970

शुक्रदेहा
śukradehā
She Who is the Embodiment of Purity 971

शुक्रपूजकपुत्रिणी
śukrapūjakaputriṇī
She Who is the Daughter of Worship with Purity 972

शुक्रस्था
śukrastha
She Who is Situated in Purity 973

शुक्रिणी
śukriṇī
She Who is Supreme Purity 974

शुक्रसंस्पृहा
śukrasaṁspṛhā
She Who is the Complete Touch of Purity 975

शुक्रसुन्दरी
śukrasundarī
She Who is the Beauty of Purity 976

शुक्रस्नाता शुक्रकरी शुक्रसेव्यातिशुक्रिणी ।
महाशुक्रा शुक्रभवा शुक्रवृष्टिविधायिनी ॥१४९

śukrasnātā śukrakarī śukrasevyātiśukriṇī
mahāśukrā śukrabhavā śukravṛṣṭividhāyinī

शुक्रस्नाता
śukrasnātā
She Who is Bathed in Purity 977

शुक्रकरी
śukrakarī
She Who is the Manifestation of Purity 978

शुक्रसेव्यातिशुक्रिणी
śukrasevyātiśukriṇī
She Who is the Supreme Purity Served by the Pure 979

महाशुक्रा
mahāśukrā
She Who is the Great Purity 980

शुक्रभवा
śukrabhavā
She Who is Pure Existence 981

शुक्रवृष्टिविधायिनी
śukravṛṣṭividhāyinī
She Who is the Giver of the Rain of Purity 982

शुक्राभिधेया शुक्रार्हाशुक्रवन्दकवन्दिता ।
शुक्रानन्दकरी शुक्रसदानन्दविधायिनी ॥ १८०

śukrābhidheyā śukrārhāśukravandakavanditā
śukrānandakarī śukrasadānandavidhāyinī

शुक्राभिधेया
śukrābhidheyā
She Who is the Supreme Wisdom of Purity 983

शुक्रार्हाशुक्रवन्दकवन्दिता
śukrārhāśukravandakavanditā
The Pure of the Pure Consider Her as the Worshiped of the Worshiped 984

शुक्रानन्दकरी
śukrānandakarī
She Who is the Expression of the Bliss of Purity 985

शुक्रसदानन्दविधायिनी
śukrasadānandavidhāyinī
She Who Aways Gives the Bliss of Purity 986

शुक्रोत्सवा सदाशुक्रपूर्णा शुक्रमनोरमा ।
शुक्रपूजकसर्वस्वा शुक्रनिन्दकनाशिनी ॥ १८१

śukrotsavā sadāśukrapūrṇā śukramanoramā
śukrapūjakasarvasvā śukranindakanāśinī

शुक्रोत्सवा
śukrotsavā
She Who Enjoys the Festivals of Purity 987

सदाशुक्रपूणा
sadāśukrapūrṇā
She Who Always Manifests Full, Complete and Perfect Purity 988

शुक्रमनोरमा
śukramanoramā
She Who is the Beauty of Purity 989

शुक्रपूजकसर्वस्वा
śukrapūjakasarvasvā
She Who is Worshiped As the Pure in All 990

शुक्रनिन्दकनाशिनी
śukranindakanāśinī
She Who is the Destroyer of the Criticism of Purity 991

शुक्रात्मिका शुक्रसम्पच्छुक्राकर्षकारिणी ।
सारदा साधकप्राणा साधकासक्तमानसा ॥ १८२
śukrātmikā śukrasampacchukrākarṣakāriṇī
sāradā sādhakaprāṇā sādhakāsaktamānasā

शुक्रात्मिका
śukrātmikā
She Who Has the Capacity of the Soul of Purity 992

शुक्रसम्पच्छुक्राकर्षकारिणी
śukrasampacchukrākarṣakāriṇī
She Who is the Cause of Attraction of the Wealth of Purity 993

सारदा
sāradā
She Who is the Giver of All (as the energy of creation) 994

साधकप्राणा
sādhakaprāṇā
She Who is the Lifeforce of Sādhus 995

साधकासक्तमानसा
sādhakāsaktamānasā
She Who Disables the Divisive Thoughts of Sādhus 996

साधकोत्तमसर्वस्वसाधिका भक्तवत्सला ।
साधकानन्दसन्तोषा साधकाधिविनाशिनी ॥ १८३
sādhakottamasarvasvasādhikā bhaktavatsalā
sādhakānandasantoṣā sādhakādhivināśinī

साधकोत्तमसर्वस्वसाधिका
sādhakottamasarvasvasādhikā
She Who is the Female Sādhu of all Excellent Sādhus 997

भक्तवत्सला
bhaktavatsalā
She Who is the Refuge of Devotees 998

साधकानन्दसन्तोषा
sādhakānandasantoṣā
She Who is Completely Pleased With Bliss 999

साधकाधिविनाशिनी
sādhakādhivināśinī
She Who is the Destroyer of All Thoughts of Sādhus 1000

आत्मविद्या ब्रह्मविद्या परब्रह्मस्वरूपिणी ।
त्रिकूटस्था पंचकूटा सर्वकूटशरीरिणी ।
सर्ववर्णमयी वर्णजपमालाविधायिनी ॥ १८४

ātmavidyā brahmavidyā parabrahmasvarūpiṇī
trikūṭasthā paṁcakūṭā sarvakūṭaśarīriṇī
sarvavarṇamayī varṇajapamālāvidhāyinī

आत्मविद्या
ātmavidyā
She Who is the Knowledge of the Soul 1001

ब्रह्मविद्या
brahmavidyā
She Who is the Knowledge of Supreme Divinity 1002

परब्रह्मस्वरूपिणी
parabrahmasvarūpiṇī
She Who is the Intrinsic Nature of Supreme Divinity 1003

त्रिकूटस्था
trikūṭasthā
She Who is Established in Three Places 1004

पंचकूटा
paṁcakūṭā
She Who is Established in Five Places 1005

सर्वकूटशरीरिणी
sarvakūṭaśarīriṇī
She Who is the Embodiment of All Places 1006

सर्ववर्णमयी

sarvavarṇamayī

She Who is the Expression of All That Can be Expressed 1007

वर्णजपमालाविधायिनी

varṇajapamālāvidhāyinī

She Who is the Giver of the Garland of All Expressions Which can be Recited 1008

ॐ

Consecration of Tantric Offerings

bhāṅga

ॐ ह्रीं अमृते अमृतोद्भवे अमृतवर्षिणि अमृतमाकर्षयाकर्षय सिद्धिं देहि कालिकां मे वशमानय । ॐ ह्रीं श्रीं क्रीं परमेश्वरि कालिके स्वाहा विजयां समर्पयामि ॥

oṁ hrīṁ amṛte amṛtodbhave amṛtavarṣiṇi amṛtamākarṣayākarṣaya siddhiṁ dehi kālikāṁ me vaśamānaya
oṁ hrīṁ śrīṁ krīṁ parameśvari kālike svāhā vijayāṁ samarpayāmi

Oṁ hrīṁ the nectar which comes forth from nectar, you who pour forth nectar, again and again bring nectar to me. Give me control of Kālikā, the Goddess Who Takes Away the Darkness. Give me siddhi, the attainment of perfection. I am One with God.

This is the mantra for the consecration of the Vijayā, a preparation of the leaves of cannabis. Then inwardly reciting the mūlamantra seven times over the Vijayā, show the Dhenu, the Yoni, the Āvāhanī, and other mudrās: (Sthāpanī, Sannidhāpanī, Sannirodhinī, Sammukhī-karanī mudrās.)

Then satisfy the Guru who resides in the Thousand-petaled Lotus by offering the Vijayā three times with the Saṁketa-Mudrā. Then worship the Devi in your heart by offering the Vijayā with the same mudrā, reciting the mūla mantra three times: **oṁ hrīṁ śrīṁ krīṁ parameśvari kālike svāhā.** Then offer oblations to the mouth of Kundalinī with the Vijayā, while reciting the following mantra:

ऐं वद वद वाग्वादिनि मम जिह्वाग्रे स्थिरीभव सर्वसत्त्ववशङ्करि स्वाहा ॥

aiṁ vada vada vāgvādini mama jihvāgre sthirībhava sarvasattvavaśaṅkari svāhā

Aiṁ Oh Goddess Sarasvatī, Who Rules over all vibrations, inspire me and remain forever on the tip of my tongue, I am One with God!

After drinking the Vijayā he should bow to the Guru by placing his folded palms over his left ear, then to Gaṇeśa by placing his folded palms over his right ear, and lastly to the Eternal Ādyā Devī by placing his folded palms in the middle of his forehead. Then he should meditate on the Devī.

wine or alcohol

ॐ एकमेव परं ब्रह्म स्थूलसूक्ष्ममयं ध्रुवम् ।
कचोद्भवां ब्रह्महत्यां तेन ते नाशयाम्यहम् ॥

oṁ ekameva paraṁ brahma sthūlasūkṣmamayaṁ dhruvam
kacodbhavāṁ brahmahatyāṁ tena te nāśayāmyaham

Oṁ There is only One Supreme Consciousness, without a second, which is both gross and subtle. Oh Divinity, destroy the sin of slaying a Brahmaṇa which became attached to wine by the death of Kacha.*

सूर्यमण्डलमध्यस्थे वरुणालयसम्भवे ।
अमाबीजमये देवि शुक्रशापाद्विमुच्यताम् ॥

sūryamaṇḍalamadhyasthe varuṇālayasambhave
amābījamaye devi śukraśāpādvimucyatām

Oh you who reside in the regions of the Sun, where the light of wisdom always shines, and your birth was in the dwelling place of the Lord of Ocean, in the churning of which this nectar was produced, who are one with the bīja mantra of the Divine Mother, be free from the curse of Śukra.

वेदानां प्रणवो बीजं ब्रह्मानन्दमयं यदि ।
तेन सत्येन ते देवि ब्रह्महत्या व्यपोहतु ॥

* Kacha was the son of Bṛhaspati and the disciple of Śukra, priest of the asuras. Kacha was burnt by the asuras, and his ashes were mixed in the wine which Śukra drank. When Śukra discovered what he had done under the influence of intoxication he cursed wine.

vedānāṁ praṇavo bījaṁ brahmānandamayaṁ yadi
tena satyena te devi brahmahatyā vyapohatu

Oh Goddess, the **oṁ** of the Vedas is the seed of the bliss of Supreme Divinity. May the sin of slaying a Brahmaṇa be destroyed by the recitation of this principle.

ॐ ह्रीं हंसः शुचिषद्वसुरन्तरिक्षसद्धोता
वेदिषदतिथिर्दुरोणसत्। नृषद् वरसदृतसद् व्योमसदब्जा
गोजा ऋतजा अद्रिजा ऋतम् ॥

oṁ hrīṁ haṁsaḥ śuciṣad vasurantarikṣasaddhotā
vediṣadatithirduroṇasat
nṛṣad varasadṛtasad vyomasadabjā gojā ṛtajā adrijā ṛtam

Oṁ Hrīṁ the Supreme Haṁsa, the swan who flies on the wings of Consciousness and Nature, dwells in the brilliant Heaven. As Vasu, the Lord of Wealth, It moves throughout the space between heaven and earth. It dwells on earth in the form of the Vedic fire, and in the sacrificer, and is honored in the Guest. It is in the household fire and in the Consciousness of man, and dwells in the honored region. It resides in Truth and in the ether. It is born in water, in rays of light, in Truth, and in the eastern hills where the sun rises. Such is the great Illuminator of Light, the Truth, which cannot be bound or concealed, the Great Consciousness Who dwells everywhere -- Supreme Divinity.

(repeat seven times)

ॐ वां वीं वूं वैं वौं वः ब्रह्मशापविमोचितायै सुधादेव्यै नमः

oṁ vāṁ vīṁ vūṁ vaiṁ vauṁ vaḥ brahmaśāpavimocitāyai sudhādevyai namaḥ

I bow to the Goddess of Nectar who is relieved of the curse of Brahma.

ॐ क्रां क्रीं क्रूं क्रैं क्रौं क्रः श्रीं ह्रीं सुधाकृष्णशापं मोचयामृतं
स्रावय स्रावय स्वाहा ॥

oṁ krāṁ krīṁ krūṁ kraiṁ krauṁ kraḥ śrīṁ hrīṁ sudhākṛṣṇaśāpaṁ mocayāmṛtaṁ srāvaya srāvaya svāhā

Remove the curse of Kṛṣṇa in the wine: pour nectar again and again. I am one with God.

ह स क्ष म ल व र युं आनन्दभैरवाय नमः

ha sa kṣa ma la va ra yuṁ ānandabhairavāya namaḥ

I bow to Ānandabhairava, the Bliss of Fearlessness.

स ह क्ष म ल व र यीं सुधादेव्यै वौषट्

sa ha kṣa ma la va ra yīṁ sudhādevyai vauṣaṭ

I bow to Sudhā Devī, to the Goddess of Wine, Purify!

ॐ ह्रीं श्रीं क्रीं परमेश्वरि कालिके स्वाहा

oṁ hrīṁ śrīṁ krīṁ parameśvari kālike svāhā

Oṁ Māyā, Increase, Dissolution, to the highest female divinity Kālī, I am One with God!

Wave lights and incense over the container of wine:

त्र्यम्बकं यजामहे सुगन्धिं पुष्टिवर्द्धनम् ।
उर्व्वारुकमिव बन्धनान्मृत्योर्म्मुक्षीय मामृतात् ॥

tryambakaṁ yajāmahe sugandhiṁ puṣṭivarddhanam
urvvārukamiva bandhanānmṛtyormmukṣīya māmṛtāt

We adore the Father of the three worlds, of excellent fame, Grantor of Increase. As a cucumber is released from its bondage to the stem, so may I be freed from Death to dwell in immortality.

ॐ अखण्डैकरसानन्दाकरे परसुधात्मनि ।
स्वच्छन्दस्फुरणामत्र निधेहि कुलरूपिणि ॥

oṁ akhaṇḍaikarasānandākare parasudhātmani
svacchandasphuraṇāmatra nidhehi kularūpiṇi

Oh Intrinsic form of the Universal Family, infuse the thrill of joy into the essence of this excellent wine, so that it produces full and unbroken bliss.

अनङ्गस्थामृताकारे शुद्धज्ञानकलेवरे ।
अमृतत्वं निधेह्यस्मिन् वस्तुनि क्लिन्नरूपिणि ॥

anaṅgasthāmṛtākāre śuddhajñānakalevare
amṛtatvaṁ nidhehyasmin vastuni klinnarūpiṇi

You are the nectar which is infinite and the embodiment of Pure Knowledge. Fill this liquid with the nectar of the Bliss of Infinite Consciousness.

तद्रूपेणैकरस्यञ्च कृत्वाऽर्घ्यं तत्स्वरूपिणि ।
भूत्वा कुलामृताकारं मयि विस्फुरणं कुरु ॥

tadrūpeṇaikarasyañca kṛtvā-rghyaṁ tatsvarūpiṇi
bhūtvā kulāmṛtākāraṁ mayi visphuraṇaṁ kuru

You alone are the form of That, the Infinite Unifying Principle. Make this respectful offering of the intrinsic nature of That, and having become this divine nectar, blossom in me.

ब्रह्माण्डरससम्भूतमशेषरससम्भवम् ।
आपूरितं महापात्रं पीयूषरसमावह ॥

brahmāṇḍarasasambhūtamaśeṣerasasambhavam
āpūritaṁ mahāpātraṁ pīyūṣarasamāvaha

Fill this sacred vessel of wine with the nectar of immortal wisdom produced from the essence of all that is in the world, and containing all kinds of taste.

अहन्तापात्रभरितमिदन्तापरमामृतम् ।
परहन्तामये वह्नौ होमस्वीकारलक्षणम् ॥

ahantāpātrabharitamidantāparamāmṛtam
parāhantāmaye vahnau homasvīkāralakṣaṇam

Lord, may this cup of Self, which is filled with the nectar of the Self, be sacrificed in the fire of the Supreme Self.

Wave lights and incense over the container of wine :

ह्रीं त्र्यम्बकं यजामहे सुगन्धिं पुष्टिवर्द्धनम् ।
उर्व्वारुकमिव बन्धनान्मृत्योर्म्मुक्षीयमामृतात् ॥

hrīṁ tryambakaṁ yajāmahe sugandhiṁ puṣṭivarddhanam
urvvārukamiva bandhanānmṛtyormmukṣīyamāmṛtāt

We adore the Father of the three worlds, of excellent fame, Grantor of Increase. As a cucumber is released from its bondage to the stem, so may I be freed from Death to dwell in immortality.

Draw a square

Tarpana

ह स क्ष म ल व र युं आनन्दभैरवाय वषट्
आनन्दभैरवं तर्पयामि नमः स्वाहा

ha sa kṣa ma la va ra yuṁ ānandabhairavāya vaṣaṭ
ānandabhairavaṁ tarpayāmi namaḥ svāhā

I offer to Ānandabhairava, the Bliss of Fearlessness, Purity! I bow. I am one with God (male)!

स ह क्ष म ल व र यीं आनन्दभैरव्यै वौषट्
आनन्दभैरवीं तर्पयामि नमः स्वाहा

sa ha kṣa ma la va ra yuṁ ānandabhairavyai vauṣaṭ
ānandabhairavīṁ tarpayāmi namaḥ svāhā

I offer to Ānandabhairavī the Bliss of Fearlessness, Purity! I bow. I am one with God (female)!

ॐ ऐं श्री गुरुं तर्पयामि नमः स्वाहा

oṁ aiṁ śrī guruṁ tarpayāmi namaḥ svāhā

Oṁ I bow to my guru with the offering of respect. I am One with God!

ॐ ऐं श्री परमगुरुं तर्पयामि नमः स्वाहा

oṁ aiṁ śrī paramaguruṁ tarpayāmi namaḥ svāhā

Oṁ I bow to my guru's guru with the offering of respect.
I am One with God!

ॐ ऐं श्री परापरगुरुं तर्पयामि नमः स्वाहा

oṁ aiṁ śrī parāparaguruṁ tarpayāmi namaḥ svāhā

Oṁ I bow to the Gurus of the lineage with the offering of respect. I am One with God!

ॐ ऐं श्री परमेष्ठिगुरुं तर्पयामि नमः स्वाहा

oṁ aiṁ śrī parameṣṭiguruṁ tarpayāmi namaḥ svāhā

Oṁ I bow to the Supreme gurus with the offering of respect. I am One with God!

three times

ॐ ह्रीं श्रीं क्रीं परमेश्वरि स्वाहा

आद्यां कालीं तर्पयामि नमः स्वाहा

oṁ hrīṁ śrīṁ krīṁ parameśvari svāhā
ādyāṁ kālīṁ tarpayāmi namaḥ svāhā

Oṁ Māyā, Increase, Dissolution, to the highest female divinity, I offer and bow to the Foremost Kālī, I am One with God!

ॐ अङ्गदेवतास्तर्पयामि नमः स्वाहा

oṁ aṅgadevatāstarpayāmi namaḥ svāhā

I offer and bow to the Gods of the body, I am One with God!

ॐ आवरणदेवतास्तर्पयामि नमः स्वाहा

oṁ āvaraṇadevatāstarpayāmi namaḥ svāhā

I offer and bow to the most worshipful Gods who have been invited as attendants to the Goddess, I am One with God!

ॐ ह्रीं श्रीं क्रीं परमेश्वरि कालिके स्वाहा सायुधां सपरिकरामाद्यां कालीं तर्पयामि नमः स्वाहा

oṁ hrīṁ śrīṁ krīṁ parameśvari kālike svāhā sāyudhāṁ saparikarāmādyāṁ kālīṁ tarpayāmi namaḥ svāhā

Oṁ Māyā, Increase, Dissolution, to the highest female divinity, I am One with God! I offer and bow to the Foremost Kālī accompanied by devoted attendants, I am One with God!

ॐ बटुकेभ्यो तर्पयामि नमः स्वाहा

oṁ baṭukebhyo tarpayāmi namaḥ svāhā

Oṁ I bow to the young people. I am One with God!

ॐ ऐं ह्रीं श्रीं वं बटुकाय तर्पयामि नमः स्वाहा

oṁ aiṁ hrīṁ śrīṁ baṁ baṭukāya tarpayāmi namaḥ svāhā

Oṁ Creation, Māyā, Increase, I bow to the young people.
I am One with God! (east)

ॐ यां योगिनीभ्यो तर्पयामि नमः स्वाहा

oṁ yāṁ yoginībhyo tarpayāmi namaḥ svāhā

Oṁ I bow to the energies of the Goddess which assist in union.
I am One with God! (south)

ॐ क्षां क्षीं क्षूं क्षैं क्षौं क्षः क्षेत्रपालाय तर्पयामि नमः स्वाहा

oṁ kṣāṁ kṣīṁ kṣūṁ kṣaiṁ kṣauṁ kṣaḥ kṣetrapālāya tarpayāmi namaḥ svāhā

Oṁ I bow to the Protectors of the field of existence.
I am One with God! (west)

ॐ गां गीं गूं गैं गौं गः गणपतये तर्पयामि नमः स्वाहा

oṁ gāṁ gīṁ gūṁ gaiṁ gauṁ gaḥ gaṇapataye tarpayāmi namaḥ svāhā

Oṁ I bow to the Lord of Wisdom. I am One with God! (north)

ॐ ह्रीं श्रीं सर्वविघ्नकृद्भ्यः सर्वभूतेभ्यो
हूं फट् तर्पयामि नमः स्वाहा

oṁ hrīṁ śrīṁ sarvavighnakṛdbhyaḥ sarvabhūtebhyo hūṁ phaṭ tarpayāmi namaḥ svāhā

Oṁ Māyā, Increase, I bow to the Beings who cause the removal of all difficulties or obstructions. I am One with God!

ॐ गृहाण देवि महाभागे शिवे कालाग्निरूपिणि ।
शुभाशुभं फलं व्यक्तं ब्रूहि गृहाण बलिं तव ॥

oṁ gṛhāṇa devi mahābhāge śive kālāgnirūpiṇi śubhāśubhaṁ phalaṁ vyaktaṁ brūhi gṛhāṇa baliṁ tava

Oṁ Oh Goddess, one of Great Parts, Śivā, Oh Energy of Infinite Goodness, the intrinsic form of the final conflagration of total dissolution; please accept this sacrificial offering, and reveal to me the good and evil fruit of action.

The Kula worshiper should sanctify the wine by repeating over it the Pāshāḍī-trika-bīja one hundred and eight times. (Mahānirvāṇa Tantra, Arthur Avalon, 8:170)

आँ ह्रीं क्रौं स्वाहा

āṁ hrīṁ kroṁ svāhā

Creation, Māyā, Dissolution, I am One with God!

Take the cup to your heart and meditate upon the presence of the deity. Then put it back upon the square and ring the bell.

If one has the desire to eat meat, it should be offered with the highest respect and appreciation, and shared with the community as a rite of worship. The offering conveys all impurities and sense of separation which are actually the offerngs to be sacrificed in worship. The entire ceremony from the slaying of the animal, to the preparation, offering and partaking, should be designed to encourage the surrender of the animalistic nature of each the participants. It is very common to substitute a squash or pumpkin for an animal, and much more respectful than the purchase of packaged meats from a grocery store.

ॐ ह्रीं श्रीं क्रीं परमेश्वरि स्वाहा एष बलिः ॐ शिवायै नमः

oṁ hrīṁ śrīṁ krīṁ pārāmeśvari svāhā
eṣa baliḥ oṁ śivāyai namaḥ

Oṁ Māyā, Increase, Dissolution, to the highest female divinity, I am One with God! I offer and bow to the Energy of Infinite Goodness with this offering.

परमं वारुणीकल्पं कोटिकल्पान्तकारिणि ।
गृहाण शुद्धिसहितं देहि मे मोक्षमव्ययम् ॥

paramaṁ vāruṇīkalpaṁ koṭikalpāntakāriṇi
gṛhāṇa śuddhisahitaṁ dehi me mokṣamavyayam

You are the cause of the end of ten million ages of time. Please accept this excellent offering and grant to me eternal liberation.

Sprinkle water over the offering.
Dhenumudrā. Worship the offering.

नमः

namaḥ
I bow.

ॐ पशुपाशाय विद्महे विश्वकर्मणे धीमही ।
तन्नो जीवः प्रचोदयात् ॥

oṁ paśupāśāya vidmahe viśvakarmaṇe dhīmahī
tanno jīvaḥ pracodayāt
Oṁ We meditate upon the bondage of the life of a beast, contemplate the Doer of all Action. May that Life-Force grant us increase.

Worship the sacrificial knife:

हूं

hūṁ
Cut the ego!

वागीश्वरीब्रह्माभ्यां नमः

vāgīśvarībrahmābhyāṁ namaḥ
I bow to the female Lord of all vibrations with her husband, the Creative Capacity. (end)

लक्ष्मीनारायणाभ्यां नमः

lakṣmīnārāyaṇābhyāṁ namaḥ
I bow to Lakṣmī and Nārāyaṇa. (middle)

उमामहेश्वराभ्यां नमः

umāmaheśvarābhyāṁ namaḥ
I bow to Umā and Maheśvara. (handle)

ब्रह्मविष्णुशिवशक्तियुक्ताय खड्गाय नमः

brahma viṣṇu śivā śākti yuktāya khaḍgāya namaḥ

I bow to Brahma, Viṣṇu, Śiva along with their Śaktis situated in this sword.

Hold the victim into the air. Take Saṅkalpa:

...pashum imam sampradade.

Return the sacrificial victim to the ground.

Meditation. Then sever the sacrificial victim with one stroke of the knife.

With क्रीं **krīṁ** place a candle on the severed head, and offer it to the Goddess.

सप्रदीपशीर्षबलिः श्रीमदाद्याकालिकायै देव्यै नमः

sapradīpaśīrṣabaliḥ śrīmadādyākālikāyai devyai namaḥ

I bow to the Goddess with this offering of a head with a light upon it.

While repeating the mūla mantra **oṁ hrīṁ śrīṁ krīṁ parameśvari kālike svāhā** sprinkle the water of the special offering three times over the Deity, and then make nyāsa of the Devī to the six parts of Her body. This ceremony is called Sakalīkaraṇa or Sakalīkṛti. Then worship again with all the sixteen offerings. These are water for washing the feet, the water for the offering, water for rinsing the mouth and for Her bath, garments, jewels, perfume, flowers, incense sticks, lights, food, water for washing the mouth, nectar (or alcoholic beverage) pāna (or mouth freshner), and obeisance. In worship these sixteen offerings are needed. (Mahānirvāṇa Tantra, Arthur Avalon, 6:77-79)

The Śrīpātra should be placed in the company of own's own virtuous śakti. She should be sprinkled in the form of a bath with the purified wine or water from the common offering. The Mantra for the sprinkling of the śakti is:

ऐं क्लीं सौः त्रिपुरायै नमः इमां शक्तिं पवित्रीकुरु ।
मम शक्तिं कुरु स्वाहा ॥

aiṁ klīṁ sauḥ tripurāyai namaḥ imāṁ śaktiṁ pavitrīkuru mama śaktiṁ kuru svāhā

Creation, preservation, all existence, I bow to Tripurā, to She who resides in the three cities. Purify this śakti, make her my śakti. I am One with God!

If she who is to be śakti is not already initiated, then the Māyā Bīja should be whispered into her ear, and other śaktis who are present should be worshiped and not enjoyed.

Let the assembled worshipers then joyously take up each his own cup filled with excellent nectar. Then let him take up each his own cup and meditate upon the Kula-Kuṇḍalinī, who is Consciousness, and who is spread from the Mūlādhāra lotus to the tip of the tongue, and, uttering the Mūlamantra, let each, after taking the others' permission, offer it as an oblation to the mouth of the Kuṇḍalī. When the śakti is of the household, the smelling of the wine is the equivalent of drinking it. Worshipers who are householders may drink (a maximum of) five cups only. Excessive drinking prevents the attainment of success by Kula worshipers. They may drink until the sight or the mind is not affected. To drink beyond that is beastly. How is it possible for a sinner who becomes a fool through drink and who shows contempt for the sādhaka of śakti to say, I worship Ādyā Kālikā, the Supreme Female Divinity? (Mahānirvāṇa Tantra, Arthur Avalon, 6:18-19)

Gharbhā Dhāna Viddhi

The System of Making Spiritual Children

Sūryārghyam

Offering to the Sun

ॐ विश्वा विश्वप्सा विश्वतः कर्त्ता विश्वयोनिजः ।

नवपुष्पोत्सवे चार्घ्यं गृहाण त्वं दिवाकर ॥ १

oṁ viśvā viśvapsā viśvataḥ karttā viśvayonijaḥ
navapuṣpotsave cārghyaṁ gṛhāṇa tvaṁ divākara

Oṁ You are the universe, the nourisher of the universe, the creator of the universe, and the womb of the universe as well. Oh Radiator of Light, you please accept this offering comprised of all nine flowers. 1

ॐ सम्पदाकृतिराकाशे क्षोभरूपी जगत्प्रभो ।

साक्षी त्वं सर्वभूतानां गृहाणार्घ्यं दिवाकर ॥ २

oṁ sampadākṛtirākāśe kṣobharūpī jagatprabho
sākṣī tvaṁ sarvabhūtānāṁ gṛhāṇārghyaṁ divākara

Oṁ You are the unattainable wealth which resides in the atmosphere, of the most beautiful form, Lord of the Worlds. You are the Witness of all the elements, Oh Radiator of Light, you please accept this offering. 2

ॐ मया च यत् कृतं कर्म साम्प्रतं फलहेतवे ।

तिमिरघ्न महातेजो गृहाणार्घ्यं दिवाकर ॥ ३

oṁ mayā ca yat kṛtaṁ karma sāmpratаṁ phalahetave
timiraghna mahātejo gṛhāṇārghyaṁ divākara

Oṁ You grant the fruit to be obtained from all of the actions which I have performed. You who Take Away the Darkness, Oh Great Light, Oh Radiator of Light, you please accept this offering. 3

ॐ नवपुष्पोत्सवे चार्घ्यं ददामि भक्तितत्परः ।
सम्पदां हेतुः कर्त्ता च गृहाणार्घ्यं दिवाकर ॥ ४

oṁ navapuṣpotsave cārghyaṁ dadāmi bhaktitatparaḥ
sampadāṁ hetuḥ karttā ca gṛhāṇārghyaṁ divākara

Oṁ This offering comprised of all nine flowers I am giving with the highest devotion. And you are the Maker of all wealth, please accept this offering, Oh Radiator of Light. 4

ॐ नमस्ते भगवन् सूर्य लोकसाक्षिन् विभावसो ।
पुत्रार्थी च प्रपन्नोऽहं गृहाणार्घ्यं दिवाकर ॥ ५

oṁ namaste bhagavan sūrya lokasākṣin vibhāvaso
putrārthī ca prapanno-haṁ gṛhāṇārghyaṁ divākara

Oṁ I bow in devotion to the Lord Sun-God, Light of Wisdom, the Seer of all the worlds (and inhabitants), the attitude of all beings. For the purpose of having a child I am extolling you. Please accept this offering, Oh Radiator of Light. 5

ॐ कमलकान्त देवेश साक्षी त्वञ्च जगत्पते ।
भक्तस्तव प्रपन्नोऽहं गृहाणार्घ्यं दिवाकर ॥ ६

oṁ kamalakānta deveśa sākṣī tvañcā jagatpate
bhaktastava prapanno-haṁ gṛhāṇārghyaṁ divākara

Oṁ With your lotus throat, Lord of all Gods, you are the Witness of All, and the Lord of the World. With this song of devotion I am extolling you, please accept this offering, Oh Radiator of Light. 6

ॐ स्वर्गदीप नमस्तेऽस्तु नमस्ते विश्वतापन ।
नवपुष्पोत्सवे चार्घ्यं गृहाणार्घ्यं दिवाकर ॥ ७

oṁ svargadīpa namaste-stu namaste viśvatāpana
navapuṣpotsave cārghyaṁ gṛhāṇārghyaṁ divākara

Oṁ Oh Light of Heaven, I bow in devotion to you. I bow in devotion to the heat of the universe. Oh Radiator of Light, you please accept this offering comprised of all nine flowers. 7

ॐ नमस्ते पद्मिनीकान्त सुखमोक्षप्रदायक ।
छायापते जगत्स्वामिन् स्वर्गदीप नमोऽस्तु ते ॥ ८

oṁ namaste padminīkānta sukhamokṣapradāyaka
chāyāpate jagat svāmin svargadīpa namo-stu te

Oṁ Oh lotus throat, I bow in devotion to you. You are the Grantor of pleasure and liberation. Lord of the shadow, Master of the Worlds, Oh Light of Heaven, I bow in devotion to you. 8

ॐ विश्वात्मा विश्वबन्धुश्च विश्वेशो विश्वलोचनः ।
नवपुष्पोत्सवे चार्घ्यं गृहाण त्वं दिवाकर ॥ ९

oṁ viśvātmā viśvabandhuśca viśveśo viśvalocanaḥ
navapuṣpotsave cārghyaṁ gṛhāṇa tvaṁ divākara

Oṁ Soul of the Universe, Friend of the Universe, Lord of the Universe, Eye of the Universe. Oh Radiator of Light, you please accept this offering comprised of all nine flowers. 9

ॐ जवाकुसुमसङ्काशं काश्यपेयं महाद्युतिम् ।
तमोऽरिं सर्वपापघ्नं प्रणतोऽस्मि दिवाकर ॥

oṁ javākusumasaṅkāśaṁ kāśyapeyaṁ mahādyutim
tamo-riṁ sarvapāpaghnaṁ praṇato-smi divākara

Oṁ With the redness of the Hibiscus flower, Oh son of Kāśyapa, of Great Splendor, Remover of the Darkness of all sin, I bow in devotion to you, Oh Radiator of Light.

give arghya:

ॐ नमो विवस्वते ब्रह्मन् भास्वते विष्णुतेजसे ।

जगत्सवित्रे सूचये सवित्रे कर्मदायिने ॥

इदमर्घ्यं ॐ श्रीसूर्यदेवाय नमः

oṁ namo vivasvate brahman bhāsvate viṣṇutejase
jagatsavitre sūcaye savitre karmadāyine
idamarghyaṁ oṁ śrīsūryadevāya namaḥ

Oṁ I bow in devotion to He whose own self is the Universe, Infinite Consciousness, Whose own self Shines, the Light of Universal Consciousness, to the Light of the worlds, to the One who indicates (or shows), to the Bearer of Light who gives all karma.

ॐ ह्रीं प्रजापतये स्वाहा

oṁ hrīṁ prajāpataye svāhā

Oṁ Māyā to the Lord of all created beings, I am One with God!

ॐ विष्णुर्योनिं कल्पयतु त्वष्टा रूपाणि पिंशतु ।

आंसिञ्चतु प्रजापतिर्धाता गर्भं दधातु ते ॥

oṁ viṣṇuryoniṁ kalpayatu tvaṣṭā rūpāṇi piṁśatu
āṁsiñcatu prajāpatirdhātā garbhaṁ dadhātu te

May Viṣṇu grant the power to concieve, may Tvaṣṭā give the form. May Prajāpati sprinkle it with blessings, and may Dhātā support the womb.

ॐ गर्भं धेहि सिनीवाली गर्भं धेहि सरस्वती ।

गर्भं ते अश्विनौ देवावाधत्तां पुष्करस्रजौ ॥

oṁ garbhaṁ dhehi sinīvālī garbhaṁ dhehi sarasvatī
garbhaṁ te aśvinau devāvādhattāṁ puṣkarasrajau

May Sinivālī support the womb, may Sarasvatī support the womb. May the Aśvins who wear garlands of lotuses support the womb.

Offer flowers:

ॐ क्लीं स्त्रीं ह्रीं श्रीं हूं "To the woman's name in the dative case" पुत्रकामायै गर्भमाधेहि स्वाहा

oṁ klīṁ strīṁ hrīṁ śrīṁ hūṁ "To the Woman's name in the dative case" **putrakāmāyai garbhamādhehi svāhā**

Oṁ Klīṁ Strīṁ Hrīṁ Śrīṁ Hūṁ grant conception "To the Woman's name in the dative case" who desires a child Svāhā, I am One with God!

ॐ विष्णो ज्येष्ठेन रूपेण नार्यामस्यां वरीयसम् सुतमाधेहि स्वाहा ॥

oṁ viṣṇo jyeṣṭhena rūpeṇa nāryāmasyāṁ varīyasam sutamādhehi svāhā

Viṣṇu! In thy excellent form give to this woman an excellent child.
I am One with God!

This ends the Ṛtu Saṅskāra which should be performed daily by both husband and wife together from the time of taking the saṅkalpa until conception.

On the night of union before physical intercourse, first the wife should perform pūjā to her husband as Lord Śiva, according to the complete system of worship. Then the husband should worship his wife as the Divine Mother.

After the husband and wife have completed the worship and honor of the divine through their spouse, the worship of communion proceeds:

touch bed with tattvamudrā:

ॐ ह्रीं आवयोः सुप्रजायै त्वं शय्ये शुभकरी भव ।

oṁ hrīṁ āvayoḥ suprajāyai tvaṁ śayye śubhakarī bhava

Hrīṁ Oh Bed, be propitious so that together we may conceive children.

touch wife's navel with a gold ring:

ॐ जीववत्सा भव त्वं हि सुपुत्रोत्पत्तिहेतवे ।
तस्मात् त्वं भव कल्याणि अविघ्नगर्भधारिणी ॥

oṁ jīvavatsā bhava tvaṁ hi suputrotpattihetave
tasmāt tvaṁ bhava kalyāṇi avighna garbhadhāriṇī

Oṁ Child of Life, let you be. Let an excellent child be born. Thus let you bring welfare and freedom from obstructions to She who supports (or bears) the womb.

Place the ring on her finger, right hand if
a boy is desired, left hand for a girl.

ॐ दीर्घायुषं वंशधरं पुत्रं जनय सुव्रते ॥

oṁ dīrghāyuṣaṁ vaṁśadharaṁ putraṁ janaya suvrate

Oṁ Oh One of Excellent Vows, long life to you, bearer of progeny, giving birth to a child!

ॐ आरुह्य भार्यया शय्यां प्राङ्मुखो वाप्युदङ्मुखः ।
उपविश्य स्त्रियं पश्यन् हस्तमाधाय मस्तके ।
वामेन पाणिनाऽऽलिङ्ग्य स्थाने स्थाने मनुं जपेत् ॥

oṁ āruhya bhāryayā śayyāṁ prāṅmukho vāpyudaṅmukhaḥ
upaviśya striyaṁ paśyan hastamādhāya mastake
vāmena pāṇinā--liṅgya sthāne sthāne manuṁ japet

Then the husband and wife should get on the bed with their heads facing either East or North. Looking at his wife, with his right hand over her head and embracing her with his left arm, he should make japa on the various places of her body.

ॐ शीर्षे कामं शतं जप्त्वा चिबुके वाग्भवं शतम् ।
कण्ठे रमां विंशतिधा स्तनद्वन्द्वे शतं शतम् ॥

oṁ śīrṣe kāmaṁ śataṁ japtvā cibuke vāgbhavaṁ śatam
kaṇṭhe ramāṁ viṁśatidhā stanadvandve śataṁ śatam

On the head of her body Kāma Bīja, Klīṁ, one hundred times; On the chin Vāgbhava Bīja, Aiṁ, one hundred times; on the throat Ramā Bīja, Śrīṁ, twenty times; and the same bīja (Śrīṁ) one hundred times each on each of the two breasts.

ॐ हृदये दशधा मायां नाभौ तां पञ्चविंशतिम् ।
जप्त्वा योनौ करं दत्त्वा कामेन सह वाग्भवम् ॥

oṁ hṛdaye daśadhā māyāṁ nābhau tāṁ pañcaviṁśatim
japtvā yonau karaṁ dattvā kāmena saha vāgbhavam

On her heart ten times Māyā Bīja, Hrīṁ, and the same twenty-five times over her navel. On the genital placing the hand, Kāma Bīja together with Vāgbhava, Klīṁ with Aiṁ.

ॐ शतमष्टोत्तरं जप्त्वा लिङ्गेऽप्येवं समाचरन् ।
विकाश्य मायया योनिं स्त्रियं गच्छेत् सुताप्तये ॥

oṁ śatamaṣṭottaraṁ japtvā liṅge-pyevaṁ samācaran
vikāśya māyayā yoniṁ striyaṁ gacchet sutāptaye

One hundred eight times he should recite, and again over his own genital the same mantra the same number of times. Pronouncing the Māya Bīja, Hrīṁ, he should part the lips of his wife's genital, and enter within.

ॐ रेतःसम्पातसमये ध्यात्वा विश्वकृतं पतिः ।
नाभेरधस्तात् चित्कुण्डे रक्तिकायां प्रपातयेत् ॥

oṁ retaḥsampātasamaye dhyātvā viśvakṛtaṁ patiḥ
nābheradhastāt citkuṇḍe raktikāyāṁ prapātayet

The Lord of all Causes and Effects of the Universe should be meditated upon at the time of discharging semen through the vaginal passage into the uterus just below the navel.

ॐ शुक्रसेकान्तरे विद्वानिमं मन्त्रमुदीरयेत् ॥

oṁ śukrāsekāntāre vidvānimaṁ mantramudīrayet

As the semen enters within, the intelligent one will recite this mantra.

ॐ यथाऽग्निना सगर्भा भूर्द्यौर्यथा वज्रधारिणा ।
वायुना दिग्गर्भवती तथा गर्भवती भव ॥

oṁ yathā-gninā sagarbhā bhūrdyauryathā vajradhāriṇā
vāyunā diggarbhavatī tathā garbhavatī bhava

As the earth is pregnant with fire, as the heavens are pregnant with the Wielder of the thunder (Indra), as all the directions are pregnant with wind, so let you also become pregnant.

After discharge, both should make japa according to their respective mantras. Thereafter obeisances should be repeated to each other:

ॐ क्रीं क्रीं क्रीं हुं हुं ह्रीं ह्रीं दक्षिणे कालिके क्रीं क्रीं क्रीं हुं हुं ह्रीं ह्रीं स्वाहा ॥

oṁ krīṁ krīṁ krīṁ huṁ huṁ hrīṁ hrīṁ dakṣiṇe kālike
krīṁ krīṁ krīṁ huṁ huṁ hrīṁ hrīṁ svāhā

The Cause Which Moves the Subtle Body to the Infinite Perfection and Beyond, cut the ego! Cut the ego! Māyā! Māyā! Oh Goddess Who Removes All Darkness, the Cause Which Moves the Subtle Body to the Infinite Perfection and Beyond, cut the ego! Cut the ego! Māyā! Māyā! I am ONE with God!

ॐ कालि कालि महाकालि कालिके पापहारिणी ।
धर्मार्थमोक्षदे देवि नारायणि नमोऽस्तुते ॥

oṁ kāli kāli mahākāli kālike pāpahāriṇī
dharmārthamokṣade devi nārāyaṇi namo-stute

Oṁ Goddess Who Takes Away Darkness, Goddess Who Takes Away Darkness, Great Goddess Who Takes Away Darkness, beloved Goddess Who Takes Away Darkness, Who Takes Away All Sin. Give the way of peace and harmony, the necessities for physical sustenance, and liberation or self-realization. Oh Goddess, Exposer of Consciousness, we bow to you.

ॐ क्रीं काल्यै नमः

oṁ krīṁ kālyai namaḥ

I bow to the Goddess Who Takes Away Darkness.

सर्वमङ्गलमङ्गल्ये शिवे सर्वार्थसाधिके ।
शरण्ये त्र्यम्बके गौरि नारायणि नमोऽस्तु ते ॥

sarvamaṅgala maṅgalye śive sarvārtha sādhike
śaraṇye tryambake gauri nārāyaṇi namo-stu te

To the Auspicious of all Auspiciousness, to the Good, to the Accomplisher of all Objectives, to the Source of Refuge, to the Mother of the three worlds, to the Goddess Who is Rays of Light, Exposer of Consciousness, we bow to you.

सृष्टिस्थितिविनाशानां शक्तिभूते सनातनि ।
गुणाश्रये गुणमये नारायणि नमोऽस्तु ते ॥

sṛṣṭisthitivināśānāṁ śaktibhūte sanātani
guṇāśraye guṇamaye nārāyaṇi namo-stu te

You are the Eternal Energy of Creation, Preservation and Destruction in all existence; that upon which all qualities depend, that which limits all qualities. Exposer of Consciousness, we bow to you.

शरणागतदीनार्तपरित्राणपरायणे ।
सर्वस्यार्तिहरे देवि नारायणि नमोऽस्तु ते ॥

śaraṇāgatadīnārta paritrāṇa parāyaṇe
sarvasyārti hare devi nārāyaṇi namo-stu te

For those who are devoted to you and take refuge in you, you save from all discomfort and unhappiness. All worry you take away. Oh Goddess, Exposer of Consciousness, we bow to you.

दुर्गां शिवां शान्तिकरीं ब्रह्माणीं ब्रह्मणः प्रियाम् ।
सर्वलोकप्रणेत्रीञ्च प्रणमामि सदा शिवाम् ॥

durgāṁ śivāṁ śāntikarīṁ brahmāṇīṁ brahmaṇaḥ priyām
sarvaloka praṇetrīñca praṇamāmi sadā śivām

The Reliever of Difficulties, Exposer of Goodness, Cause of Peace, Infinite Consciousness, Beloved by Knowers of Consciousness; all the inhabitants of all the worlds always bow to Her, and I am bowing to Goodness Herself.

मङ्गलां शोभनां शुद्धां निष्कलां परमां कलाम् ।
विश्वेश्वरीं विश्वमातां चण्डिकां प्रणमाम्यहम् ॥

maṅgalāṁ śobhanāṁ śuddhāṁ niṣkalāṁ paramāṁ kalām
viśveśvarīṁ viśvamātāṁ caṇḍikāṁ praṇamāmyaham

Welfare, Radiant Beauty, Completely Pure, Without Limitations, the Ultimate Limitation, the Lord of the Universe, the Mother of the Universe, to you Caṇḍi, to the Energy which Tears Apart Thought, I bow in submission.

सर्वदेवमयीं देवीं सर्वरोगभयापहाम् ।
ब्रह्मेशविष्णुनमितां प्रणमामि सदा शिवाम् ॥

sarvadevamayīṁ devīṁ sarvarogabhayāpahām
brahmeśaviṣṇunamitāṁ praṇamāmi sadā śivām

Composed of all the Gods, removing all sickness and fear, Brahma, Maheśvara and Viṣṇu bow down to Her, and I always bow down to the Energy of Infinite Goodness.

विन्ध्यस्थां विन्ध्यनिलयां दिव्यस्थाननिवासिनीम् ।
योगिनीं योगजननीं चण्डिकां प्रणमाम्यहम् ॥

vindhyasthāṁ vindhyanilayāṁ divyasthānanivāsinīm
yoginīṁ yogajananīṁ caṇḍikāṁ praṇamāmyaham

The dwelling place of Knowledge, residing in Knowledge, Resident in the place of Divine Illumination, the Cause of Union, the Knower of Union, to the Energy Which Tears Apart Thought, we constantly bow.

ईशानमातरं देवीमीश्वरीमीश्वरप्रियाम् ।
प्रणतोऽस्मि सदा दुर्गां संसारार्णवतारिणीम् ॥

īśānamātaraṁ devīmīśvarīmīśvarapriyām
praṇato-smi sadā durgāṁ saṁsārārṇavatāriṇīm

The Mother of the Supreme Consciousness, the Goddess Who is the Supreme Consciousness, beloved by the Supreme Consciousness, we always bow to Durgā, the Reliever of Difficulties, who takes aspirants across the difficult sea of objects and their relationships.

ॐ महादेव महात्राण महायोगि महेश्वर ।
सर्वपापहरां देव मकाराय नमो नमः ॥

oṁ mahādeva mahātrāṇa mahāyogi maheśvara
sarvapāpaharāṁ deva makārāya namo namaḥ

Oṁ The Great God, the Great Reliever, the Great Yogi, Oh Supreme Lord, Oh God who removes all Sin, in the form of the letter "M" which dissolves creation, we bow to you again and again.

ॐ नमः शिवाय शान्ताय कारणत्रय हेतवे ।
निवेदयामि चात्मानं त्वं गतिः परमेश्वर ॥

oṁ namaḥ śivāya śāntāya kāraṇatraya hetave
nivedayāmi cātmānaṁ tvaṁ gatiḥ parameśvara

Oṁ I bow to the Consciousness of Infinite Goodness, to Peace, to the Cause of the three worlds, I offer to you the fullness of my soul, Oh Supreme Lord.

त्वमेव माता च पिता त्वमेव त्वमेव बन्धुश्च सखा त्वमेव ।
त्वमेव विद्या द्रविणं त्वमेव त्वमेव सर्वम् मम देवदेव ॥

tvameva mātā ca pitā tvameva
tvameva bandhuśca sakhā tvameva
tvameva vidyā draviṇaṁ tvameva
tvameva sarvam mama deva deva

You alone are Mother and Father, you alone are friend and relative. You alone are knowledge and wealth, Oh my God of Gods, you alone are everything.

कायेन वाचा मनसेन्द्रियैर्वा बुद्ध्यात्मानवप्रकृतस्वभावत् ।
करोमि यद्यत् सकलम् परस्मै नारायणायेति समर्पयामि ॥

kāyena vācā manasendriyairvā
buddhyātmā nava prakṛta svabhavat
karomi yadyat sakalam parasmai
nārāyaṇāyeti samarpayāmi

Body, speech, mind, the five organs of knowledge (five senses) and the intellect; these nine are the natural condition of human existence. In their highest evolution, I move beyond them all, as I surrender completely to the Supreme Consciousness.

ॐ पापोऽहं पापकर्माहं पापात्मा पापसम्भव ।
त्राहि मां पुण्डरीकाक्षं सर्वपापहरो हरिः ॥

oṁ pāpo-haṁ pāpakarmāhaṁ pāpātmā pāpasambhava
trāhi māṁ puṇḍarīkākṣaṁ sarvapāpa haro hariḥ

Oṁ I am of sin, confusion, duality; my actions are of duality; this entire existence is of duality. Oh Savior and Protector, Oh Great Consciousness, take away all sin, confusion, duality.

ॐ मन्त्रहीनं क्रियाहीनं भक्तिहीनं सुरेश्वरि ।
यत्पूजितं मया देवि परिपूर्णं तदस्तु मे ॥

oṁ mantrahīnaṁ kriyāhīnaṁ bhaktihīnaṁ sureśvari
yatpūjitaṁ mayā devi paripūrṇaṁ tadastu me

Oṁ I know nothing of mantras. I do not perform good conduct. I have no devotion, Oh Supreme Goddess. But Oh my Goddess, please accept the worship that I offer.

त्वमेव प्रत्यक्षम् ब्रह्माऽसि । त्वामेव प्रत्यक्षम् ब्रह्म वदिष्यामि ।
ऋतम् वदिष्यामि, सत्यम् वदिष्यामि । तन मामवतु, तद
वक्तारमवतु । अवतु माम्, अवतु वक्तारम् ॥

tvameva pratyakṣam brahmā-si
tvāmeva pratyakṣam brahma vadiṣyāmi
ṛtam vadiṣyāmi, satyam vadiṣyāmi
tana māmavatu, tada vaktāramavatu
avatu mām, avatu vaktāram

You alone are the Perceivable Supreme Divinity. You alone are the Perceivable Supreme Divinity, so I shall declare. I shall speak the nectar of immortality. I shall speak Truth. May this body be your instrument. May this mouth be your instrument. May the Divine always be with us. May it be thus.

ॐ सह नाववतु सह नौ भुनक्तु । सह वीर्यं करवावहै ।
तेजस्विनावधीतमस्तु । मा विद्विषावहै ॥

oṁ saha nāvavatu, saha nau bhunaktu
saha vīryam karavāvahai tejasvināvadhītamastu
mā vidviṣāvahai

Oṁ May the Lord protect us. May the Lord grant us enjoyment of all actions. May we be granted strength to work together. May our studies be thorough and faithful. May all disagreement cease.

ॐ असतो मा सद् गमय । तमसो मा ज्योतिर्गमय ।
मृत्योर्मा अमृतं गमय ॥

oṁ asatomā sad gamaya tamasomā jyotirgamaya
mṛtyormā amṛtaṁ gamaya

Oṁ From untruth lead us to Truth. From darkness lead us to the Light. From death lead us to Immortality.

ॐ सर्वेषां स्वस्तिर्भवतु । सर्वेषां शान्तिर्भवतु । सर्वेषां पूर्णं भवतु । सर्वेषां मङ्गलं भवतु सर्वे भवन्तु सुखिनः । सर्वे सन्तु निरामयाः । सर्वे भद्राणि पश्यन्तु । मा कश्चिद् दुःख भाग्भवेत् ॥

oṁ sarveṣāṁ svastir bhavatu sarveṣāṁ śāntir bhavatu
sarveṣāṁ pūrṇaṁ bhavatu sarveṣaṁ maṅgalaṁ bhavatu
sarve bhavantu sukhinaḥ sarve santu nirāmayāḥ sarve
bhadrāṇi paśyantu mā kaścid duḥkha bhāgbhavet

Oṁ May all be blessed with the highest realization. May all be blessed with Peace. May all be blessed with Perfection. May all be blessed with Welfare. May all be blessed with comfort and happiness. May all be free from misery. May all perceive auspiciousness. May all be free from infirmities.

गुरुर्ब्रह्मा गुरुर्विष्णुः गुरुर्देवो महेश्वरः ।
गुरुः साक्षात् परं ब्रह्म तस्मै श्रीगुरवे नमः ॥

gurur brahmā gururviṣṇuḥ gururdevo maheśvaraḥ
guruḥ sākṣāt paraṁ brahma tasmai śrīgurave namaḥ

The Guru is Brahmā, Guru is Viṣṇu, Guru is the Lord Maheśvara. The Guru is actually the Supreme Divinity, and therefore we bow down to the Guru.

ॐ ब्रह्मार्पणं ब्रह्म हविर्ब्रह्माग्नौ ब्रह्मणा हुतम् ।
ब्रह्मैव तेन गन्तव्यं ब्रह्मकर्मसमाधिना ॥

oṁ brahmārpaṇaṁ brahma havirbrahmāgnau brahmaṇā hutam
brahmaiva tena gantavyaṁ brahmakarma samādhinā

Oṁ The Supreme Divinity makes the offering; the Supreme Divinity is the offering; offered by the Supreme Divinity, in the fire of the Supreme Divinity. By seeing the Supreme Divinity in all actions, one realizes that Supreme Divinity.

ॐ पूर्णमदः पूर्णमिदं पूर्णात् पूर्णमुदच्यते ।
पूर्णस्य पूर्णमादाय पूर्णमेवावशिष्यते ॥

oṁ pūrṇamadaḥ pūrṇamidaṁ pūrṇāt pūrṇamudacyate
pūrṇasya pūrṇamādāya pūrṇamevāva śiṣyate

Oṁ That is whole and perfect; this is whole and perfect. From the whole and perfect, the whole and perfect becomes manifest. If the whole and perfect issue forth from the whole and perfect, even still only the whole and perfect will remain.

ॐ शान्तिः शान्तिः शान्तिः

oṁ śāntiḥ śāntiḥ śāntiḥ

Oṁ Peace, Peace, Peace

aśīrbād - blessings

ॐ श्रीर्वर्चस्वमायुष्यमारोग्यमाविधात् पवमानं महीयते ।
धान्यं धनं पशुं बहुपुत्रलाभंशतसंवत्सरं दीर्घमायुः ॥

oṁ śrīrvarcasvamāyuṣyamārogyamāvidhāt
pavamānaṁ mahīyate
dhānyaṁ dhanaṁ paśuṁ
bahuputralābhaṁśatasaṁvatsaraṁ dīrghamāyuḥ

You are blessed with the Highest Respect, with Wealth, with Life, with Freedom from disease and freedom to be One with the Greatness; with food, with wealth, with animals and with many children, and with a long life of one hundred years.

मन्त्रार्थाः सफलाः सन्तु पूर्णाः सन्तु मनोरथाः ।
शत्रूणां बुद्धिनाशोऽस्तु मित्राणामुदयस्तव ॥

mantrārthāḥ saphalāḥ santu pūrṇāḥ santu manorathāḥ
śatrūṇāṁ buddhināśo-stu mitrāṇāmudayastava

May the meanings of the mantras bring excellent fruit, and may the journey of your mind be full and complete. May all enmity be removed from your intellect, and may friendship continuously rise.

आयुष्कामो यशस्कामो पुत्र-पौत्रस्तथैव च ।
आरोग्यं धनकामश्च सर्वे कामा भवन्तु मे ॥

āyuṣkāmo yaśaskāmo putra-pautrastathaiva ca
ārogyaṁ dhanakāmaśca sarve kāmā bhavantu me

May you enjoy life, may you enjoy fame, children and grandchildren throughout the generations; may you all live without disease, with abundance of wealth, and may all your desires be fulfilled.

visārjaṇ

removing the divine energy

ॐ इतः पूर्व प्राणबुद्धिदेह धर्माधिकारतो ।

जाग्रत् स्वप्नशुषुप्तयवस्थाशु मनसा ॥

oṁ itaḥ pūrva prāṇabuddhideha dharmādhikārato
jāgrat svapnaśuṣuptayavasthāśu manasā

Oṁ Thus the full and complete intelligence of the Life Force, the Cause of Dharma, the Way of Truth to Perfection, has been given. Waking Consciousness, dreaming (or thinking) Consciousness, and Consciousness in dreamless sleep (intuitive Consciousness) in which all thoughts are situated.

वाचा कर्मणा हस्ताभ्यां पध्भ्यामूद्रेण शिश्ना

यत् कृतं तद्युक्तं यत् स्मृतं तत् सर्वं ब्रह्मार्पणं भवतु स्वाहा

vācā karmaṇā hastābhyāṁ padhbhyāmūdareṇa śiśnā
yat kṛtaṁ tadyuktaṁ yat smṛtaṁ tat sarvaṁ brahmārpaṇaṁ bhavatu svāhā

All speech has been offered with folded hands raised in respect while bowing to the lotus feet. That activity, that union, that memory, all of that has been offered to the Supreme Divinity. I am One with God!

मां मदीयञ्च सकलं श्री चण्डिका चरणे समर्पये ।

ॐ तत् सत् ॥

māṁ madīyañca sakalaṁ śrī caṇḍikā caraṇe samarpaye
oṁ tat sat

All of me and all that belongs to me entirely, I surrender to the feet of the respected caṇḍikā, She Who Tears Apart Thought. The Infinite, That is Truth.

ॐ ब्रह्मार्पणं ब्रह्म हविर्ब्रह्माग्नौ ब्रह्मणा हुतम् ।
ब्रह्मैव तेन गन्तव्यं ब्रह्मकर्मसमाधिना ॥

oṁ brahmārpaṇaṁ brahma havirbrahmāgnau brahmaṇā hutam
brahmaiva tena gantavyaṁ brahmakarma samādhinā

Oṁ The Supreme Divinity makes the offering; the Supreme Divinity is the offering; offered by the Supreme Divinity, in the fire of the Supreme Divinity. By seeing the Supreme Divinity in all actions, one realizes that Supreme Divinity.

ॐ पूर्णमदः पूर्णमिदं पूर्णात् पूर्णमुदच्यते ।
पूर्णस्य पूर्णमादाय पूर्णमेवावशिष्यते ॥

oṁ pūrṇamadaḥ pūrṇamidaṁ pūrṇāt pūrṇamudacyate
pūrṇasya pūrṇamādāya pūrṇamevāva śiṣyate

Oṁ That is whole and perfect; this is whole and perfect. From the whole and perfect, the whole and perfect becomes manifest. If the whole and perfect issue forth from the whole and perfect, even still only the whole and perfect will remain.

क्षमास्य (Visārjaṇ mudrā)

kṣamāsya

Please forgive me.

ॐ शान्तिः शान्तिः शान्तिः

oṁ śāntiḥ śāntiḥ śāntiḥ

Oṁ Peace, Peace, Peace

Kālī Pūjā Mudrās

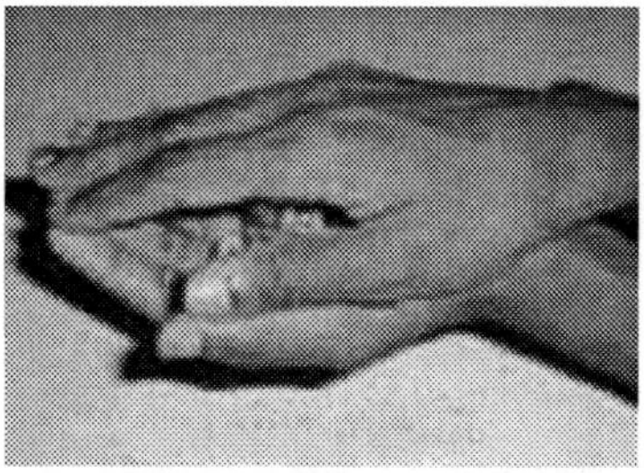

The Saṅkalpa Mudrā is used for stating the date, time and place, the performer, proposed activity and purpose, prior to the commencement of worship.

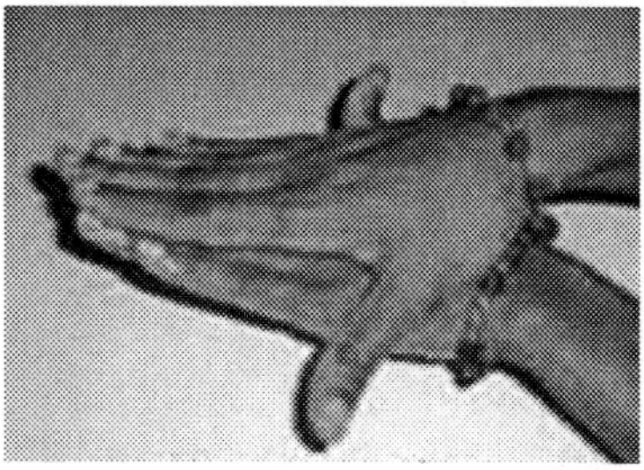

The Matsyā Mudrā is the mudrā of the fish, which symbolizes swimming across the ocean of worldliness without fear. Shree Maa tells us to be like the fish at the bottom of the pond. He is always in the mud, but never dirty.

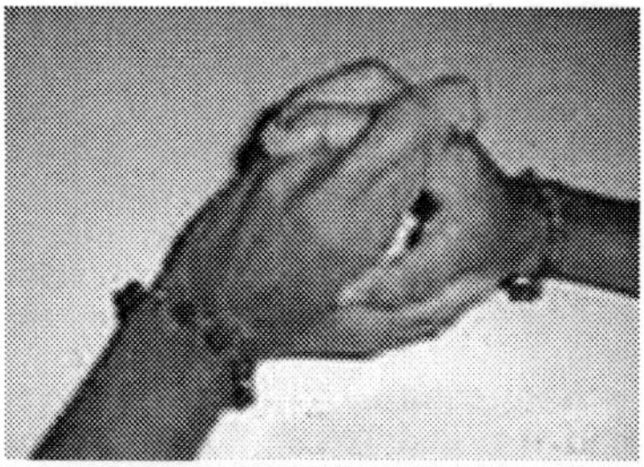

The Dhenu Mudrā is the mudrā of the cow, which indicates the one who pours forth nourishing goodness in abundance.

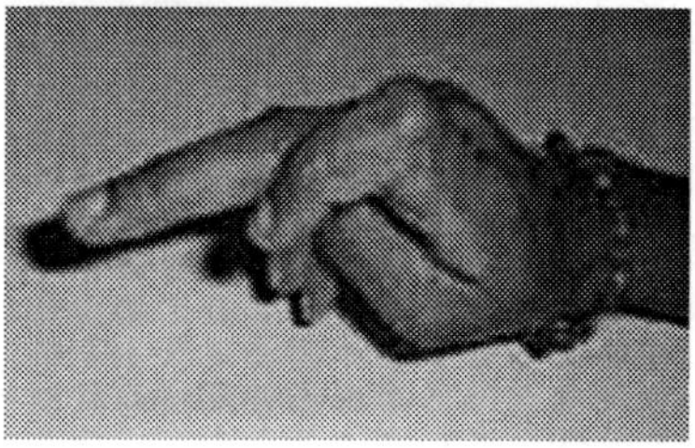

The Aṅkuśa Mudrā is the mudrā of the goad or curved sword, which symbolizes prodding seekers on towards their ultimate goal, or cutting down the iniquities of the ego.

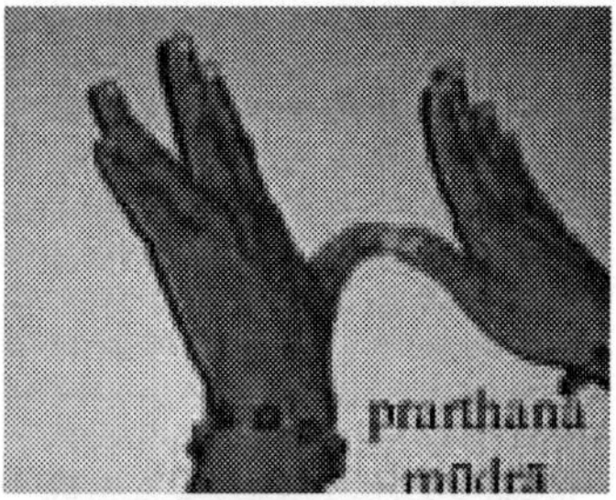

The Prārthanā Mudrā is the mudrā of prayer, and the worshiper who demonstrates this mudrā prays for purity and clarity.

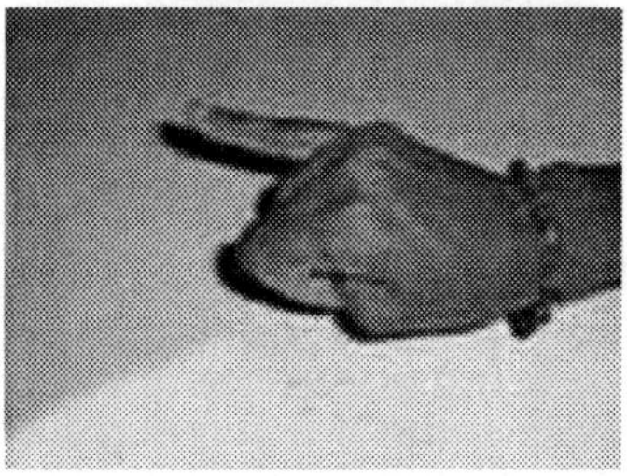

The Lelihāna Mudrā literally means "Sticking Out." It is the mudrā which indicates, "It is You and only You who is our salvation."

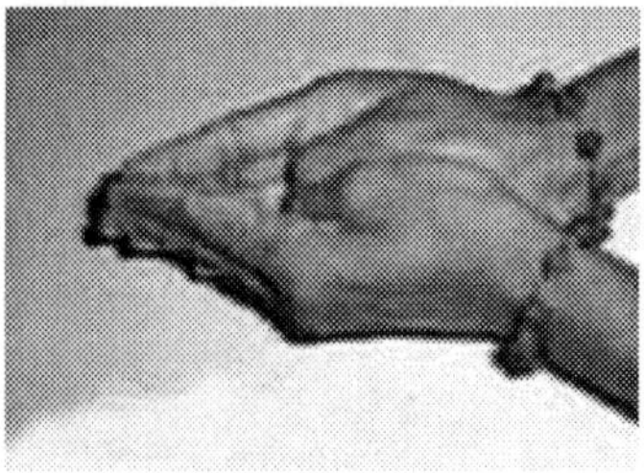

The Āvāhanī Mudrā is the mudrā of invitation. It is used to invoke the deity into the presence of the worshiper.

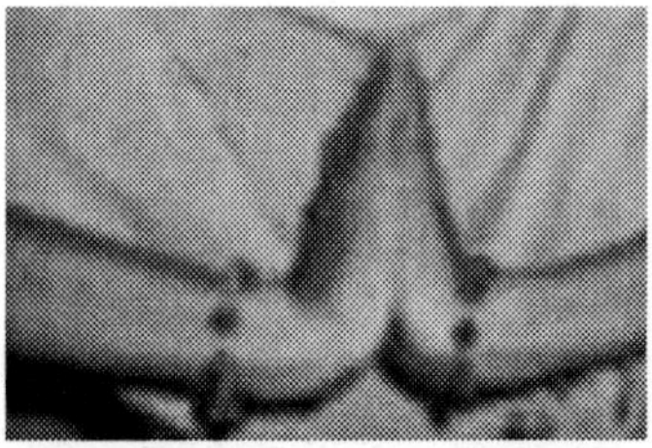

The Stāpanī Mudrā is the mudrā of establishment. The worshiper actually places the presence of the deity into his or her heart.

The Sannidhāpanī Mudrā is the mudrā which indicates apology for any inconvenience it may cause the deity to be summoned in this manner. We understand that many devotees are requesting Her presence. Even still, we request Her to pay attention to our worship, and apologize for Her inconvenience.

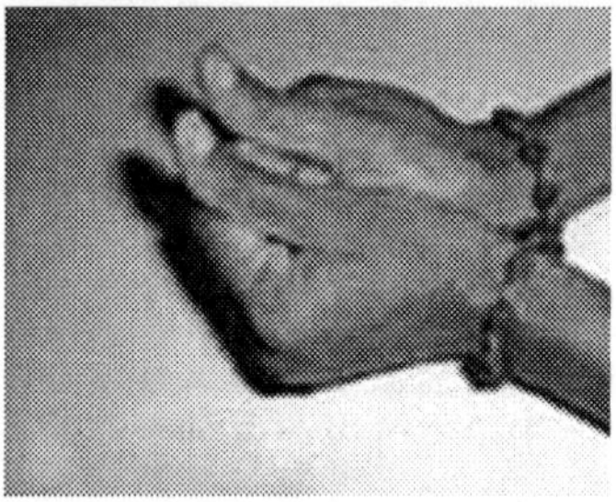

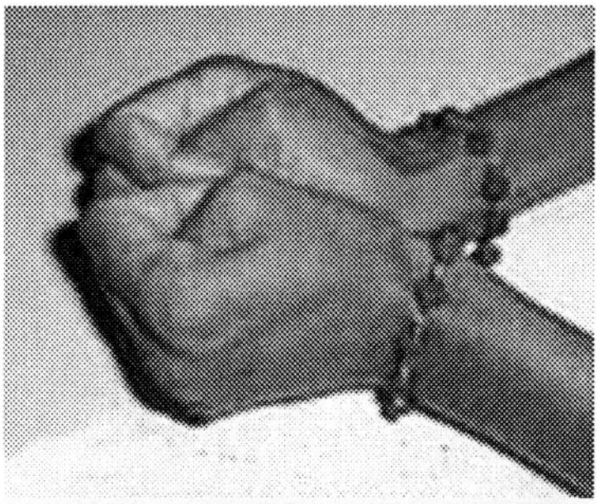

The Sambodhinī Mudrā symbolizes that "I am binding You with all my power not to leave me until this worship is completed. For so long as I pay attention to You, You must stay and receive it."

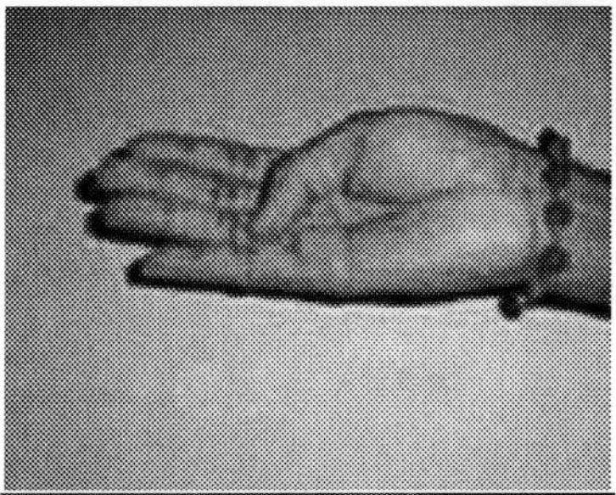

The Tattva Mudrā is the mudrā of the Principle. It refers to the establishment of divinity within, and most often indicates those places on the body which are different seats of the various energies.

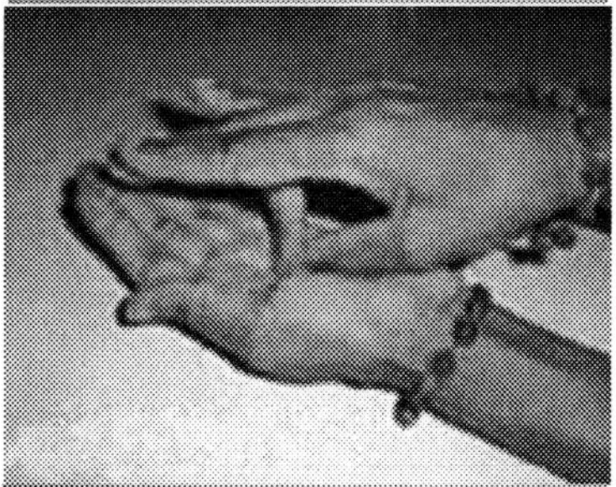

The Tarpana Mudrā is the mudrā of offering. Tarpana usually is performed in ceremonies respecting ancestors who have passed on, in respect of the Guru, the Sun, or any other deity. With the thumb and ring finger we offer a pinch of whatever offering is being made. In the Pitri Shraddha the offering is sessamee seeds in water. In the Kālī Pūjā it is wine.

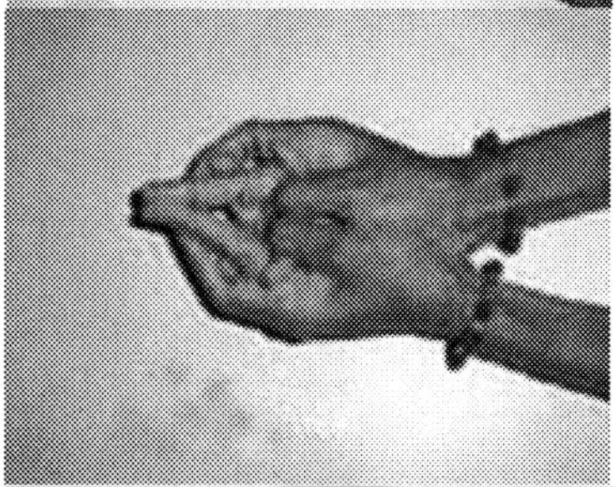

The Yoni Mudrā symbolizes the womb of creation. It shows that She is the origin of all beings, and as Mother She nurtures Her creation.

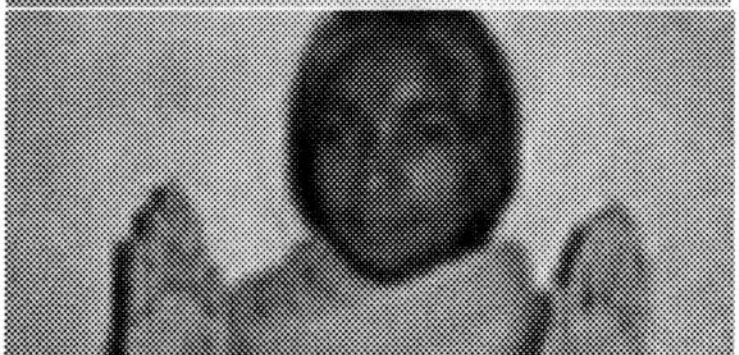

The Upasaṁhāra Mudrā is a call to all divine beings to assemble. "May all Gods and Goddesses make their presence manifest, right here, right now."

Books by Shree Maa and Swami Satyananda Saraswati

Annapūrṇa Thousand Names
Before Becoming This
Bhagavad Gītā
Chaṇḍi Pāṭh
Cosmic Pūjā
Cosmic Pūjā Bengali
Devī Gītā
Devī Mandir Songbook
Durgā Pūjā Beginner
Ganeśa Pūjā
Gems From the Chaṇḍi
Guru Gītā
Hanumān Pūjā
Kālī Dhyānam
Kālī Pūjā
Lakṣmī Sahasra Nāma
Lalitā Triśati
Rudrāṣṭādhyāyī
Sahib Sadhu
Saraswati Pūjā for Children
Shree Maa's Favorite Recipes
Shree Maa - The Guru & the Goddess
Shree Maa, The Life of a Saint
Śiva Pūjā Beginner
Śiva Pūjā and Advanced Fire Ceremony
Sundara Kāṇḍa
Swāmī Purāṇa
Thousand Names of Ganeśa
Thousand Names of Gayatri
Thousand Names of Viṣṇu and
Satya Nārāyaṇa Vrata Kathā

Cassette Tapes and CDs by Shree Maa

Chaṇḍi Pāṭh
Durgā Pūjā Beginner
Lalitā Triśati
Mantras of the Nine Planets
Navarṇa Mantra
Oh Dark Night Mother
Oṁ Mantra
Sādhu Stories from the Himalayas
Shree Maa at the Devi Mandir
Shree Maa in the Temple of the Heart
Shiva is in My Heart
Shree Maa on Tour, 1998
Śiva Pūjā Beginner
Śiva Pūjā and Advanced Fire Ceremony
The Goddess is Everywhere
The Songs of Ramprasad
The Thousand Names of Kālī
Tryambakaṁ Mantra

Please visit us on the
World Wide Web at http://www.shreemaa.org

5950 Highway 128
Napa, CA 94558 USA
Phone and Fax: 01-707-966-2802